MARCHING AHEAD!

MARCHING AHEAD!

RAM NAIK

PRABHAT PRAKASHAN

ISO 9001: 2008 Publishers

Published by
PRABHAT PRAKASHAN
4/19 Asaf Ali Road,
New Delhi-110 002 (INDIA)
Tele : +91-11-23289777
e-mail: prabhatbooks@gmail.com

e-mail: vishakha@ramnaik.com

ISBN 978-93-86231-63-5
MARCHING AHEAD
by Ram Naik
e-mail: me@ramnaik.com

Translated by
Dilip Chaware

Designed by
India Printing Works, Mumbai
e-mail: anand@ipworks.in

Paperback Edition
First, August 2016

Reprint
March 2017

Price
₹ 400.00 (Rupees Four Hundred only)

Printed at
Deep Colour Scan, Delhi

Dedication!

Charaiveti! Charaiveti!! चरैवेति! चरैवेति!!

Marching Ahead!

'Charaiveti' चरैवेति! is a Sanskrit term. Translated, it says: "One should constantly move forward, success only comes your way when you do." This has proved true in my own case.

In my journey through life and career, I have gained numerous colleagues who have devotedly stood by me in every situation. It is only with their support that I am able to reach this station in my life. I dedicate my memoir to them with a grateful heart.

—Ram Naik

प्रधान मंत्री
Prime Minister

New Delhi
May 4, 2016

Hon'ble Shri Naik jee,

I am indeed happy to receive your book 'Charaiveti! Charaiveti!!' along with the letter. Your contributions in the politics of Maharashtra and also at the national level are really commendable. You have gained invaluable experience while discharging social and political responsibilities over a long period. I am happy that this treasure of experience is reaching readers in the form of a book. I do hope that Hindi, Gujarati, English and Urdu editions of 'Charaiveti! Charaiveti!!' will get positive response from the readers.

With heartiest compliments,

Yours,

(Narendra Modi)

Shri Ram Naik
Governor, Uttar Pradesh
Raj Bhavan, Lucknow

FOREWORD

There are some relations that are difficult to describe in a few words. My relation with Shri Ram Naik jee or, Rambhau, as he is widely known, is one such very close and personal relationship. I do not know where to start from. When I think of Ram Naik jee, a number of happy memories come to mind – a friendly and kind 'uncle' with whom I loved spending time during my childhood, a passionate social worker caring for the poor and the needy, a dedicated political leader who cut his teeth on the streets of Mumbai and built the party brick by brick, a no-nonsense Union Minister committed to serving people; and now the Governor of Uttar Pradesh, India's most populous state.

Ram Naik jee belongs to a generation of leaders, who never imagined that the seeds they planted would grow into such a large and vibrant tree. Selflessly, he immersed himself in the noble task of nation-building; blissfully unaware of the pedestals of success he would scale in the years to come. To my mind, Rambhau has truly lived the ideals espoused in the book 'Charaiveti! Charaiveti!!' – 'Marching Ahead!' his entire life. A true *Nishkaam Karmayogi*, he has been associated with the party right from its Jana Sangh days. A doughty fighter known for his upright idealistic nature, he soon made a mark for himself both within the party and with the general public at large.

During the emergency, the Rashtriya Swayamsevak Sangh (RSS) and the Jana Sangh faced the brunt of the Government clampdown. When it was lifted in 1977 and it was certain that there were to be elections, it was decided by the top brass that the Jana Sangh would merge with other opposition parties to form the Janata Party. A meeting of the party was held in Lonavala, a tourist hill spot near Mumbai, where Ram Naik jee played a prominent role being the Organising Secretary of Mumbai Jana Sangh. While returning to Mumbai, he met with a car accident and suffered major injuries to his backbone. He was admitted to Tilak (Sion) hospital, which was near our home. My mother used to send food for him everyday, and since those were summer holidays, I often went to deliver it. As a 12-year-old boy, I looked forward to these visits where Ram Naik jee, even in his traction-bed, evidently suffering from immense pain, would be at his jovial best. One day, however, probably due to the intense heat and election-fever at home, and the typical hospital smell, I fainted in the hospital. I woke up lying in the bed next to Rambhau himself, with him concerned for my well being more than for himself. To my family's embarrassment, he would berate himself for having caused my fainting! I must mention here that it is to Ram Naik jee's credit that despite his near-death experience, he would lift the mood of the ward and the patients and staff at the hospital with his humorous demeanour.

It is in those days of political struggle and adversity that an association was forged between Rambhau and my late father, Shri Ved Prakash Goyal. The culture of our party has been of sharing and brotherhood. Their common ideology, simplicity and ability to endure the toughest of times with cheerfulness, endeared them to each other. In 1989, Rambhau led the BJP's rise in Maharashtra and became a Member of Parliament from the North Mumbai constituency. He was allotted a small bungalow No. 42 at Ashoka Road, New Delhi. My father, who was the National Treasurer of the Bharatiya Janata Party, and was required to be in Delhi often, was a permanent guest of Shri Ram Naik jee and enjoyed his hospitality every time he visited Delhi. In fact, this large-hearted man reserved his second bedroom for Papa and would ensure his comfort, conveniences and home-cooked delicious vegetarian food.

It was in 1991 that Shri Bhaurao Deoras jee entrusted me the responsibility to assist the National General Secretary (Organisation) of the BJP for managing the Lok Sabha elections from Delhi. I literally took it for granted that Rambhau's residence would be home during this period. I do not recall even asking him for his permission to live there! Without any notice, I ensconced myself in his home and commandeered every facility there for myself. For four months, or probably longer, since the National election had to be postponed due to the unfortunate assassination of Shri Rajeev Gandhi jee, Rambhau's home almost became a party *karyalaya*. Since I was handling the travels of all the senior leaders for campaign rallies, and for the first time, we were extensively using aircrafts, I had to get on to the phones very early each morning, often before sunrise, contacting different leaders all over India. Those were the days of landline phones and I had installed 12 telephone lines in the hall, where I would sit on the ground talking on 2 or 3 phones at the same time, often for hours on end, and the house would buzz with the tensions and small joys of an election control room. May be that was the time I developed the habit of multi-tasking and talking to two persons simultaneously, a habit I have still not got over. Even the most quintessential of party loyalists would have lost their patience at this disturbance in their house but not Ram Naik jee, whose humour and kindly nature helped us forget the daily frustrations and pressures.

In 1991, another happy event took place in my life. I was introduced to Seema, sometime in September after the elections, and we decided to marry in December 1991. Those were conservative times and we would often meet at Rambhau's home under his stern but fatherly gaze and parental affection. It almost feels like divine providence that the two most important events of my life, personal and political, are connected to Shri Ram Naik jee.

Rambhau is a person who has never been attracted to power. People of his spartan lifestyle and austere worldview always attract power and position, as people trust them. In 1999, Prime Minister Shri Atal Bihari Vajpayee jee gave this giant of a man his political due and appointed him Union Minister for Petroleum and Natural Gas. His efforts to clean up the sector are legendary and his tenure is remarkable for eliminating the LPG shortage in the country. In my work as Minister for Power, Coal and New & Renewable Energy, I draw inspiration from him and following his example have succeeded in eradicating coal and electricity shortages in the country. My father too served as Union Minister for Shipping under Vajpayee jee. The functioning of both the ministries – Petroleum and Shipping is closely interlinked and their friendship, forged over a lifetime of political struggle and hardship, helped smoothen the thornier issues with both working seamlessly to serve the people of India.

There is one episode in Rambhau's life that is testimony to his grit, determination and tenacity. In 1994, he was detected to have cancer, which can test the capacity of even the best of men. I remember accompanying Atal jee and my father to meet him, in what was a very poignant moment for me. In 1977, I had been a young boy, with a lesser understanding of the concerns of the world, but 17 years later as a young man, the seriousness of the situation deeply affected me. I am personally witness to Rambhau's remarkable discipline and undaunted spirit to combat and defeat the emperor of maladies, when a lesser person would have easily given up. He followed his dietary and medical restrictions religiously, to the extent that even Atal jee's visit was with the doctor's approval and within the prescribed time following all procedures.

The Bharatiya Janata Party went through a difficult time in 2004. Perhaps, to use the word 'difficult' for Rambhau is most inappropriate for he can make the toughest of mountains look conquerable. He went about serving the people in the same diligent manner, as was his wont as an MP. Cut from the same cloth as Shri Rambhau Mhalgi jee, who is remembered as an ideal MP, Shri Ram Naik jee too is meticulous in his work. Known as a perfectionist, he prepares for every meeting with a written agenda and specific notes. He personally takes down notes for his reference and draws upon his remarkable memory to solve any problem. As a Parliamentarian, he started the path-breaking initiative of giving an annual report card to his constituents known as *'Karyavratta'*. He continued this commendable practice even after he was no more an MP, and to this day as a Governor. This focus on transparency and accountability has motivated me in my work as a Minister to regularly report my activities and the outcomes of my work to the people at large, both by way of real-time data in the form of mobile apps – GARV (rural electrification), UJALA (LED bulbs distribution), Vidyut PRAVAH (price and availability of power), URJA (information to urban consumers) etc., and through periodical report cards. Rambhau is a role model for any people's representative wishing to serve his constituents.

The party naturally engaged Ram Naik jee in different roles, given his unbiased, affable and honest personality. He was appointed as the Chairman of the Disciplinary Committee of the party (2004-07) and his genial nature ensured complaints were handled with tact and diplomacy. He was the Convener of the M.P.s. & M.L.A.s Training Cell (2007-10) and also the Convener of the Good Governance Cell (2010-14). His work would often bring him to Delhi where my father got the opportunity to reciprocate his generous hospitality. He would stay at Papa's house until 2008, and this familial practice continued even when I became a Rajya Sabha MP in 2010.

When Shri Ram Naik jee asked me to write the foreword to 'Marching Ahead', the English version of 'Charaiveti! Charaiveti!!', I was humbled. It has been a moving experience to describe a man who is no less than a father figure to me. In this book, Rambhau has covered only a small part of his vast political and personal experiences for which, even multiple books would not suffice. His love for people that comes naturally to him is evident in this book. His philosophical bent of mind and his commitment to our party's ideology are well reflected. I congratulate him for sharing his wisdom and experiences with the younger generation, to guide them through the trials and tribulations of political life.

—Piyush Goyal
Minister of State
(Independent Charge) for Power,
Coal, New & Renewable Energy,
Government of India
Email: piyushgoyalbjp@gmail.com

PREFACE

In December 2014, I was approached by a popular Marathi daily, 'Sakal', requesting me to record my recollections in the form of a fortnightly column for its Sunday edition. It was suggested that the compilation may deal with my memories, sweet or bitter, and my experiences of different events and people. I was hesitant about this assignment as I did not consider myself a born writer.

My life's mission has always been, and still is, social work and my entry into electoral politics was a diktat by my party leadership. The only book I had written before this is a slim Marathi publication, 'Gatha Sangharshachee' and its English version 'The

Saga of Struggle', which depicts my struggle to ensure that justice was received by the project-affected persons of the Tarapur Atomic Power Project near Mumbai. All other 'literary' works were confined to the writing about the annual railway budget or regarding a colleague or leader in connection with some particular incident. Moreover, I was not sure as to how readers would receive these memories.

While I remained double minded about accepting this assignment, Shriram Pawar, the Group Editor of the newspaper, assured me that my vast and multi-faceted experiences in the world of politics had much to offer to the readers. He also mentioned that other contributors to the column included Sharad Pawar, Manohar Joshi and Sushilkumar Shinde – all three Maharashtra's former Chief Ministers. In effect, that would make me the odd man out. Besides, I considered that all three were junior to me in age, although they were my political contemporaries. Shriram's conviction about my memoirs' potential and positive impact on the readers prevailed and I decided to go ahead.

By nature, I am reluctant to speak about myself. But when my column began appearing on Sundays, the readers' response was overwhelmingly positive. It encouraged me to write about myself for a whole year. After this, despite Sakal's desire that I should continue, I had to discontinue this assignment, primarily due to the paucity of time. I realised then that even at eighty-two, time is a hard task master and does not provide much respite to me to undertake such assignments.

My reason for stopping the column was 'Charaiveti' – keep working, marching ahead and remain busy. This triple motto has governed my life and I continue to adhere to it.

The Editor of 'Sakal' had required that my columns be an introspection of my journey through life and politics and my resultant metamorphosis. But does a human being metamorphose as a result of a solitary factor? The obvious answer is 'no'. Life has taken me through many twists and turns. Although a middle-class salaried employee, I plunged full-time into politics by resigning from my secure job, first with the government and then in the corporate sector. Later in life, cancer mounted an unexpected attack on my body, which I overcame and have since continued to move forward with my work.

The prime force that sculpted me was my father, popularly known as 'Naik Master'. He died when I was only nineteen and in my final year of B.Com. But I continued to forge ahead. Besides my father, those who have guided me through difficult situations included some veterans, colleagues, and at times, even the man on the street. In light of this, I decided to depict some of the major events in my life and try to contemplate the future through the various incidents that have impacted my personality.

I began my public life with a resolve to work for the people. I have kept walking on this path despite the obstacles that were strewn along the way. It is true that everyone's life has its own distinct limitations and boundaries. I continued to write my column, though I was aware that a daily newspaper's life span is just for that day. Neither my friends, readers, nor I would have liked this collection to go into oblivion, as most newspaper writings do.

With this in mind, it was suggested that my memoirs be compiled and published in the form of a book. I sought the feedback about my column from a noted publisher, Anand

Limaye, of 'India Printing Works' Mumbai. His enthusiastic response was instant. Not only did he announce his decision to publish this book, but was also insistent that it reaches the public at the earliest.

This book is the collection of some select recollections of my sixty years in public life. I believe that the life of a social worker must be completely transparent and keeping with this philosophy, I have expressed my deepest thoughts through these recollections.

I began contributing my recollections to the 'Sakal' when I had already shifted to Lucknow as the Governor of Uttar Pradesh. I needed a vast number of references and pictures, a daunting task my daughter Vishakha undertook. It is due to her prompt assistance that these writings have emerged as a cohesive and comprehensive compilation. My hectic schedule had made it difficult for me at times to honour the deadline, but the editorial team at 'Sakal' accommodated me to the fullest possible extent. It is because of their cooperation that this book has become a reality.

Over the years, I have been blessed with so much affection from the people, known to me and unknown. I trust that they will accord to this modest effort the same warmth and affection.

—Ram Naik

September 2016
Raj Bhavan, Lucknow – 226027

POST SCRIPT

My memoirs in 'Charaiveti, Charaiveti' were originally published in Marathi. During my long social and political life in Mumbai, I had interacted with people from various linguistic backgrounds.

Following the release of the original Marathi version, my friends and well-wishers suggested that it also needs to be published in Hindi, Gujarati, Urdu and English. Responding to their suggestion, I have consented to the English translation being published.

I am obliged to my friend, Shri Dilip Chaware, for his excellent translation from the original Marathi into English and to Prabhat Prakashan, the publishers for bringing out this book in such a short time and so beautifully.

—Ram Naik

Raj Bhavan, Lucknow – 226027
Email – me@ramnaik.com

TRANSLATOR'S TRIBUTE

Shri Ram Naik is Rambhau for everybody, including us journalists. Rambhau's political ascendance is almost synced with my career as a journalist. I came to Mumbai in 1977 when Rambhau was becoming known. I have travelled on the back-seat of his two-wheeler, have seen him working from his tiny two-room Goregaon flat, wondered how little Nishigandha and Vishakha could study in that cramped kitchen as there would not be an inch of space in the house full of people and files. Like everybody else, I was amazed to witness the massive infrastructure created by a team of dedicated workers at the time of the birth of the Bharatiya

Janata Party under Rambhau's leadership. When I joined The Times of India, Mumbai, Rambhau was already a name to reckon with. Rambhau and Kunda Tai have not changed at all over these 40 years. Simplicity, uprightness and sincerity are the three virtues that are at a premium in Indian politics today. Rambhau has them in abundance. I reported Rambhau's numerous speeches made on the floor of the Assembly, in Party conclaves and during elections. I have covered him as a prominent MP and Union Minister. I was stunned, like countless others, when he was down with cancer or due to his defeat in 2004. Yet, I had a confidence, just like all others, that Rambhau will recover. He did not belie our faith in him.

I am gratified since Rambhau approached me to translate his memoirs from Marathi to English. I have come across many new nuggets of information through these writings. I have tried my best to articulate Rambhau's emotions and sentiments in this English translation. However, I am aware of my limitations and imperfections. I hope that I have been able to do justice to the original masterpiece.

—Dilip Chaware

September 2016

PROFILE OF RAM NAIK

Birth	16 April, 1934 (Akshay Truteeya) at Sangli, Maharashtra
Family	Wife Kunda, daughters Dr Nishigandha and Vishakha
Mother/father	Smt. Indira/ Shri D.V. Kulkarni aka Naik Master
School education	Shri Bhavani Vidyalaya, Atpadi, District Sangli, Maharashtra
Higher education	B.Com. (1954) – Brihan Maharashtra College of Commerce, Pune LL.B. (1958) – K.C. College, Mumbai
Employment	• Upper Division Clerk in Accountant General's Office, Mumbai (1954-57) • Company Secretary in Khira Steel Works, Mumbai (1957-69) • General Manager, ABMEF Consultants (1974-77)
Political career	• Started as a local worker of Bharatiya Jana Sangh, Mumbai (1959) • Full-time worker of Bharatiya Jana Sangh as Mumbai Organising Secretary (1969-74) • Janata Party (JP) Mumbai President (1978-80) • Bharatiya Janata Party (BJP) Mumbai President for three terms (1980-1985, 1991-1993) • Elected to Maharashtra Legislative Assembly for three consecutive terms from Borivali Constituency in Mumbai (1978, 1980, 1985) • Elected to Lok Sabha from North Mumbai Parliamentary Constituency for five consecutive terms (1989, 1991, 1996, 1998, 1999) • Member, BJP National Executive Committee (since BJP's inception in 1980 till appointment as UP Governor in 2014) • Chairman, BJP National Disciplinary Committee (2005-07) • Convener, BJP MPs/MLAs/MLCs Development Cell (2007-10) • Convener, BJP Good Governance Cell (2010-14)
Minister	• Minister of State for Railways (Independent Charge), Home, Planning and Programme Implementation, Parliamentary Affairs (1998-99) • Minister of Petroleum and Natural Gas (1999-2004) (only incumbent to hold this charge for a full five-year term)
Retirement from electoral politics	Announcement on 25 September, 2013 on the occasion of birth anniversary of Pandit Deen Dayal Upadhyaya
Governor, Uttar Pradesh	22 July, 2014

CONTENTS

CHARAIVETI! CHARAIVETI!!
चरैवेति! चरैवेति!!
MARCHING AHEAD!

Our ancient scriptures have explained a philosophy which is helpful in day-to-day life. One of the couplets in the 'Aitareya Sukta' mentions how Indra, Emperor of Gods, came in a human form before a ruler and enlightened him on how to proceed on the path of self-development. In the sermon, Indra advises the ruler to keep walking, moving ahead, so that good fortune will come his way.

आस्ते भग आसीनस्य
उर्ध्वम् तिष्ठति तिष्ठतः
शेते निपद्य मानस्य
चराति चरतो भगः। चरैवेति! चरैवेति!!

"One who is sitting, his fortune sits as well.
One who is standing, fortune halts for him.
One who sleeps, his fortune goes to sleep.
But one who keeps walking, his fortune leaps forward.
Hence, keep moving, keep marching ahead!!"

Citing an example, Indra adds:

चरन्वै मधुविन्दति
चरन्स्वादुमुदुम्बरम्
सूर्यस्य पश्य श्रेमाणं
चरैवेति! चरैवेति!!

"Honeybees collect honey by working ceaselessly.
Birds have to fly around for sweet fruits.
The Sun is worshipped as he never sleeps,
keeps moving forward.
Therefore, Oh Man! Keep moving! Keep marching ahead!!"

MARCHING
AHEAD!
चरैवेति! चरैवेति!!

Shri Bhavani Vidyalaya, Atpadi and its first Headmaster Naik Master & father who sculpted son Ram's character and personality

THE SLEEPING CAPSELLER - A GREAT TEACHER

South of Maharashtra, in the district of Sangli, lies a perennially drought-affected little village known as Atpadi. It was here that my parents raised me, since my birth in Sangli on April 16, 1934. They were not to know that the child they brought into the world would go on to become the Governor of Uttar Pradesh, the largest state in their home country of India.

During my childhood, it was mandatory for every student to perform *'Surya Namaskar'*, which had been popularised by Bhavanrao Pant Pratinidhi, the King of Aundh Sansthan (Princely State). Indians have worshipped *Surya*, the Sun God since time immemorial. The *Surya Namaskar* is a set of twelve powerful *yoga asanas*, or postures that provide the body with a good cardiovascular workout. Literally translated as sun salutation, these postures are a good way to keep the body in shape and the mind calm and serene.

Today, eight decades later, my memories of Atpadi have not faded in the least. It will always be the place closest to my heart. In my mind's eye, I can relive my years as a child so many years ago. It makes me feel like a schoolboy once again. Oftentimes I tread down this nostalgic path, especially when people enquire of me as to my good health at this advanced age, or my victory over the dreaded cancer.

Pant Pratinidhi had an obsession. He expected everyone to perform the *Surya Namaskar* daily. He was convinced that this was the surest path to good health and had adopted it so that the people in his Princely State maintained good health and retained it as they advanced in age.

So, the answer to the query regarding my health is this great secret: I attribute it to the consistent practice of the *Surya Namaskar* since my early childhood.

Ram Naik handing over cooking gas agency allotment letter to wife of Kargil martyr Suresh Chavan, a son of Atpadi

In the schools run by the Sansthan, every first period was dedicated to the performing of the *Surya Namaskar*. My headmaster was a strict disciplinarian, who brooked no excuses from the students in this regard. They were not allowed to attend school if they did not participate in performing this *asana*. A striking factor was that the headmaster who emphasised

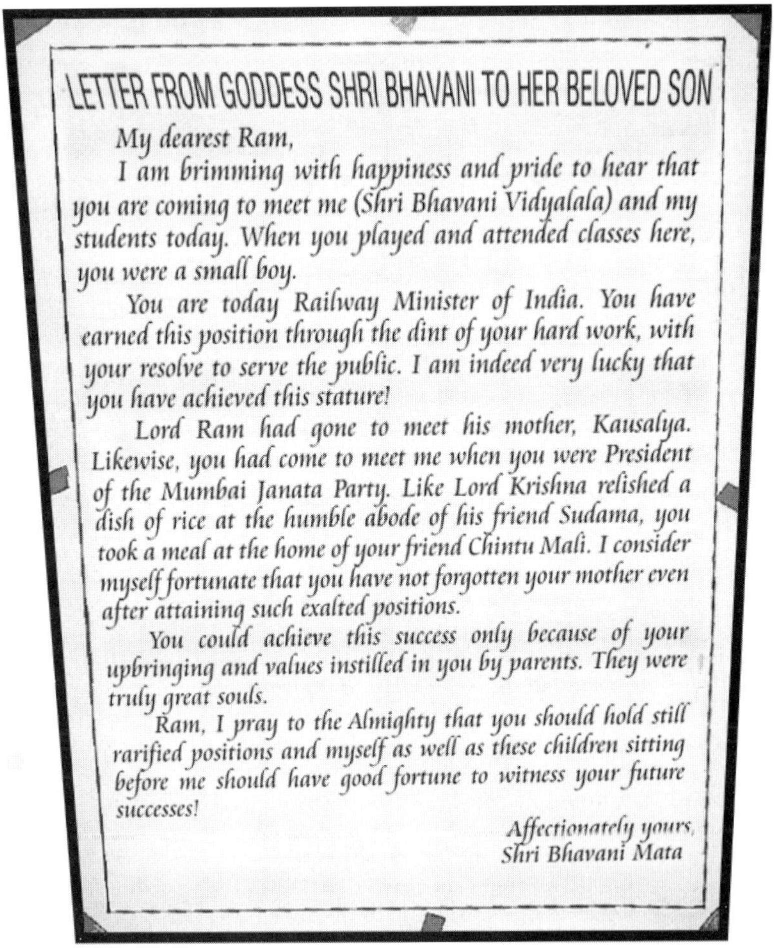

LETTER FROM GODDESS SHRI BHAVANI TO HER BELOVED SON

My dearest Ram,

I am brimming with happiness and pride to hear that you are coming to meet me (Shri Bhavani Vidyalala) and my students today. When you played and attended classes here, you were a small boy.

You are today Railway Minister of India. You have earned this position through the dint of your hard work, with your resolve to serve the public. I am indeed very lucky that you have achieved this stature!

Lord Ram had gone to meet his mother, Kausalya. Likewise, you had come to meet me when you were President of the Mumbai Janata Party. Like Lord Krishna relished a dish of rice at the humble abode of his friend Sudama, you took a meal at the home of your friend Chintu Mali. I consider myself fortunate that you have not forgotten your mother even after attaining such exalted positions.

You could achieve this success only because of your upbringing and values instilled in you by parents. They were truly great souls.

Ram, I pray to the Almighty that you should hold still rarified positions and myself as well as these children sitting before me should have good fortune to witness your future successes!

Affectionately yours,
Shri Bhavani Mata

Welcome plaque erected for past student Ram Naik at Shri Bhavani Vidyalaya when he was felicitated in 1998

that 'health is wealth' and implemented this motto in letter and spirit, was nobody else but my father – popularly known by all as 'Naik Master'.

It is true that though my generation was born in a drought-affected village, we all earned our good health through the consistent practice of the *Surya Namaskar* throughout our lives. It is this regimen that has endowed me with a robust constitution and healthy immunity, except during the interval when I underwent treatment for cancer. These days the *Surya Namaskar* is usually performed only on the birth anniversary of Swami Vivekananda. It is my sound conviction that all children and young people should imbibe the practice of this *asana* as a regular part of their daily routine at the start of their day for good health.

Nothing is Impossible

Just as I had developed good health during my childhood, I was also inculcated with another important attribute, that of self-confidence. I grew up to believe that nothing is impossible in this world. In a way, I undertook the job of creating a dictionary in which the word 'impossible' did not exist. I have lived by that rule and toiled hard and sincerely to reach my present position today. I believe that every human is endowed with the ability to think likewise and so be able to reach his highest potential.

In school, I was endeared to my teachers owing to my perseverance and willingness to work hard to complete any assignment entrusted to me. This affection was certainly not due to my father's position as the headmaster. I got no partial treatment because of him – he treated me just as he did other students and not as his son.

The King of Aundh was also a connoisseur of the art of painting and was himself a distinguished painter. He had made art another compulsory subject in school besides the *Surya Namaskar*. And indeed, art is a beautiful and creative subject. Brushes, pencils and paints can lead to one's discovery of oneself in a way. It was this subject that draws my mind back to one of the most challenging situations of my young life.

My drawing teacher had insisted that I appear for the elementary drawing examination at Pandharpur, the great pilgrimage centre in Maharashtra and India, thirty kilometres away from Atpadi. Clearing this examination was considered an achievement. I was shaken by my teacher's edict. Although I had been selected by the school as a gifted student, I was under tremendous mental pressure. I was worried that my reputation as a model student would be ruined if I did not pass the examination with flying colours. Our drawing teacher, Kalal Master, had pinned his hopes on me and it was he who accompanied me to Pandharpur for the examination.

The moment I saw the question paper, I was petrified. We had been asked to draw a sleeping capseller and monkeys. I began with drawing a large tree. I followed this up with monkeys sitting on its branches, wearing caps. By now, I was beginning to regain some semblance of composure. But it was momentary. While I had first assumed that I would complete the drawing in record time – a crisis developed. I realised that I could not draw the face of the sleeping capseller, no matter how hard I tried. I struggled for a while, erasing and drawing again, eventually giving up when it appeared that if I went this way any longer, the drawing paper would be in tatters.

I sat for a while, my mind racing, wondering how I could overcome this predicament in time. My mind seemed to have gone blank and I wondered what would happen if I failed this examination. Would I lose my reputation? Would it prove that the confidence placed in me by Kalal Master had been misplaced?

Pressure was now mounting. I had to complete the examination in time. Then suddenly a ray of inspiration; I aborted the attempt to draw the face of the sleeping capseller and instead drew a figure in a sleeping posture, his face covered by a blanket. To indicate that there was indeed a man asleep under the blanket, I drew his feet protruding from beneath. I had fulfilled the criteria and the drawing showed a man sleeping under the tree with his feet visible. Miracle of miracles; I cleared the examination.

I attribute this success to my presence of mind, the belief that nothing is impossible, and my imagination. These forces had coalesced at the right moment, in the right place, in such a manner that, at that momentous challenge, I learnt two lessons: First, that anyone can find a way if he can overcome fear, keeping his mind calm and serene, so as to be able to think clearly. Secondly, fate may not necessarily prove to be a friend every time, one has also to make serious concerted efforts, which could possibly be a tough struggle.

Not only was the elementary examination held at Pandharpur, every important examination was too. The journey had seemed inordinately long in those days and the means of transportation were limited. There was just one trip of a public transport bus everyday from Atpadi. Teachers escorted students to Pandharpur for various examinations, each student carrying his tiffin and some ration. The previous night would be spent in a dharmashala, which is a free dormitory and the troupe would return to Atpadi as soon as the examination was over.

However, going for a darshan of Vithoba, the diety of Pandharpur was inevitable and our teachers would discharge this responsibility with great enthusiasm.

Lesson of Equality

I may have been around twelve years of age when I appeared for the seventh standard examination held at Pandharpur. The temple of Vithoba was not open for the downtrodden (scheduled castes) in those times. Therefore, not a single Dalit friend could accompany us and this broke my heart. Inside the temple, a group of priests pounced upon us for offerings of money. I questioned this practice. "Why this discrimination at the feet of God? And why do priests loot the devotees?" I would ask.

Being a mere boy, I felt helpless to take a stance against this form of discrimination. While other students were accustomed to such situations, to some extent at least, it was all unfamiliar to me. It made me uncomfortable and I felt a twinge of conscience at the blatancy of it all. As our school was outside the village borders and our house was nearby, I had never witnessed such caste discrimination. Moreover, my father was also a social reformer. So there was no question of practising it.

Near our school were the homes of the Vadar (stone-breakers) and Ramoshi (an outcast community) families. Their children would play with us. Their drinking water well often dried up quite early every summer and my father would allow them to draw water from the well in the

Ram Naik & wife Kunda happily repeating marital vows in front of Vithoba; the temple is now open to all!

school. It was my visits to Pandharpur that woke me up to the blatant social discrimination.

On my return, I recounted the entire sad episode to my father, who advised me: “If you don’t like it, don’t practise it. However people may choose to behave, you should behave according to your own conscience and do whatever your mind dictates.” My father had been practising what he preached and lived by this credo.

This enlightened upbringing under his supervision was supplemented by the Rashtriya Swayamsevak Sangh (RSS). I would attend a ‘shakha’ held by ‘Nawathe Master’, a teacher from our school. My personality and career have been sculpted through the discipline and social awareness instilled in me by the RSS.

(February 8, 2015)

❐

Ram Naik firmly believes in the values instilled by RSS since childhood

Deputy Prime Minister L.K. Advani presenting a scroll of honour to noted freedom fighter and famous singer-composer Sudhir Phadke at Pune for the role he played along with a band of patriots in the liberation of Dadra & Nagar Haveli from Portuguese rule. (L-R) Ram Naik, Babasaheb Purandare and Pune MP Pradeep Ravat

A GALAXY OF FRIENDS AND WELL-WISHERS

It is true that my father and the RSS have played a major role in sculpting my personality. I must, however, also acknowledge my debt to many well-wishers whom I encountered during my childhood and youth. They have given me so much that I consider it imperative to express my gratitude at the very outset. Many of them have gone on to earn great fame and reputation with their own achievements. I consider myself blessed and fortunate to have been a recipient of their love and affection.

I learned cycling when I was quite young. It was my elder brother's friend who taught me and my younger brother the joys of cycling. Our teacher was Vyankatesh Madgulkar, an accomplished and famous Marathi author. His elder brother, Gajanan Digambar Madgulkar, popularly known as 'Gadimaa', became a legend in his lifetime with his immortal composition 'Geet Ramayan' and other numerous stories, screenplays and songs that he wrote for films. It was thanks to my father that I benefited from these two enterprising brothers for they were his students. It must be said to their credit that although they became highly accomplished individuals within their own spheres, they never did forget their obligation to their Guru. Gadimaa even accommodated me in the outhouse of his bungalow Panchavati in Pune when I shifted to that city for higher education.

Ram Naik felicitated with the 'Gadimaa Snehbandh Award' on 14 December 2012 by Maharashtra State Cultural Development Board's Managing Director Lakshmikant Deshmukh, while Gadima's son Anand Madgulkar and veteran music director Yashwant Deo looking on

'Gadimaa' and 'Babujee'

Gadimaa, singer and music composer Sudhir Phadke, and film director Raja Paranjape were aptly called a triumvirate of the Marathi film industry. Together they enjoyed tremendous popularity and success by producing excellent movies in quick succession. I was privileged to witness several of their meetings while I resided at the Panchavati. Gadimaa was a Congress supporter while Sudhir Phadke or 'Babujee', as he was known, was a staunch RSS worker. Of course, this did not hinder their friendship in any way, despite their frequent stormy political skirmishes. Gadimaa introduced me to Babujee as 'Your Jaatwala' (belonging to your caste) due to my association with the RSS, and, since then, Babujee always treated me as his younger brother. These rare individuals have been cast from a different mould – they valued friendship above everything else.

Eventually, I shifted from Pune to Mumbai and began my career as a political activist working for the Bharatiya Jana Sangh – the forerunner of the Bharatiya Janata Party. During this time I once met Gadimaa, who was then a Member of the Legislative Council (MLC), having been nominated by the Governor of Maharashtra to that august house. Boosting my morale, he said, "I have become an 'Aamdar' (a Member of the Legislature), you will become a 'Naamdar' (a minister)." At that time, the Jana Sangh had just four MLAs and hardly any space in the political scenario of Maharashtra. Gadimaa's blessings and prediction became a reality, when three decades later, in 1998, I became Minister of State in Prime Minister Shri Atal Behari Vajpayee's cabinet. Gadimaa's words echoed in my mind as

Internationally renowned water expert Dr. Madhav Chitale (L) and his wife Vijaya (R) with Ram Naik and his wife Kunda at Raj Bhavan

I recalled his prediction and I was thrilled, yet humbled, at his astute prophecy.

Babujee was an altogether different personality. He composed the music for 'Geet Ramayan', which Gadimaa had written and he sang many of the songs himself, which are popular even today. Babujee produced many a popular record in quick succession, which became long-running hits on the popularity charts.

In 1960, I was travelling with my wife Kunda, whom I had just married. Babujee saw me at the Karjat railway station and called out to me by my first name. My wife was very impressed that such a great personality knew me personally! Babujee, the epitome of politeness and protocol, had called out to me in this informal manner as his greeting had come from the bottom of his heart, which was for a fellow RSS worker. The bond we shared and our mutually respectful relationship that existed between us during his life was recognised when I was honoured with an invitation for the celebration of the Diamond Jubilee of 'Geet Ramayan' by his son Shridhar. This invitation was a recognition of our enduring bond.

In 1998, I was a Minister of State for Railways. At that time, Babujee was busy producing the epic film 'Savarkar', depicting the life and battles fought by the patriot. He required a meeting with me in that connection. Although he was well aware that I would have rushed to his side had he just made a telephone call, he decided to visit my office himself without any prior intimation during the hours reserved for meeting the general public. Anticipating my reaction, he embraced me warmly, saying, "I have come for my work. Your official status must be respected."

Notwithstanding his polite nature, he could become quite steely when he wanted. That was how he refused to accept the *Padmashree*, a civilian honour, instituted by the Government of India, which he rightly felt was not according to his stature. Even so, he did not publicise his refusal, as he did not wish anyone to feel slighted. Seniors and elders like Babujee have bestowed so much upon me that I shall never be able to enumerate it.

Friends from RSS

I lived in Pune between 1950 and 1954 during my college education. Besides my academic education, which was a B.Com. degree, there were many invaluable lessons I picked up along the way.

Ram Naik inaugurating the Chitale Bandhu Mithaiwale hostel for girls in Pune. Donors Rajabhau Chitale and his wife (at his right) and Nanasaheb Chitale and his wife (at his left) flanked him

When I became a 'Swayamsevak' (voluntary worker) of the Vaidikashram Shakha (Branch) of the RSS, Rambhau Mhalgi was our regional secretary. He was later to be regarded as an accomplished Parliamentarian – both in the Assembly and the Lok Sabha (lower house of Indian Parliament). Whenever my performance is compared with that of Rambhau's, I am aware that the seeds of my future were sown during my time at that RSS Shakha.

I developed some lifelong friendships at Pune's Deccan Gymkhana RSS Shakha. Though I was a commerce student, I could integrate very easily with an engineering student in no time at all. Today, he is famous the world over as an expert on water – Madhav Chitale. He and I had developed a habit of quenching our intellectual thirst through arguments and counter-arguments. This habit earned me three other distinguished friends. Yashwantrao Lele, who later became close associate of Appa Pendse – a familiar name, who devoted his life to nurturing talent from school levels by establishing – 'Dnyan Prabodhini' a great institution of learning in Pune. Another friend of mine, Sharad Bhide, later turned out as a pillar of the co-operative consumer movement. And last but not the least was Ramdas Kalaskar, who is remembered as an editor of 'Ekata' (Unity) a Marathi monthly. All of us were of the same age group though I was the youngest and the bond of our friendship continued to strengthen.

Later, Ramdas was deputed to West Bengal to spread the working of the Jana Sangh in order to counter the Naxalite movement. At his suggestion, I was selected as the Organising Secretary of the Mumbai Jana Sangh. This was the first leap on my political graph. Despite their middle-class economic situation, these and many other such friends had the largeness of heart to spend from their own pockets, when they were told that one from amongst them, i.e. me was planning to enter into the politics of elections. These friends and well-wishers inculcated in me the awareness that one must repay society as much as possible.

Collegemates

I had joined the Brihan Maharashtra College of Commerce (BMCC), Pune for my B.Com. degree. To date it remains one of the prime commerce colleges in the state. There was such an abundance of talent in the college that my pride at being the topmost student of my village school soon dissipated. Though full of gifted students, we never did experience the kind of cut-throat competition so prevalent today.

One of my friends had beautiful handwriting. Coupled with his mastery of various subjects – his notebooks proved more valuable to me than even the textbooks. He was instrumental in helping me and other students like me to clear the examinations. This intelligent personality was none other than C.G. Vaidya, who later on became the Principal of our college, the BMCC, and continued to hold that position for a long time.

My fellow students, who later distinguished themselves as educationists, included the Principal of Modern College, Pune M.B. Limaye, the Principal of Baramati College, Dr. Godha, the Principal of Gokhale College, Nashik, Dr. M.S. Gosavi, Pune University management faculty Dean Dr. Prof. Gopal Pethe, the famous accountancy tuition classes mentor, Dada Ganpule, and several others. Thanks to the support of these friends, I was elected to the Commerce Association of the BMCC, although I was not in Pune at the time of the election. To top it all, the blazer I wore for a photograph after my election was borrowed from a friend. I am overwhelmed when I think back on my memories of them.

A Sweet Bond

There was one person I immediately established a rapport with, due to our similar ideological values; Rajabhau Chitale! He was from the famous Chitale family, who were distributors of milk and ran a string of sweetmeat shops. Today, their products are in demand in several countries. Rajabhau, who had a lion's share in establishing the brand 'Chitale Bandhu Mithaiwale', was of the firm belief that there is no substitute for hard work. Our mutual readiness to toil cemented our relationship.

During the 1950s, Rajabhau's day began at dawn, with the daunting task of delivering milk to the doorsteps of customers as soon as it reached Pune from Bhilawadi in Sangli district. Storage of milk was unheard of in those days. Rajabhau himself would load his bicycle with cans of milk and distribute them from door to door. I too was up early every morning, making several rounds on a bicycle to deliver newspapers. The fact that we both woke up early, making our respective deliveries on our cycles further endeared us to each other.

I subsequently shifted to Mumbai while Rajabhau stayed in Pune. There was no instant social media at the time, such as there is today. Even a landline was a rarity and was very expensive to use. As it was, both of us were completely immersed in building our respective careers. Despite this, during my quick visits to Pune, I would invariably peep into the Chitale shop to meet Rajabhau if he was inside. On his part, Rajabhau had close contacts with many MPs and ministers. But even so, he would still approach me to get any social project done through me as a matter of protocol. He was very insightful and could measure up a person easily, nurturing relationships wherever deserved.

In 1994, when I was afflicted with cancer, Rajabhau rushed to Mumbai on hearing the news. Although he had surmised that the expenditure for my cancer treatment would be borne by the government since I was a Member of Parliament, he was worried that the allied expenses would be quite substantial too. He told me that his presence in Pune was required to handle the business and, thrusting a demand draft in my hand, murmured, “Let me know if anything is needed.” I had never shed a tear on account of the dreaded cancer, but this selfless gesture on his part made my eyes moist. Even at that momentous point in my life, I was struck by the transparency of the Chitale Brothers. Despite his being such a big-shot, he had come with a demand draft and not cash since the firm was known to be absolutely honest in paying up its income tax and other taxes. This fact had been validated by the income tax authorities earlier and was then endorsed by Rajabhau.

Anybody who knows Pune and the Chitale Brothers is not likely to believe that they would present anyone anything free of charge. However, I must have been an exception since Rajabhau, till the very end of his life, would enquire regarding my whereabouts every Diwali and send over a can of Shrikhand, which is a sweet made of seasoned curds, milk and saffron – whether I was in Mumbai or Delhi. This sweet little secret tends to shock many, even today.

Rajabhau would approach me on many occasions for social causes. No doubt, some of them concerned sweet-meat makers; but let me now reveal that Rajabhau could have claimed the credit for establishing the first girls' engineering college in Maharashtra. The project in Pune had been stalled within the corridors of bureaucracy in Delhi. Rajabhau asked me to intervene and take up the issue. When I began making enquiries into the same, I learnt the sad truth that the Secretary of the Ministry of Human Resources Development had not even been aware of the name 'Maharshi Karve Stree Shikshan Sanstha' – the very first educational institution in Asia to open a school and a college for destitute women over 120 years ago by the legendary social reformer Dr. D.K. Karve. This ignorance was the reason for the stonewalling. When I met the HRD minister and explained the situation, the project's path was cleared. In the course of time, the Chitale Brothers even

Ram Naik over joyed with unexpected visit of (L to R) Yashwantrao Lele, Sharad Bhide and Jyotsna Bhide on the occasion of his 50th anniversary of wedding

got constructed a hostel for the institution and, of course, Rajabhau did not forget to invite me for its inauguration.

I have been blessed with a host of friends and well-wishers who have kept the cause of social consciousness aflame in my mind. I have always tried to repay this debt by discharging my obligations to the best of my ability.

(February 22, 2015)

❒

Ram Naik's favourite Goregaon abode 'Shivsmriti' illuminated to celebrate the golden jubilee of the housing society

THE QUEST FOR SHELTER

My childhood was spent in Atpadi, in the district of Sangli, while my college days were spent in Pune. But, now I am a true Mumbaikar and I can never forget that it was the support and warmth of the people of Mumbai that helped me attain my position.

The memory of my first visit to Mumbai, however, is filled with tragedy and the memory disturbs me even today.

During my last year of B.Com., out of the blue, I received a message that I was needed in Mumbai immediately. I was in the midst of my terminal examination and for that reason, my father had advised me not to accompany him and mother to Mumbai; studying and examinations being more important. But he himself had to rush to Mumbai, since his chronic ulcer problem had been aggravated and surgery was necessary.

In those days, it was not an easy surgery, as it is today. Still no one suspected that it would prove fatal for him. And so, my first visit to Mumbai was straight to the KEM Hospital and from there, directly on to the crematorium at Dadar, to bid my father a final goodbye. Completing all the formalities and rituals of my father's death, I returned to Pune.

But this incident had caused me to develop quite an aversion towards Mumbai. However, four months after completing my B.Com. examination, I was forced to return to Mumbai out of compulsion, but with a heavy heart, since I had to shoulder the responsibility of our household.

First Shelter

I had been introduced to the family of my father's friend during his last rites. On the strength of this sketchy acquaintance, I arrived at Batuk Mansion in Thakurdwar – the home of Prabhakar Joshi, son of my father's deceased friend Shankar Joshi. It was a middle-class residential locality in South Mumbai. Prabhakar's mother, Uma Kaku (aunt) extended her warm hospitality, accommodating me in that tiny block. Those who know Mumbai, will understand how difficult it is to entertain a guest in one's house, even for a short while! Moreover, my father was no more and I was unemployed and, therefore, in no position to make any monetary contribution.

Besides sheltering me and treating me with warm affection, Uma Kaku trained me in the life-styles of Mumbai.

On one occasion I remember her advising me; "If you go to someone's house and refuse the offer of a cup of tea, you will create an awkward situation for that family, because everyone cannot afford to offer guests a cup of milk. Therefore, learn to drink tea." I followed this advice closely in letter and spirit. The first time I tasted tea, I was twenty. I also learned to put others first in different situations.

My very first job was with the government sector. I joined the office of the Accountant General (AG) at Ballard Estate as a clerk. It was time now to move out of the Joshi household, since I had begun earning for myself. After all, one should not overstay one's welcome. I decided to shift elsewhere, whatever the facilities. I soon found accommodation as a paying guest in Khetwadi, Girgaon, in the home of the well-known violinist, Pandit Paluskar.

Pandit Paluskar was a teacher at the Sangeet Vidyalaya in Benares, better known as Varanasi. His wife, son and daughter lived in Khetwadi's Gowardhan Niwas. The common verandah was used for sleeping out at night. If it rained, I had permission to sleep inside. Otherwise, I would only enter their tenement to bathe. I had just begun working and was shouldering the responsibility of my mother and younger brother, who were in Pune. I had very little option, but to make the best of the situation.

My friend Sharad Bhide too by then started working in Mumbai. During our days off, we used to take long tram rides via various routes to while away time and get to know Mumbai enroute.

My daily routine consisted of completing my morning toiletries, after which I would eat a meal at Tambe's restaurant nearby, packing a few chapattis and a cooked dry vegetable dish for my afternoon snack, before heading off to the office. After office hours, I walked to the LL.B. classes at K.C. College in Churchgate.

During all this, my work for the RSS had continued. I met Nana Apte, a staunch Swayamsevak, at the Girgaon Shakha. As per RSS practice, we would visit the home of one *Swayamsevak* or the other. When no such visit was planned, we would gather at Nana's home. I would play with his little son Vinay, who later went on to become a famous stage and film personality. Still, he too continued the relationship till his demise at a comparatively young age a couple of years ago. It was during this period that I began to understand life in a *chawl* and was on my way to becoming a part of Mumbai's inclusive culture.

RSS Shelter

Shortly thereafter, arrangements were made for my stay at Ishwar Bhuvan, the RSS office near Churchgate. The premises were turned into the advertisement section of the Sangh Parivar weekly, 'Vivek'. RSS meetings were held here in the evenings. Once the meetings were concluded, it converted into the domain of another *Swayamsevak* and myself. But for me, it was a great luxury in comparison to my previous accommodation.

However, whenever an RSS meeting was to be held at night and I was not required to be there, I would carry my books to Marine Drive to study, sitting on a bench under a street lamp.

The only problem in the accommodation was that it did not have toilet or bathroom facilities. True, there was a latrine for the servants working in that building, but it was so dirty, that I could not get myself to use it. I learned that the public toilet at Churchgate railway station was a better option. Still, having a bath was another problem that I faced. I soon made friends with a garage owner just outside the station and began bathing from a tap there. Thus, I became privy to the difficulties faced by slum-dwellers in Mumbai.

This part of my life was a huge learning curve. I was spending my days without any mental anguish; in fact, I was enjoying the experience. Actually, I didn't have any spare time to consider the drawbacks and discomforts, which were a part of my daily life. Going to office in the morning and college in the evening, then holding night shakhas at an open public ground known as Azad Maidan, for the boys working at various restaurants, consumed most of my time and kept my mind well occupied. My means of transport was a bicycle. For a change, I would occasionally go to the old MLAs' Hostel for a square meal, which cost ten annas (a rupee then was 16 *annas*). If anyone had predicted then, that one day I would be visiting this very hostel as an MLA, I would have laughed at him. My days went by in this manner.

One morning, I received a call for an interview from the reputed Khira Steel Furniture Company, for the post of an accountant. Back then, the practice of holding campus interviews, which is so commonplace now, did not exist. But Pune University had started up an Employment Bureau for its graduating students and I had enrolled myself with it. The responsibility of selecting candidates for this post was entrusted by Khira Company to the great management expert, Dr. N.H. Athreya, whose books on the art and science of management are still popular. Athreya had carefully shortlisted the candidates from different places and had selected my name from Pune University. I had represented the BMCC in basketball and kho-kho tournaments and was a Students' Representative as well. Athreya had taken into account all these factors.

At that time, working for the government and the RSS simultaneously was a difficult task. But I was bent on working for social causes and the RSS. When I appeared for an interview, despite holding a secure government job, my interviewers seemed taken aback. They asked me why I was opting for private company employment, when I already had such a steady government job? When I responded candidly, company owner, Jayanandbhai Khira laughed and I was selected for the job. He was a recognised Congress sympathiser, appointing an RSS activist, so that he would be able to work for the RSS. The Congress and the RSS were at loggerheads even then, as they are now. But Khira had proven his liberal credentials by offering me the job. His only expectation was that I do my work in the office with sincerity, which I did and my progress got accelerated.

As the Khira factory was at Santacruz in the western suburbs of Mumbai, I decided to shift my accommodation to the suburbs.

It was around 1957 that I began living with a south Indian family at Jogeshwari as a paying guest. Here, I came in contact with Vishwa Hindu Parishad activist, Bhaskarrao Mundale and Marathi entrepreneur, Balasaheb Ghalsasi, as well as other like-minded social workers. When I was promoted as Chief Accountant at Khiras, I decided to hire independent accommodation, regardless of its size. I was soon able to rent two small rooms at Gogate Wadi in Goregaon.

School at Home

But before I could shift there, my friend Sharad Bhide was transferred from Mumbai. He had rented a two-room tenement in a *chawl* called 'Happy Home', in Jayprakash Nagar, a middle-class locality in Goregaon. Sharad handed it over to me. In turn, I handed over the small rooms, I had rented at Gogate Wadi to Smt. Mrunalini Chirmule, an active lady associated with the Sangh Parivar, for opening a Balwadi, which is a nursery school.

Till then, she had been running the Balwadi from her own residence. We sowed the seed of an educational institution, and named it 'Sanmitra Mandal' (Circle of Good Friends). Its founder-president was the local Jana Sangh Councillor, Prof. G.B. (Balasaheb) Kanitkar, who later on served brilliantly as an MLC. The institution is a reputed Marathi-medium school today and its board of trustees does not represent any family or enterprise. The common thread is the ideology of the trustees, who ensured that the institution operated as smoothly as well-oiled wheels, which it has for the past fifty-eight years.

Balasaheb was a prominent Jana Sangh leader and a member of the Mumbai Municipal Corporation (BMC) at the time. I had come into contact with him earlier for his civic electioneering. Now that I had shifted to Goregaon, the Sangh Parivar indicated that I should concentrate more on Jana Sangh work. Gradually, my political career began its ascent.

Dream Home

As I began to settle down in Goregaon, I dreamed of buying my own accommodation, just like any young man would. Several friends were thinking along similar lines. We had big dreams and were ready to think out of the box to realise them. We were determined to work hard towards this end. The only factor lacking was money.

In those days, the majority of Mumbaikars lived in rented accommodations. A few lucky ones would have owned their independent home. Though we desired our own homes, it was almost impossible to afford one. It was around this time that a visionary builder and developer constructed and sold several affordable flats in the buildings for middle-class families. His name was Baburao Paranjape. This initiative considerably boosted the concept of cooperative housing.

My friends and I decided to go beyond this concept. A senior citizen in our locality had bought a plot of land on which he was to build his house, but he changed his mind. A dozen of us like-minded individuals came together and purchased the plot from him. Sadanand Vaidya, a civil engineer among us, supervised the building construction. Being with Khira Company, I undertook the responsibility of purchasing materials, like cement, iron, timber and electrical fittings at wholesale rates.

The two-room flats were planned in such a manner, that the insides of the common walls were utilised for constructing kitchen racks, while the exteriors were converted into cupboards with mirror on its doors. The

Original 12 members or their offsprings gathered to celebrate the golden jubilee of 'Shivsmriti'

quality of the materials was so exceptional, that not a single mirror has since been replaced in the last fifty-five years. Another member, Vasant Oak, who worked in the water supply department of the Municipal Corporation (BMC), installed the water connections. Lakshman Ghangrekar, who was in the BMC's estate department, looked after the assessment of the property. Electrician Kashinath Athalye, took on the responsibility of installing the wiring. Since we needed to minimize expenditure, we built latrines with twin entrances from two adjoining flats. Each flat was 'customised', in that the kitchen platform in every flat was built as per the height of the respective housewife. Wire nets were fixed for drying clothes.

We named our housing society 'Shivsmriti'. This may have perhaps been the first of Mumbai's cooperative housing societies that was constructed without involving a builder. The cost of each flat was a mere ₹ 10,000. But all I had was ₹ 1,000. I had to avail of a loan to raise the rest of the required amount.

It was a major challenge and achievement to own a house in the 1960s and by the time I was in my thirties, I was a proud house owner. Our housing society became the talk of the town for quite a while. I realised that with sheer determination and grit, one is able to create virtually anything out of a zero. Good like-minded company helps to expedite the process.

That experience had been a turning point in my life – an eureka moment if you will. It has always proved useful for me, as it helps to remind me that anything is possible if we do not give up. Though I now own a four-room flat in Mumbai, my mind keeps returning to the Shivsmriti flat. It was a dream house that became a tangible reality. My best moments of happiness were experienced in Shivsmriti, rather than in the Raj Bhavan at Lucknow.

Ram Naik's childhood home in the compound of Shri Bhavani Vidyalaya, Atpadi displaying a new name board though the original structure is unchanged

Stable During Instability

After a childhood spent in three different accommodations at Atpadi, in Pune I had to repeatedly shift from one place to another, in six-monthly terms, during my four years there because of the paucity of funds and out of compulsion. I had stayed at six different places in Pune, before shifting into Gadimaa's Panchavati bungalow. Furthermore, I shifted my residence to seven places in Mumbai and three in Delhi. Today, I reside at the Raj Bhavan, Lucknow.

But every shift brought with it a new learning experience and forged new and often long-lasting relationships; all of which have moulded my personality through the years.

In all, I have resided at twenty different places over the past eighty years. Although unstable in terms of shelter, I have remained stable in terms of character – still looking forward and moving ahead.

(March 8, 2015)

❐

Ram Naik, a full timer of Jana Sangh, holding a megaphone in a meeting addressed by Motiram Lahane, with Vasantkumar Pandit, Jhamatmal Wadhvani and Wamanrao Parab

TWISTS AND TURNS IN MY LIFE

Life often takes unexpected turns and the direction one has in mind is completely transposed. My life has witnessed many such twists and turns and every bend has posed a new challenge. I have had to face them all and continue to move ahead. Through it all, my wife Kunda has stood by me through thick and thin. In fact, marrying her also proved to be a major turning point in my life. Though this turn was not unexpected, it is nonetheless true that it has proven to be a boon.

Kunda is the daughter of the late K.N. Dharap, a staunch supporter of the Hindu Mahasabha and a renowned legal eagle. When Swatantryaveer

Vinayak Damodar Savarkar was arrested as an accused in connection with the Mahatma Gandhi assassination case, Dharap was among those who helped Savarkar by offering legal assistance and guidance. Savarkar himself had gone to Dharap's house in Girgaon, Mumbai, after his acquittal. Kunda was Dharap's youngest child. Coming from such a venerated family, her presence filled my abode with joy and satisfaction. She paved the path for my progress and development by her unstinting support and encouragement.

Water Conference (*Pani Parishad*)

I was more involved in the Jana Sangh work than in my family. I had been shouldering fresh responsibilities in the party. Around the time we were settling down in Goregaon, the Socialist Party leader, Mrinal Tai (a way to call 'sisterly figure') Gore launched her agitation by demanding that water supply be given to the people. Banners appealing to people to join this novel move were put up all around. Water is of concern to everybody. Therefore, my co-workers in Jana Sangh and I felt that we should set aside our political ideology and join this conference. Our presence astonished the Socialist organisers and Mrinal Tai, since the Jana Sangh and Socialist-Communist ideologies were at loggerheads. However, they welcomed our involvement as it would strengthen the agitation. I was appointed as the treasurer of the Water Conference, which projected Mrinal Tai as a crusader at the national level, for which she became famously known as 'Paniwali Bai'. The strategy for uniting and involving all towards a common cause and objective was inculcated in me due to the experience I gained at the Water Conference.

Jana Sangh Full-Timer

The RSS and the Jana Sangh had adopted the practice of enlisting aspiring young men, based on their performance, to work full-time for the organisation. If selected, the financial requirements of their households were taken care of, to some extent by the organisation. In 1968, I was asked to work for the Jana Sangh on a full-time basis. In a way, this was an acknowledgement of my performance. An additional factor was my keen interest in social work. While I was eager to convey my acceptance, I was equally concerned about the turn my life would take if I took this step. I was the only earning member of my family, which included my mother, wife and two small daughters. Kunda's support was expressed in these practical words of wisdom; she said: "Anyway, you are rarely at home. If you give up your job and take up the party work, we might have your company, even if for a brief while." But her support came with a rider. She said, "Politics is full of uncertainties. We have two daughters and even though the party will take partial responsibility of our household, let me earn a living too, so that we could be financially stable." I acquiesced in this condition. She passed her B.Ed. examination within a year and joined as a school teacher in the Mumbai Municipal Corporation. Though I was head of the family, it was Kunda, who unstintingly accepted this burden, providing me with a solid support system and enabling me to continue with my social activism.

I worked full-time for the party for six years and decided to take up a job once again after this interlude. I was offered the post of manager in one of the firms run by the successful industrialist, Jhamatmal Wadhvani, the then president of the Mumbai Jana Sangh. Convinced that I could juggle my time and efforts between the organisation and the job assignment, I joined the firm.

Black Days of Emergency

At the time, the Jana Sangh's electoral symbol was an earthen lamp, also known as 'Deepak'. A strong chain of workers had developed over the years through their commitment to make the party known to every family throughout Mumbai. Dr. Vasantkumar Pandit, Jamatmal Wadhvani, Ved Prakash Goyal, who later became a Union Minister, Prof. Balasaheb Kanitkar, Wamanrao Parab, Babanrao Kulkarni, Nanubhai Patel, Jayawantiben Mehta and Malatibai Naravane were some of the shining stars of the party. All of us had been working together in united coordination.

Prime Minister, Indira Gandhi was the most dominant political leader at the time. She imposed the internal emergency on the night of June 25, 1975. Detention of workers of various anti-Congress political parties and social organisations was rampant. Workers of the Jana Sangh in Mumbai too were under scrutiny. The veterans to whom I looked to as guides were jailed. Just two of us, Babanrao Kulkarni and I, had not been arrested. It is common knowledge that workers of various opposition parties had suffered during those dark days and all those who opposed the emergency shared similar circumstances.

Babanrao and I had been given the task of keeping in touch with family members of the jailed Jana Sangh workers, as well as with other opposition parties, with a view to organising an anti-Emergency agitation in Mumbai. During this period, our friendship was cemented. One afternoon, we drafted two statements against the Emergency. Babanrao was assigned the task of getting the drafts and some other material secretly printed the next day. After tying up all ends, we bade each other goodbye at Dadar railway station. I rode my scooter to Goregaon, while Babanrao took a suburban train for Mulund in the eastern suburbs of Mumbai. I had barely stepped inside my home when I received a telephone call informing me that Babanrao had suffered a heart attack in the train. Fellow commuters rushed him to hospital, but it was too late – he did not survive. It was such a sudden shock!

While trying to assimilate the distressing news of Babanrao's sudden demise, I realised he had been carrying the anti-Emergency drafts with him, besides some other papers that contained the name of the printing press and other confidential material in a briefcase. I was perturbed by the possible future scenario. Since he had died in a train, the involvement of the police was inevitable. Should the police seize this cache, our agitation against the Emergency would receive a major set-back.

Trying to control my emotions, I called Babanrao's neighbour, Sharad Chavan, who was then a news-reader with All India Radio. I quickly apprised him of the situation and urged him to try to spirit away the bag. Though a government employee, Chavan decided to take this risk. He promptly bought an identical looking bag, rushed to the hospital and adroitly exchanged them unnoticed by anyone. The anti-Emergency fight had trained us to keep the nation's interest above all, even grief of the demise of a close friend and associate.

Life-threatening Accident

The Emergency almost cost me my life. General

elections were declared after the Emergency was lifted. Various political parties had been fighting the Emergency and in early 1977, decided to team up and fight general elections. We defeated Smt. Indira Gandhi and a coalition government was formed. Later, all these parties decided to come under one banner – the Janata Party. Before the Janata Party was formally recognised, the last meeting of the Mumbai Jana Sangh was held at Lonavala, a pristine hill station between Mumbai and Pune. Following the meeting, I was returning to Mumbai in an old jeep, along with some colleagues, while seated next to the driver. We stopped briefly at Panvel to buy watermelons. On resuming the journey, Advocate Chandrabali Singh, who was President of the North Mumbai Jana Sangh, switched places with me, so that I could get some fresh air. He took my place next to

Janata Party President Chandrashekhar addressing a meeting in Mumbai organised by Ram Naik and attended by leaders like Pannalal Surana, Kushabhau Thakre, Madhu Dandavate, Babanrao Dhakne, Nanubhai Patel, Pramila Dandavate and Motiram Lahane

the driver, while I occupied his seat at the front window. But, even before we had travelled a couple of kilometres ahead, a lorry coming at us from the wrong side of the road, caused our jeep to overturn, as our driver tried to avoid the impending collision. Chandrabali died on the spot. He had taken my seat as if to invite death and save me!

My spinal cord was badly injured and I was hospitalised at the Lokmanya Tilak Municipal Hospital in Sion for over a month and a half. My neck was set in traction and I was suffering excruciating pain. But, in every cloud, there is a silver lining. For during my convalescence, I realised that there were many people who cared for my well-being. They had come to know of me through my social work. I was barely in my early forties and hardly a veteran, nor was I so well-known either. Still, my visitors included such esteemed personalities like the RSS Chief, Balasaheb Deoras and Union Health Minister, Raj Narain, who had just defeated Indira Gandhi in the Lok Sabha election. Whenever such VIPs were slated to visit, the hospital was always in apple pie order. Relatives of fellow patients revelled in these visits and would jocularly remark, "Let more such visitors come to meet you!"

Shrikant Sarade, a middle-class Bharatiya Mazdoor Sangh worker, came every night after his day job to attend to me. Ved Prakash Goyal, Balasaheb Ghalsasi and other colleagues would send food every morning and evening. They had extended a helping hand, so that my wife would be spared the trouble of cooking and carrying food for me, as the hospital was almost twenty kilometers away from our residence. This accident brought home to me the fact that I had acquired quite an extended family due to my social work and I was enthused to work more.

A huge gathering of women commuters at launching of 'Ladies Special' suburban train by Minister of State for Railways Ram Naik in Mumbai

After being discharged from hospital, I was strapped with a heavy collar covering my body from neck to chest. Thus decorated, I went about my daily tasks.

Contestant for Election

Around that time, elections to the Maharashtra Legislative Assembly were announced. I had already been elected President of the Mumbai Janata Party unit. Prior to that, I was the Organising Secretary of the Mumbai Jana Sangh. There was an unwritten convention in the Jana Sangh that its Organising Secretaries did not contest elections. So, when we began our preparations for the elections, it did not occur to me that I should be contesting. But the opinion of the local Member of Parliament (MP) was taken into consideration while distributing seats on a Party basis. Mrinal Tai was the MP of our area in North Mumbai, which covered the long belt between Goregaon and Palghar in the districts of Mumbai and Thane and she offered the Borivali assembly seat to the erstwhile Jana Sangh faction of the Janata Party.

Vasantrao Bhagwat, who was the Maharashtra Jana Sangh Organising Secretary, suggested that I contest from Borivali. This suggestion came most unexpectedly. One reason being that I had been working as Organising Secretary for the Jana Sangh and was not mentally prepared to enter the fray. The other, was that I had been asked to contest from Borivali and not from my residential locality, Goregaon, which had been a bastion of the Socialist Party for decades. We all had immense faith in Bhagwat's political sagacity. But even so, my wife too was apprehensive of this new development. Eventually, I decided to contest. This was a different phase of my life and it proved to be very significant. It was this election that shot me into the limelight.

When one witnesses the ruthless competition for securing party nominations these days, one can't help feeling that those were truly different times. For me, the first opportunity to contest the 1989 Parliamentary elections also came my way without asking for it. In the assembly, Prof. Ram Kapse and I had earned the enviable reputation of being the studious and sincere members of the House. We were referred to as 'the two Ramas of the BJP'. I had been elected to the Assembly thrice in a row in 1978, 1980 and 1985, and had made ample preparation for the 1990 Assembly election, which was due shortly.

Life of a Parliamentarian

Meanwhile, elections to the Lok Sabha were declared in the year 1989. In most places, the Janata Party and the newly-born Bharatiya Janata Party (BJP) had finalised an electoral understanding by deciding which seat each Party would contest, for which the other Party wouldn't field a candidate.

But this didn't happen in Maharashtra. Hence the BJP was forced to contest separately. The Industrialist, Shri Virendra Shah was almost finalised as our candidate for the North Mumbai Lok Sabha seat. However, he decided at the eleventh hour that he would not contest. For the Janata Party, the candidate Mrinal Tai Gore was a certainty. She had played a major role in ousting the Jana Sangh from the Janata Party, which was formed by merging four parties: the Jana Sangh, the Socialist Party, the Congress (O) and the Bharatiya Lok Dal. Given her image, the BJP needed a candidate who would be able to challenge her on an equal footing.

I was the MLA from the Borivali Assembly constituency, which was the largest in terms of the number of voters in the North Mumbai Lok Sabha constituency. Therefore, the rank and file felt that I was the suitable candidate, equipped to undertake this daunting task and give her a tough fight. On the other hand, due to the colossal image that preceded her, there was a school of thought at the national level that the BJP should not contest against her.

On my part, I was quite content working at the state level in Mumbai and in the Assembly and was therefore rather reluctant to contest the Lok Sabha election. Once again, Vasantrao Bhagwat, the BJP State Organising Secretary, exercised his powers of persuasion on me and for a change, Kunda remarked, "If you go to Delhi, you will be away for six months in a year, but in the Lok Sabha, you will be able to work much more. Go ahead!"

The contest between Mrinal Tai and me made headlines for I won the election with a margin of over a hundred thousand votes!

This was yet another turn that catapulted me to another milestone in my life. This victory gained me the reputation amongst the voters as being an alert MP. It was due to my initiative that the two Houses of Parliament began singing 'Vande Mataram' at each session, 'Bombay' was renamed 'Mumbai' and the government sanctioned the MP Local Area Development Scheme, popularly known as 'MP Fund'. These initiatives made me a household name nationwide.

Ministership

In 1998, I was elected to the Lok Sabha for the fourth consecutive term when Shri Atal Bihari Vajpayee took over as the Prime Minister. Everybody was confident that I would get a berth in his Council of Ministers. Though that did happen, I was accommodated as a Minister of State and not as a Cabinet Minister. There were strong reactions in the media and also among the general public that such an experienced, dedicated worker and an effective MP was made a junior minister. However, I was aware that Atal jee was walking a tight rope while forming a coalition government. Therefore, I accepted this assignment without expressing any displeasure.

Atal jee appointed me as a Minister of State for Railways, taking into account my association with that subject. Moreover, I was also made Minister of State for Parliamentary Affairs, Planning and Programme Implementation. After some time, the Home Ministry too was added to my portfolio and responsibilities as Minister of State.

When Railway Minister, Nitish Kumar resigned abruptly following a rail mishap, Atal jee entrusted independent charge of the Railway Ministry to me. Notwithstanding the fact that I had worked as an Opposition member over the past twenty years, I handled the responsibility as a Minister satisfactorily, bringing to light the fact that even a Minister of State could do much, against the general perception that such a Minister is often made to 'accommodate' politically, without being given serious responsibilities.

Within a year, the nation faced a mid-term Parliamentary election in 1999 and Atal jee returned as Prime Minister. In acknowledgement of my performance as Minister of State, he appointed me Cabinet Minister and entrusted me with a major portfolio, Petroleum and Natural Gas. This was a delicate and highly inflammable responsibility, since it concerned millions of families across the nation. I had some superficial knowledge of the petroleum and natural gas sector and was aware that diesel was cheaper than petrol, that there was a shortage of cooking gas and that adulteration in petrol and diesel was rampant. However, years of sincere and consistent performance in handling any assignment given to me, proved useful in this Ministry.

Changing the landscape in this sector became my goal. I ended the long wait that consumers faced for cooking gas all over the country and initiated the use of ethanol in petrol. I invested abroad for our oil production. Exploring off-shore gas was another major achievement which proved successful. The petroleum sector was truly revolutionised under my watch.

Unexpected Defeats

'Ram Naik' had become a brand name on the basis of

my performance. Piped gas supply in millions of kitchens in Mumbai had been my initiative. Vehicles were now running on CNG. In light of these achievements, no one, especially I, foresaw an electoral defeat in 2004 by cine star Govinda.

This was one of those unexpected curved balls life throws at us and it was an awkward turn in my career. But, I remained true and judicious to my political and social work, continuing to move ahead with an upbeat and positive attitude in the face of this unexpected setback.

I was defeated again in 2009, but continued unabated in my work as before. The reason for this grit and determination was my vow, "I may have lost an election, but not my fortitude."

All the same, as the next general elections approached, I felt that I had enough. It was time to let someone else avail of the opportunity to contest. So, in 2013, convinced that one can work just as well outside the electoral sphere as in, I announced my retirement from electoral politics on September 25, 2013 – the birth anniversary of Deen Dayal Upadhyaya, towering Jana Sangh leader. This unexpected declaration did not go down well with my colleagues and well-wishers. Although it was evident that the 2014 elections would turn out in favour of the BJP, I remained steadfast in my decision.

I knew I could utilise my time appropriately in the capacity of offering advice if sought, or as mediator between people and government. But once again, my life took yet another unexpected turn – I am now Governor of the largest state in India – Uttar Pradesh.

Let's see where this turn leads to...

(March 22, 2015)

❐

Ram Naik being administered oath of office as Governor of UP by Chief Justice Hon'ble Dhananjay Chandrachud of Allahabad High Court

लाइट हाउस

Ram Naik a ray of hope for Leprosy-Affected Women

EMPOWERING LEPROSY AFFECTED PERSONS

Bharatiya Janata Party's leader late Rambhau Mhalgi, who was considered a model representative of the people, would often say, "A model public representative is one who represents those who have voted for him, against him, those who did not exercise their franchise and those who are yet to become voters." These words are etched in my mind.

As mentioned earlier, I was elected from the Borivali Assembly Constituency in 1978, winning with a large margin, securing more than seventy percent of the votes in most polling booths. The principal reason for this win was the pro-Janata Party wave after the Emergency.

However, there were two exceptions. While I had received just two votes in one such booth, the other booth had also recorded only three votes for me. When I looked into the details of this discrepancy, it appeared that the first booth had the leprosy-affected persons (LAPs) registered as voters. The second booth was in the Gorai-Manori villages, which were across the creek from Borivali. These villages had no contact with Borivali and the voters were mostly Christians and the fishermen community known as Kolis. I vowed to change this scenario by liaising with them.

The reason why the LAPs did not vote in my favour was most unexpected and it completely threw me off guard. Most of them were involved in distilling illicit liquor, for want of proper employment. I am a teetotaler and moreover belong to the RSS, who shun alcohol. My opponents had spread the rumour that, if elected, I would shut down their distilling activity.

Most people avoid any contact with LAPs, due to age-old misconceptions. Even accepting a glass of water from them was unthinkable. Interestingly enough, the illicit brew they distilled was not taboo and consumed by others without hesitation. Still, nobody would offer them any employment. The only viable option left open to them was to beg, or dabble in the manufacture of distilled illicit liquor.

I witnessed this sad reality first-hand and decided to concentrate my efforts in their economic rehabilitation. It is my belief that LAPs too have a right to live with dignity and that they should be empowered to exercise it effectively.

Their colony was on the banks of the Dahisar river in the Borivali constituency. The very next year after my election, there was a huge flooding of the river. Two residents of the colony were washed away and all the belongings in about twenty hutment units were annihilated. I was heart-broken at this disastrous spectacle and it only renewed my conviction to work towards their rehabilitation. And through my work to improve their lot, I managed to convey my concern for them. I can legitimately state this after staying on course for over thirty-five years now.

Until that time, there were barely any political leaders or workers who visited their colony. My visit at my own initiative proved to be an asset and a strong foundation for my future work. Within no time, we had built an emotional bond. Gradually, I constructed drainage, pathways and latrines and drilled tube wells in the colony. I approached the government to declare it a 'notified slum', so that some facilities from the government's social budget could be given towards it. Even then, the need to empower them economically had not been fulfilled and I persisted with my efforts to include them in the social mainstream.

Vasantdada, Myself and LAPs

LAPs, who are disfigured due to their affliction, or are otherwise rendered physically challenged, are not accepted by the society, or given any chance for gainful employment. Their only means of survival are the meagre financial sop doled out by the government as an alternative to begging. When the government launched the Sanjay Gandhi Niradhar Yojana (scheme for the derelict), the LAPs began receiving a grant of ₹ 60 (about a US dollar) per month from the scheme. But within a few days, this grant was terminated by the Tehsildar (local revenue official). I decided to call on the Chief Minister of Maharashtra, Vasantdada Patil to appeal to him to redress this injustice.

Ram Naik introducing leprosy affected persons of Mumbai to Maharashtra Chief Minister Vasantdada Patil at Mantralaya, the State Government headquarters

An appointment was fixed at Mantralaya, the headquarters of the Maharashtra government. However, the delegation of the LAPs was prohibited from entering the elevator that took us up to the Chief Minister's office. I was told by the security personnel that I was to go up alone but not the delegation of LAPs. Expectedly, the delegation felt hurt and dejected. Enraged at this blatant rebuff, I took a firm stand stating that if they were not allowed up with me, I was not going up either. This led to an aggravating state of stalemate. Vasantdada Patil knew me and my stance on punctuality. At the appointed time for our meeting, his secretary asked the authorities why I had not arrived. When he learnt of the situation, he briefed the Chief Minister about it, since it was beyond his purview to intervene. Vasantdada, though a Congress party Chief Minister, was familiar with the pulse of the people. Though I was in an Opposition party, he forthwith ordered that the authorities allow the delegation accompany me to the scheduled meeting. This created quite a stir and some chaos ensued, since such a situation had never arisen before. The delegation led by me, was ushered into the Chief Minister's cabin. This was the

Ram Naik presenting a memorandum to President Smt. Pratibha Patil at the Rashtrapati Bhavan, New Delhi, to seek empowerment of leprosy affected persons, accompanied by (L-R) Venugopal of Kasturba Graam Kushth Ashram, Dr Sharatchandra Gokhale President of International Leprosy Union (ILU), Padmashree Awardee Dr P.K.Gopal, Uday Thakar of Hind Kushth Nivaran Sangh and Ram Belavadi of ILU

first time that any LAP had entered this seat of power. This was the maiden step in my political career towards gaining social acceptability, even for deprived sections.

The residents of Sanjay Nagar, the colony of LAPs, were overwhelmed with this development. Later, this was to become a routine affair. Many more organisations for the welfare of LAPs from across the state began to approach me through these residents. It was now part and parcel of my informal portfolio and responsibility to accompany LAPs to the authorities. They regarded it as their matter of right to contact me. These continued interactions which gradually exposed the problems they faced, caused me to appreciate their dire predicament and permanently cemented the emotional bond between us.

Petition to Rajya Sabha

The World Health Organisation (WHO) has statistically established that leprosy is not a communicable disease and moreover, visible leprosy is not spread through physical contact. Nonetheless, even in the 21st century, it is a tragic reality that society at large views leprosy as some kind of curse or aberration. Efforts to empower LAPs for full and permanent rehabilitation are needed on a vast scale. In fact, though such efforts are being made at the global level, they are a more pressing need for a country like India. Several voluntary organisations and activists have been working in this direction and I was invited for one such event – a Conference of LAPs in Maharashtra.

I suggested that we approach the Parliament with our grievances, demanding the empowerment of LAPs, so that they have a free and fair opportunity to be able to lead a dignified life. As part of this suggestion, I submitted that we should approach the Petition Committee of the Parliament, which was welcomed by all participants. Most people are unaware of this Parliamentary device: Petition to

Ram Naik and Rajya Sabha MP Ved Prakash Goyal with delegation of Leprosy Affected Persons after handing over a petition to Vice President and Chairman Rajya Sabha M. Hamid Ansari at Parliament House

Parliament. It is seldom used and, therefore, the procedure for drafting such a petition remains relatively obscure.

Prominent participants in the conference included Dr. Sharadchandra Gokhale, President of the International Leprosy Union with its headquarters in Pune, Dr. P.K. Gopal of 'Idea India' from Tamil Nadu, Shri Uday Thakar of Panvel, Maharashtra-based Hindu Kushtha Nivaran Sangh (Organisation of Leprosy Eradication) and Shri Bhimrao Madhale of the Maharashtra Kushtha Sanghatana (Leprosy Organisation), which operated from Borivali. All had indepth knowledge of this subject and had acquired vast experience over the years. During my interactions with them, I was privy to some shocking facts. For instance, leprosy was considered a communicable disease and the spouse of a leprosy patient was entitled to a divorce. Though the situation has changed medically, some necessary amendments to the law are still pending. After much deliberation, we concluded that seventeen major laws required amendment, if there was going to be any future hope for the empowerment of the LAPs. Incorporating these proposals and certain other important demands, we drafted the Petition to Parliament (Rajya Sabha).

Although I was not an MP any longer, I was familiar with the procedure in the Parliament. Through my senior colleague and Rajya Sabha member, Shri Ved Prakash Goyal, we presented our Petition to the Rajya Sabha Chairman, Shri M. Hamid Ansari on December 5, 2007. The Petition Committee of the Rajya Sabha visited various colonies of LAPs across the nation, consulted various Central and State authorities and also held discussions with us.

Based on this study, the Committee tabled their report in the Rajya Sabha on October 24, 2008. Subsequently, the government submitted its response and an Action Taken Report was presented to the Rajya Sabha on November 22, 2010. Following this, we launched efforts to prevail upon the Central and State governments for its implementation. Prime Minister, Dr. Manmohan Singh did not grant us time to meet with him, though we sent him four letters of request for the same. In the absence of any response from him, we called twice on President, Smt. Pratibha Patil. She directed the government to meet us, but the Singh government ignored her too. Now that Shri Narendra Modi is Prime Minister and since the matter has been discussed with him twice, on July 9, 2014 and on February 10, 2015, a ray of hope is emerging that soon some proactive decision will be taken.

International Leprosy Union

After taking up the cudgels for LAPs, I came across many veterans involved in this work. I am basically a political activist. Therefore, my initial concern was limited to redressing the grievances of colonies of LAPs in the constituency, or occasionally taking up the demands of their organisation. But I found that there was much more that needs to be addressed in this situation and the horizon of this work kept expanding with these interactions.

Unexpectedly, I received a request from Dr. S.D. Gokhale, aged eighty-eight at the time. He was the Founder-President of the International Leprosy Union and former editor of 'Kesari', a Marathi daily founded by Lokmanya Tilak in Pune. Dr. Gokhale was a man of large stature and such a workaholic that few could surmise his real age. He was looking out for an able successor, so that his advanced years would not impede the working of the Union. He urged me to take up the responsibility, assuring me that he would be available for consultation whenever required. His argument that it would be in the interest of the Union to hand over the responsibility to someone capable moved me and won me over. Of course, this was an honour for me. It proved beyond a shadow of doubt that Dr. Gokhale was intrinsically involved in this work for the LAPs and his concern that it should continue uninterrupted only endorsed that fact. His work ethics and forward-thinking vision are a model for every social activist. As for me, I was completely overwhelmed that a political worker like me was considered suitable for an assignment that needed deep compassion and a selfless attitude. That a scholar and sage like Dr. Gokhale considered me a candidate with those attributes, worthy to carry the baton after him, only strengthened my resolve to do my best for the LAPs. It was a moment of pride for me.

(From L to R) Justice (Retd.) Chandrashekhar Dharmadhikari, Vice President M. Hamid Ansari and Ram Naik with women leprosy workers in award function at Pune, Maharashtra.

Sadly, he died within a month of my acceptance. It seemed as if he was waiting for someone he could rely on to continue the mission that he held close to his heart. Having taken up this new responsibility, I decided to go full steam ahead for the LAPs in India and I held this post for almost two years.

The country has around seven hundred such colonies. There are some dedicated women who live in these colonies and work for the inhabitants. As President of the Union, I selected ten such women from across the country and invited Vice President, Shri M. Hamid Ansari to felicitate them in Pune, on April 10, 2013. Their selfless work needs recognition and may encourage others to do the same. Presently, I am continuing to work towards persuading the Central government to formulate a policy for the empowerment of LAPs.

After taking the oath as Governor of the state of Uttar Pradesh, I resigned as President of the International Leprosy Union, since my constitutional position stipulates that I should not hold any other post. My successor in the Union is Dr. Vikas Amte, the son of legendary activist Baba Amte, who spent his life uplifting the LAPs. I am assured that Dr. Vikas will take the baton forward with equal fervour.

LAPs in Uttar Pradesh

After I took over as the Governor, a large number of people began calling on me. They included many North Indians settled in Mumbai or Delhi, or those who had come in contact with me during my stint in the Railway or Petroleum Ministries. However, it was a pleasant surprise when I was felicitated by the organisations of leprosy patients in Uttar Pradesh. I discovered at this interaction, that the recommendations made by the Petition Committee of the Rajya Sabha were yet to be implemented in Uttar Pradesh. I felt that in the event the State government needed more time for implementing the many recommendations for the LAPs, the financial grant to them be enhanced in the interim. I discussed this matter with the Chief Minister of Uttar Pradesh. Accordingly, Chief Minister, Shri Akhilesh Yadav announced on the occasion of the World Leprosy Eradication Day on January 30, 2015 that the grant be increased to ₹ 2,500 per month for each such individual. This announcement was received with much satisfaction by myself and the LAPs.

Ram Naik welcoming leprosy affected persons at the Raj Bhavan, Lucknow

On our nation's Independence Day on August 15, it is customary for a Governor to invite people from various walks of life for an 'At Home' at the Raj Bhavan. Last year, I invited office-bearers of the organisations of LAPs. While this precedent raised many an eyebrow, there were many more who welcomed this initiative.

Bond with Maharashtra

Figuratively, my umbilical cord is attached to Maharashtra. I have been in contact with the government of Maharashtra with regard to various problems faced by the LAPs. Some have been resolved, while there are still others awaiting concrete steps by the government. The Kalyan-Dombivali Municipal Corporation pays a subsistence allowance of ₹ 2,500 per month to the LAPs within its jurisdiction. The amount is ₹ 1,500 for the Pimpri-Chinchwad Municipal Corporation, whereas ₹ 1,000 is paid by the Municipal Corporations of Pune and Mumbai. I am aware that as the Governor of Uttar Pradesh, it would not be in accordance with the norms for me to interact with the Maharashtra government due to constitutional constraints. Notwithstanding this, I met the Maharashtra Chief Minister, Shri Devendra Fadnavis on March 8, 2015 while in Mumbai. I broached the subject and conveyed to him my sentiment that matters which could not be finalised over the last few years now needed an urgent solution. The priority, of course, was the empowerment of LAPs.

During one's lifetime, one pursues many causes, but there may be a certain cause which one is happy to take up, whether it concludes with the desired outcome, or otherwise. In my case, I have derived this satisfaction from the efforts I have been making for LAPs over the years. It is often said that a politician automatically counts the votes some tasks generate, even when he undertakes it without any such allurement. Thinking in this manner is perhaps a reflex action for most politicians. But it needs to be understood that the number of LAPs in the Borivali Assembly constituency which I represented thrice and later for five times in Mumbai North Parliamentary Constituency is barely over a thousand; yet their cause remains uppermost in my mind.

Whereas I received just two votes from the colony of LAPs in 1978, I can proudly state that I am now attached to all LAPs across India and this has become a lifelong bond that goes beyond politics.

(April 5, 2015)

❐

Leprosy affected women felicitating Ram Naik in a function organised by Dyneshwar Kushta Seva Samiti, Indore, Madhya Pradesh

Ram Naik inaugurating a luggage compartment reserved for women in Mumbai suburban train amidst a group of overjoyed fisherwomen

THE FISHERMEN'S FRIEND

I completed my eighty-first year this April 16, 2015, according to the Gregorian calendar. It falls on 21st April, i.e. Akshayya Tritiya as per the Hindu calender. This birthday would have special significance and treated as 'Sahasra Chandra Darshan' as person witnesses 1,000 full moons till this birthday.

I love celebrating my birthday over a leisurely meal with my family. There is no time or place for banners, hoardings, newspaper advertisements, or felicitations in my public life. I celebrated this special birthday in similar fashion at Lucknow, though I missed one item on the menu; the pomfret of Satpati.

Satpati is a fishing hamlet on India's western coastline and a voters' pocket loyal to me. Every year on my birthday, I would receive a basket of pomfret from the fishermen of Satpati. Although this could not be sent to me in 2015 at Lucknow, I received their greetings and was very content with their sincere messages. The fishermen's leader, Rajendra Meher remarks affectionately, "You must have been born at Satpati in your earlier life."

Building the Bond

My intimate relationship with the fishermen's community is such that it will be hard for the new generation to believe that at my first election in 1978, I secured just three votes from Manori, the fishermen community village across the Borivali-Marve creek. But the picture has undergone a complete transformation over the years. Even when defeated in the Lok Sabha elections twice, the fishermen had voted for me en bloc and I am reminded how I had taken the first step to bond with this community.

I ferried to Manori and Gorai, the two tiny villages across the creek, after the 1978 victory. I realised that the journey was not safe. The only means of transport was a small watercraft, which was packed with passengers travelling in both directions at all times. Getting to Borivali or Malad from the two villages was quite hazardous for college students, the working class and fisherwomen, who were compelled to ride the craft cruising on diesel, or occasionally on kerosene. Security precautions were unheard of. Although within the Mumbai Municipal Corporation limits, these villages lacked most basic amenities, such as drinking water and school buildings. The villagers had to depend on old wells, where as even slum dwellers in Mumbai were provided with water taps. The villages had just a few wells and potable water was scarce, since the villages were adjoining the creek. Moreover, the problem was aggravated as the villages had a mixed population of Hindus and Christians and the escalation of tense situations was frequent. I happened to visit Manori in a bid to assuage the feelings of both sides when one such dispute broke out.

The local priest, Father D'Souza, invited the villagers to meet me to discuss their problems without any inhibitions. Eventually the relationship developed in such a manner, that the villagers began to contact me as and when needed, even arriving at my doorstep at times. I got tube wells drilled at Gorai and Manori and extended my assistance in constructing a school building.

Water Transport by BEST

The Brihanmumbai Electric Supply and Transport (BEST) Undertaking is famous for ferrying millions of commuters day in and day out throughout Mumbai. However, the Manori-Gorai belt was deprived of any such transport facility due to the creek that lay in between. I felt it incumbent upon me to help resolve this dilemma, formulating a plan to end the dangerous passage across this creek. I argued that as the BEST undertaking was obliged to provide transport facilities to the people of Mumbai, it was also obligated to operate a safe water transport facility for these residents too. Although the idea was out of the box, the logic was unassailable. After persistent follow-up, BEST began operating a launch service. It was a relief to know that the villagers were provided a safe and reliable transport facility and were no longer in danger

Ram Naik inaugurating a water supply through sub-sea pipeline at Manori-Gorai amidst local fisherwomen who greeted him gleefully

while crossing the creek. This service has now become a part of their daily life.

Although I achieved this success, my efforts for arranging a supply of piped drinking water for them were proving futile. Considering the small population, the Mumbai Municipal Corporation's budget would not permit installing a pipeline across the creek to carry water to Manori and Gorai. Municipal Commissioner, Shri Sadashiv Tinaikar refused point blank to do so. During this clash of opinions, I met fishermen's leader Shri Bhai Bandarkar, who belonged to the Peasants and Workers Party (PWP) – the BJP's staunch opponent. Laying aside our ideological and political differences, we worked in close tandem to achieve this basic necessity for the welfare of the fishermen.

Piped Drinking Water Reaches Manori and Gorai

I began my first term as an MP in 1989 and became a Union minister a decade later. Still, Manori and Gorai were nowhere close to receiving a supply of piped drinking water. By this time, the estimated expenditure for installing a pipeline had exceeded ₹ 4 crore (40 million). The proposition for the project seemed to be receding, becoming more unfeasible. The Petroleum Ministry had witnessed my predecessors using their influence to get a lot of their personal work done during their reign in office.

When I took office in 1999, my first visit was to the Bombay High off-shore oilfield, about 300 kms. off the coast of Mumbai. From my vantage point in the helicopter, I could see huge pipelines carrying crude oil and natural gas to the urban storage outside Mumbai. Returning to Mumbai, I spotted the tiny villages of Marve and Manori from the air. My mind was once more in high gear. 'If oil and gas can be transported across such great distances, why should it be difficult to carry water just a short distance of three kilometers to Marve-Manori in an underwater pipeline?' I thought to myself.

I discussed this possibility with the Indian Oil Corporation, which was under my charge. IOC Chairman, Dr. Pathan informed me that it was a viable project and could be achieved. Public-sector oil companies shoulder many projects under their corporate social responsibility (CSR) initiative. I suggested that IOC should install an underwater pipeline for supplying drinking water to the two villages. In a short while, Dr. Pathan executed the job in a time-bound manner. This was a victorious milestone in the history of water management in Mumbai. Shri Bhai Bandarkar attended this programme despite his poor health and advancing age. Addressing the villagers while seated on a chair, he announced, "Ram, you have performed a miracle. You have brought the Ganges to my village. Now I am free to die." I was overwhelmed by this generous accolade.

Diesel Rebate

When I was elected to the Lok Sabha in 1989, I came to know many of the problems faced by fishermen. My Parliamentary constituency had several fishing villages and a substantial population of the Koli community. Most of these fishermen used their small crafts for fishing, with diesel or kerosene as fuel and were therefore hit hard by rising oil prices. Huge foreign trawlers were allowed to enter the fishing sector in India. These foreign trawlers were exempted from the excise duty on diesel, which meant that they were buying diesel at a cheaper rate than the Indian fishermen were. As soon as I was elected, I demanded in the Lok Sabha that Indian fishing crafts also be given the same concession in excise. Finance Minister, Prof. Madhu Dandavate had been then elected to the Lok Sabha from the Konkan region, which is situated along the sea coast. He understood this to be a legitimate request and acquiesced to it. Thereafter, it was announced that a rebate of 35 paise (100 paise make a rupee in India's official currency unit) would be paid for every litre of diesel.

Coincidentally, I became Petroleum Minister a decade later and proposed that the rebate amount be enhanced to

Ram Naik greeting Phillip Mastan, a fisherman of Vasai's Pachu Bandar after his miraculous escape from a raging storm in sea, accompanied by (R-L) Kedarnath Mhatre, Harendra Patil, Smt. Manisha Choudhary and Janardan Loyli.

₹ 1.50 per litre. This was sanctioned by Prime Minister Atal Bihari Vajpayee. In 2004, the Congress Government, led by Dr. Manmohan Singh came to power and his government agreed to increase the refund amount by another three rupees per litre, in view of the increased international price of diesel. However, this announcement had a catch; the rebate was to be made available only to those fishermen who were below the poverty line (BPL) – a cut-off line that is revised by the government from time to time. The fact of the matter was that no fisherman owning a craft could be included in the BPL category. Therefore, in effect, the rebate facility had no impact on their livelihood.

In 1992-93, the government had issued licenses to foreign trawlers for deep-sea fishing. I had raised my voice against this in the Lok Sabha, since the decision was detrimental to the interests of Indian fishermen and on this issue I was supported by several MPs belonging to different political parties. In response to this, the

Ram Naik resuming his crusade for fishermen after his recovery from cancer, accompanied by fishermen's leader Bhai Bandarkar and Communist firebrand leader Smt. Ahilya Ranganekar, Motiram Bhave, Rambhau Patil, etc.

government appointed the 'Murari Committee' – an inquiry committee, and nominated me as one of its members. I toured the country and participated in the Committee's work wholeheartedly. The government accepted some of the recommendations made by the Committee, thereby providing the fishermen with some succour.

About this time in 1994, while the fishermen were agitating for their demands, I had been afflicted with cancer, which rendered me inactive as I was bed-ridden. But, as soon as I had completed my chemotherapy cycles, I declared my intention to resume all my duties and activities. The first public function in which I participated was a march by the fishermen to press their demands. My presence was lauded by Shri Bhai Bandarkar, fishermen's leader, Thomas Kocherry and Communist leader, Ahilya Tai Ranganekar.

Ram Naik being tied with 'rakhis' by fisherwomen who regard him as a brother

Coconut Day

A people's representative is required to attend various public events. In my constituency, the festival of 'Coconut Day' is considered very special. This is the day when fishermen resume their fishing activity after the monsoon hiatus. It is also a day when we celebrate 'Raksha Bandhan' – band of protection. Every lady, young or old, ties this band around the wrist of her brother. If she has no blood brother, she accords this honour to someone she regards as a brother. Given the complexion of my constituency, every year coconut day celebration was for me, invariably in the Vasai-Satpati coastal belt. My wrist and forearm were so liberally adorned with these bands, or *rakhis*, as they are commonly referred to, that there was hardly any place to accept bands from all the Koli womenfolk who were eager to show me their affection with this tradition. It convinced me all the more that I had to do something concrete for these sisters.

Mumbai's suburban trains often witnessed frequent verbal duels between the fisherwomen carrying baskets full of fish that dripped water down the backs of office-goers sharing the compartment with them. The daily overcrowding in the trains made such clashes inevitable, but, both parties were helpless to resolve this immutable situation and a solution was needed urgently!

On studying the problem, I realised that each suburban train had a compartment reserved for carrying luggage in its front and rear carriages. As there were a large number of male commuters carrying heavy loads, it was difficult for fisherwomen to enter such compartments and perforce, they had no option but to enter the ladies' compartment, fish baskets et al. The solution to this predicament involved time management. After becoming Railway Minister, I ordered that the luggage compartments in all suburban trains in the 'Up' direction be reserved for fisherwomen during rush hours, as their travel with their fish baskets was committed to specific hours of the day. This congenial solution was eagerly welcomed by the fisherwomen and office-going women alike, further strengthening my brotherly bond with the fisherwomen.

Tarapur Atomic Power Station (TAPS)

Tarapur is a bustling town on the western coast of Thane (now Palghar) district. It has the country's first atomic power station, which had been set up several decades ago. Due to the new extension of a project producing 1,080 mw electricity, a large number of residents were displaced. They are called project-affected persons or PAPs. After witnessing the difficulties faced by the fishermen's community, I insisted that a separate policy be formulated for the fishermen affected by TAPS. In the case of the fishermen, merely providing alternative housing would not be sufficient. If they were housed at a long distance away from the sea on which their livelihood depended, it would be a major impediment to their daily earnings. I posed this question before the government, but there was no positive response. A writ petition was filed in the Mumbai High Court for their proper rehabilitation in 2004. I intervened in the case, personally arguing in the fishermen's favour for over ten years. But, now as Governor of Uttar Pradesh, I am unable to appear in court myself due to constitutional constraints. I have urged the Prime Minister and the Maharashtra Chief Minister in our one-to-one meetings to facilitate amicable solution. Likewise, I have also requested the Chief Justice of the High Court for speedy disposal of the writ petition.

Ram Naik lifted by fishermen of Arnala to take him to their village

Electricity in Arnala Fort

Vasai tehsil has many fishermen's villages and I developed a special relationship with the fishermen of Arnala fort, which has a chequered history.

The fort did not have a proper jetty and during high tide, the path leading to the fort is knee-deep in water, so that one has to wade through to approach it. I have visited the fort on numerous occasions. The welcome accorded to me by them was unique; as soon as I used to be ready to alight from the boat, the fishermen used to gather around and hoist me onto their shoulders. I embark on land in this royal manner. I cannot find it in myself to refuse this courtesy, as doing so would be seen as spurning their affection. Though the Arnala fort is just a few kilometres away from Mumbai, it had been bereft of electricity for over fifty years after Independence. The reason for this was akin to that of Manori. The power company was not in a position to construct towers in the water to carry electric cables. I used my stint as Petroleum Minister to fulfil this long-awaited convenience for Arnala fort as well. The Oil and Natural Gas Corporation (ONGC) undertook the task of constructing the towers as part of its CSR activity and soon Arnala fort was illuminated.

There had been no procession for me and my wife when we were married. However, for the inauguration of the electrification, the residents of Arnala carried my wife and me in a huge procession, amidst bursts of music and revelry. It moves me even today when I recall these moments.

Diwali in Satpati

The affection shown to me was of quite a different kind

at Satpati, a place famous for its catch of pomfret, a fish native to its waters, which is also exported. Until visiting Satpati, I had never seen such huge pomfrets. They are quite a handful! The dwellings of the fishermen at Satpati were along the coastline like any fishing community. However, the problem faced by them was unprecedented; the coast had been suffering here due to the constant erosion of the sand. This gradual erosion resulted in flooding of homes during high tide. The only possible solution was a breakwater embankment that needed to be constructed to prevent water from entering inland. But, the State Government did not respond to repeated petitions in this regard. I asked Bharat Petroleum and Maritime Board officials to inspect the location for any suggestions to an alternative. Bharat Petroleum spent ₹ 3 crore (30 million) to construct a bund wall, eventually resolving this long standing problem.

When I arrived for the celebrations of the inauguration of the wall, I saw that the front yard of each house had been decorated with a huge rangoli, which is an art form in India, created during all Indian festive occasions. Patterns are created on the floor using materials, such as coloured rice, dry flour, colourful sand or flower petals. Village streets were similarly decorated. I was escorted to the dais under a shower of flowers. After I became the Governor, fishermen's organisations from all around felicitated me at Satpati.

I recall an interesting incident that took place at Satpati: After my first election, I would tour the constituency, stopping for lunch at the home of one of the supporters. Though I dined many a time at Satpati, I found that every meal served to me was strictly vegetarian. After about a year, I remarked to a local office-bearer, "Satpati appears to be tremendously influenced by Pandurang Shastri Athawale. Are all of you strict vegetarians?" Athawale, a spiritual leader, had been spreading the message of non-addiction for several decades and his disciples had a fair share of fishermen. Realising the intent behind my query, one of the villagers replied hesitatingly, "As you are a Brahmin, we presumed that you would not approve if we eat fish in your presence. Therefore, we eat vegetarian food whenever you are here." When I informed them that I enjoyed fish, they were relieved and thereafter there was no dearth of fish delicacies during my tours – a practice that has since continued, though I am more touched by their enthusiasm and affection, rather than by what they serve me as food.

I am unable to fathom the reason for this relationship. I feel that these bonds have transgressed generations to have endured to this day.

Separate Ministry for Fishing

Although fishing is referred to as 'farming on water,' facilities like financing at 4 percent interest, or supply of capital made available to farmers are not extended to fishermen. It is estimated that nearly 1.5 million families are employed daily through fishing. If one compares fishing with agriculture, it is apparent that the contribution of fishing in gross domestic product is quite high; at 5.4 percent, even though the number of persons engaged in fishing is quite small. It is estimated that the annual catch of fish in India is nearly 9.6 million tonnes. In 2014, the value of fish exports was over ₹ 30,000 crore. The fish production in India is higher than in any other country, except for China, and there is yet vast potential to enhance it.

Ram Naik inaugurating 10th conference of the Indian Fisheries & Aquaculture Forum at Lucknow

But, for more than a decade, some major demands of the fishermen are still pending with the government. They include financing at 4 per cent of interest, resumption of rebate on diesel and a Maritime Protection Act. I inaugurated the open session of the Indian Fisheries Aquaculture Forum at Lucknow on November 12, 2014 as Governor of Uttar Pradesh. During the deliberations, one of the resolutions was a demand for a separate ministry for fishing. I pressed this demand on February 10, 2015 when I called on Prime Minister, Shri Narendra Modi. I am hopeful that a positive decision will soon be taken in this regard.

(April 19, 2015)

❐

Ram Naik with Rajasthan High Court Chief Justice Hon'ble Sunil Ambani, Chief Minister Vasundhara Raje and Maharashtra's Minister of State Vidya Thakur after sworn in as Governor of Rajasthan (additional charge)

THREE GENERATIONS OF WOMEN CO-WORKERS

I visited Kashi, also known as Benares or Varanasi, several times after taking over as the Governor of Uttar Pradesh. Kashi is the most sacred city for Hindus, famous for many things, among them the beautiful saris woven in its environs and which are a great attraction for visiting this ancient city. I never brought a sari for my wife Kunda from Kashi and she never did complain either. We have now completed 55 years of our married life. It would not be stretching the truth at all to admit that she has had expectations that I would buy her a sari on my own, but she consoles herself: "I get a sari from you only if you are accompanied on a tour by your women co-workers, whom you call your sisters. Otherwise, I am not lucky enough to get one."

This is a bitter truth and I must confess my failure on this front. But, the women co-workers who accompanied me on tours were aware of my this weakness. They would take money from my wallet and buy a sari for my wife as part of their own shopping. The first-ever sari I bought for her was nearly twenty years after our marriage. Kunda was dumbstruck with this maiden purchase I had made. This was after the conclusion of the winter session of the State Legislature at Nagpur, the second capital of Maharashtra. Nagpur is famous as a hub of textiles, especially handloom production. I pretended that I had selected and bought the sari myself. But twenty years of marriage meant she read me like an open book and knew me only too well! I was as incapable of selecting such an exotic sari, and Kunda knew it too well. I had to finally confess that it had been bought by Smt. Kusum Tai Abhyankar, a famous Marathi author, who had also been elected to the Legislative Assembly in 1978. It was Kusum Tai who had made the purchase without bothering to take my opinion or consent. My wife was so delighted that she called up Kusum Tai in Ratnagiri to thank her. Alas, Kusum Tai is no more. In later years, whenever I took a sari home for Kunda, she would remark, "Oh! It seems Jayawantiben Mehta was with you for the meeting," or "This looks like the choice of Malati Bai Naravane." Both these co-workers were popular as devoted party activists.

In my prolonged socio-political journey, numerous women co-workers have stood by me like a rock. Many have played a significant role in my development. Sumati Bai Suklikar from Nagpur and Prof. Malati Bai Paranjape of Pune were my seniors in the Jana Sangh. They occupy a special place in my heart. Their upright but kind nature was evident from their faces. Easily described as efficient and model housewives, both were fiery speakers and could captivate an audience instantly at party or public meetings. They were equally adept speaking in Marathi and Hindi and stood out due to their middle-class lifestyle. Their contribution in popularising the Jana Sangh's election symbol – the earthen lamp, '*Deepak*' is invaluable. They toured the country, held meetings and led agitations. Even in the present era of social awareness, women activists face so many difficulties while away from home on tours. It can only be imagined how women workers like Sumati Bai and Malati Bai must have managed in those old days, sometimes spending their own money for the party work.

After a late-night meeting, Sumati Bai would retire at a party worker's home, rest for a few hours and would be up and start working in the kitchen even before the housewife had woken up. She always extended a helping hand in domestic chores in the homes she stayed endearing herself to family effortlessly.

Unlike today, the practice of staying in hotels did not exist then and villages did not have any hotels either. I have seen Malati Bai touring long distances and managing on mere morsels of food. I expressed my gratitude towards her leadership a couple of years ago by extending some help in publishing her autobiography after her death. I am grateful that I have had an opportunity to return her unstinting support with some help in this venture.

After the BJP was formed in 1980, I became acquainted with Raj Mata Vijayaraje Scindia, who was a contemporary of Malati Bai. Her simplicity was astonishing. Vijayaraje neither flaunted her royal lineage, nor threw her weight

Raj Mata Vijayaraje Scindia visited an exhibition of paintings of noted artist Vasudeo Kamat at the request of Ram Naik

around. Always clad in snow-white attire and without any ornaments, she would address you in such a soft-spoken, genteel manner, that one could not but respect and admire her. When I was elected to the Lok Sabha, my interactions with her increased.

Many prominent leaders came to enquire about my health when I was afflicted by cancer in 1993. Vijayaraje's visit to my home during this period is memorable. Accompanied only by her trusted aide, Sardar Angre, she took off her footwear before entering my tiny apartment. My daughter, conversant with the Delhi culture, timidly suggested that it would be all right if Raj Mata entered with her footwear on. Vijayaraje laughingly quipped, "I am a Shinde (Marathi version for Scindia). I am aware that the outside footwear is not brought inside home in Maharashtra." She sat on a plastic chair opposite my bed, enquired about my health and advised my wife affectionately how my daily food intake could be enriched. She behaved like a concerned elder sister and not as a royal personage. Her daughter, presently Chief Minister of Rajasthan, Vasundhara Raje Scindia, is

Ram Naik at a conference of cooking gas consumers organised by BJP Womens Front, alongwith (L-R) Shalinitai Kulkarni, Maltibai Naravane, Jaywantiben Mehta and Pushpa Wagle

an accomplished party colleague in her own right, but she treats me respectfully as a co-worker of her mother.

I recall a touching incident about Vasundhara jee; I was appointed by the President as a Governor for Rajasthan for a short while in addition to my duty as UP Governor. My wife was accompanying me on our air journey to Jaipur where I was to take oath as Governor. Vasundhara jee, as a Chief Minister, had come to welcome us at the airport. When she found out that my wife had a problem in walking, she said, "Don't call for a wheelchair, I will support you." This noble gesture touched everyone around.

I received much respect and affection from my women co-workers since they trusted me implicitly and looked up to me as a dependable colleague. In stark contrast, a woman political worker in Mumbai of the present generation recently enquired of me; "Are we making progress in the

Ram Naik along with MLA Dr. Vinita Samant at the inauguration of the first two-storey public toilet constructed through his MLA Fund

true sense? Nowadays, going for a meeting at night is scary. Going unescorted is not advisable; and if a male colleague accompanies us, rumours are likely to abound. We don't know what to do." In earlier days Chirmule Tai of Goregaon would often comment; "When Rambhau accompanies us, there is no worry. He drops us home." On my part, I was not doing anything extraordinary. Still, it is a fact that women know what and whom to avoid due to their natural instinct. All of them regard me as a brother. The value of clean character in public life becomes evident through such incidents. My political career is interspersed with such pleasant memories. When I was an MLA, the husband of a woman MLA had told her, "Choose the room next to Rambhau's in the MLAs' Hostel at Nagpur and I shall not have to worry about you." I am gratified that my character speaks for me in such a glowing manner.

Of course, seasoned women political workers can look after themselves. Their no-nonsense nature, frank attitude and character are so formidable, that male co-workers view them only with reverence. I vividly remember working with such co-workers as Jayawantiben Mehta, Malatai Bai

Ram Naik in a relaxed chat with crusader Mrinal Gore returning to Goregaon in a suburban train after campaigning against each other

Naravane, Pushpa Wagle and Shalini Tai Kulkarni in Mumbai. Their dexterity in caring for hearth and home as well as remaining involved in political work during the 1970s can be easily compared with today's multi-tasking women achievers in the corporate world. I still feel that those co-workers will fare better in comparison.

Besides Jayawantiben and Kusum Tai, I frequently remember two women MLAs who had been elected along with me to the Assembly – Dr Vinita Samant (wife of fiery labour leader Dr. Datta Samant) and Shalini Tai Patil (wife of former Chief Minister Vasantdada Patil). We belonged to rival Parties. I am not very talkative by nature, so our conversations were usually very brief. Shalini Tai was a great admirer of my work ethics and my middle-class lifestyle. It is common knowledge that every election needs fund raising, though some funds arrive without soliciting. Their value is beyond measure for a candidate. For each of my MP elections, Shalini Tai would send ₹ 10,000 as a goodwill gesture. The warm sentiment behind this contribution is priceless.

Dr. Vinita Tai once approached me with a personal request. That was the time Dr. Datta Samant had a stranglehold over Mumbai. Still she called me up and said, "Please do something for me as a brother, but don't tell anybody, least of all Dr. Samant." It was some family matter due to which Datta Samant had severed relations with a very close family member. The son of this person was unable to get admission in a particular school, which was in my constituency. Had Vinita Tai telephoned the school herself, the matter could have been settled immediately. But she was caught in a dilemma – for while she was eager to help the family member, she had to ensure that her husband was not offended and had, therefore, not to know of her intervention in the matter. She trusted me and so had approached me in this delicate matter. In later years, I met Dr. Datta Samant time and again but never disclosed this incident. Though we were in opposing camps, Vinita Tai

Lok Sabha Speaker Sumitra Mahajan at a birthday celebration of Dr Nishigandha, Ram Naik's daughter

would openly say, "Ramubhau is my brother." This remark would perplex the most people present. This is one of the many longstanding relationships built during my political and social career.

Socialist leader Mrinal Tai Gore played a major role in shaping my political and social life. In the Water Conference held in Goregaon, we worked together despite our opposing ideologies. However, except for that occasion, or during the formative days of the Janata Party, we had always worked as opposing political factions. Still, we never transgressed the limits of decorum even while articulating our ideological and political opposition to each other.

In a way, I have been instrumental in Mrinal Tai's retirement from electoral politics. When I became an MP by defeating her in 1989, she declared that she would no longer contest any election. Nonetheless, we held each other in high esteem. On many occasions, we would tear into each other at election rallies and then return together to Goregaon from Vasai in a suburban train, chatting amiably on various subjects. When she got to know about my cancer affliction, she promptly rushed to meet me. Later, she herself was gripped by cancer and would discuss with me issues concerning medical treatment. I wholeheartedly participated in the festivities organised to celebrate her eightieth birthday. Such healthy opposition is becoming a rare commodity in our present political milieu.

Another revered personality from whom I learnt so much was Communist leader Ahilya Tai Ranganekar, who was a Municipal Councilor and later also an MP from Mumbai Central-North.

After my election as an MP, I came in close contact with many women MPs from different states. Senior Communist

MP Geeta Mukherjee always greeted me affectionately despite representing different parties. Mamata Banerjee, the present West Bengal Chief Minister would greet me by asking, "How are you, Dada?" just like a family member would do. My close friend and associate Ram Kapse would remark mischievously, "It is a wonder that all these firebrand women are so friendly with you." In the Lok Sabha, I used to be flanked by Kapse and Pune's MP, Anna Joshi. Both were skilled at cracking jokes at the most unexpected occasions and managing to keep a straight face. Their company made even boring House proceedings quite amusing. We conversed in Marathi so that most other members would not understand what was going on.

But there was an honourable exception and it came from none other than Sumitra Mahajan, present Speaker of the Lok Sabha. She sat in the row behind us and could hear our conversations. Born at Chiplun in Maharashtra, Sumitra Tai once admonished us, "I can't control my laughter when I hear you. But the members sitting near me don't understand Marathi, so they stare at me as I begin giggling all of a sudden, even when the House is discussing some serious matter. So, please stop this funny business, or all of us will be in trouble one day."

Elected consecutively eight times as an MP from Indore in Madhya Pradesh, Smt. Sumitra Tai's bond with Marathi and Maharashtra is intact. Her brother, Arun Sathe, is a prominent BJP worker in Mumbai. This added another dimension to our relationship. We began complementing each other's arguments while participating in the House discussion. This camaraderie proved invaluable when I was the Petroleum Minister and she was appointed my Minister of State. Though discords between a Cabinet Minister and his Minister of State are commonplace in Delhi, Sumitra Tai and I worked together in perfect tandem, without any such discord. During our tenure, the Ministry posted amazing results.

I had been a member of the BJP national executive committee from day one and, thus was in constant touch with a large number of BJP women leaders. Prominent among them were MPs like Sushma Swaraj and Uma Bharti. I recall a nationwide agitation of women organised by the Party in Delhi in 1992-93 against price rise. Hundreds of activists were arrested. They included BJP women workers from Maharashtra. These women were released from detention after 10 pm that night. Most of them were first-time visitors to Delhi. They could not decide where to go at such a late hour, as they had planned to return to Mumbai the same evening after the demonstrations. Seeing their plight, a police officer offered to transport them to any one address of their choice. The women couldn't remember the BJP office location, so they requested the officer to drop them off at my residence. By the time they arrived at my place, it was well past 11 pm. More than a dozen of them were now at my residence and were extremely exhausted, looking forward to some good rest and food. I used to live alone and occasionally my wife or daughter would come to Delhi. In a way, the residence was barely stocked with food. Coincidentally, my daughter Vishakha was in Delhi that day, but my kitchen was not stocked with enough food items for so many. And there was yet another coincidence; veteran BJP leader, Ved Prakash Goyal, who is the father of present Union Energy Minister, Piyush Goyal had also come to stay with me the same night. In spite of the cold winter evening, he took them out for dinner. Somehow, we managed to make sleeping arrangements for the women. Jayawantiben Mehta arrived the next morning. Donning the hat of a homemaker by shedding her leadership one, she got busy in the kitchen, roped in my daughter to help and cooked a hearty lunch for all the women herself. The next evening they were on their way to Maharashtra, with rail tickets we had purchased for them. All these women were glad that they had decided to choose my residence in their hour of need.

I have helped and encouraged several third-generation women workers in the BJP Mumbai unit. In later years, they rose to great heights through sheer hard work and dedication. Shaila Patange-Samant became the first lady full-timer when I was the President of the Mumbai BJP. Dr. Medha Somaiya, wife of BJP MP, Kirit Somaiya, immersed herself in working for the Party and has created her own space. This began during my term. I was quite happy when a large number of women corporators – members of the Mumbai Municipal Corporation – were elected from my Parliamentary constituency.

The initial lot included present Minister of State in Maharashtra, Vidya Thakur, who had also become Mumbai's Deputy Mayor. The list goes on, but let me mention just a few names. Another Deputy Mayor was Shailaja Girkar. Other such achievers include Asawari Patil, Beena Doshi, Sunita Yadav and Ujwala Modak, who are corporators at present; former corporators include Shilpa Mithbaokar, Daksha Patel, Parul Mehta and Suchitra Naik. I am indeed happy to record the sterling performance of Manisha Chowdhary, who was first elected as a corporator and is now an MLA from my North Mumbai area. On their part, these women publicly acknowledge my role in their success.

Some of my women co-workers have established a loving and longstanding friendship with my wife and daughters. I must mention the name of present Governor of Goa, Mridula Sinha among them. She would visit my residence in Delhi to meet Jayawantiben Mehta whenever the latter was in the national capital. An accomplished Hindi writer, Mridula jee never forgot to send my wife some chosen books after learning that my wife Kunda had done her MA in Hindi and Marathi. On one occasion, Mridula jee had come to Mumbai to meet Hema Malini in connection with a Hindi movie. Though I was in Delhi, she came to my house to rest, considering it her own home. This visit of Mridula jee has provided Kunda with own daily a material to taunt me. She remarks, "Mridula jee also is happy with just a ten-minute afternoon nap just as I am...."

New women entrants to politics often approach me for advice. They repose their confidence in me, they candidly share with me their political and domestic problems. Lakhs of women rail commuters in Mumbai also have a special corner in their hearts for me since I started 'Women's Special' suburban train services. This initiative is the first anywhere in the world. I shall write about it later.

(May 3, 2015)

❐

Ram Naik inaugurating a hand-pump drilled from his MP Fund in Vasai tehsil

FOR THE CONVENIENCE OF WOMEN

My wife Kunda and I celebrate fifty-five years of married life today on 17 May, 2015. What my wife has given me need not be discussed at this juncture, nor is it relevant here. However, thanks to my wife's sincere support, I have been able to view womenfolk and their daily difficulties from a different perspective. This has happened without my making any deliberate effort to develop such an insight. As an offshoot of this sensitivity, I have been able to provide relief to women at large, both politically and socially. I can state with humility that many of the things I did for women proved to be path-breaking.

Mumbai chawls (lower and middle class housing complexes) have a unique culture. They prepare you for managing – a distinct symbiosis and one automatically imbibes the virtue of community living in chawls. The initial days of our married life were spent in a chawl. Over the years of our lives together, Kunda had to make many compromises due to my way of life, but she has never complained. However, one of these many adjustments proved quite daunting for her; it was the use of a common toilet in the chawl. Brought up in an affluent family, she found going to the common facility quite embarrassing. Because of her reservations the gravity of this situation dawned on me and I began to understand the problems of women in Mumbai.

Basic Amenities for Women

My pilot project to construct two-storeyed toilets in Mumbai slums was born out of this realisation. I was the first to use the MLA fund to create this basic amenity. The absence and shortage of toilets in the slums had been troubling my mind ever since I realised my wife's discomfort. Both women and men alike had been experiencing this inconvenience.

Given the paucity of space in Mumbai, the idea of constructing two-storeyed toilets seemed to me to be a sensible option in tackling this problem. Those not familiar with slum life in Mumbai will find it impossible to believe, but it is a fact that local women came well dressed, as if for a festival when the first such toilet was to be inaugurated at the Sukarwadi slum in Borivali. It was a very welcome amenity in Mumbai slums.

Another daily household difficulty experienced throughout India is the non-availability of enough water. The brunt of this problem is faced mostly by women, millions of whom are compelled to carry pails and buckets of water for daily domestic requirements. Men generally avoid doing this work for a variety of reasons. As a result, countless women suffer from back problems, having to lift heavy loads.

As a witness to this ordeal, I decided to redress it to the best of my ability. Utilising my MLA and MP funds, I installed tube wells wherever possible in my constituency. Women were spared from this back-breaking work and the practice of storing water. This achievement may appear insignificant for those who may not have experienced such a shortage. I am happy to say that I have earned the blessings of thousands of housewives for providing this basic amenity.

Misery of Working Women

Every wife and mother has to tackle multiple challenges everyday. The enormity of such challenges is quite intimidating in a bustling city like Mumbai. This statement

Ram Naik presenting 'Veer Bala' (Bravery) award to Jaybala Ashar who lost both legs when attackers threw her out of a running Mumbai suburban train

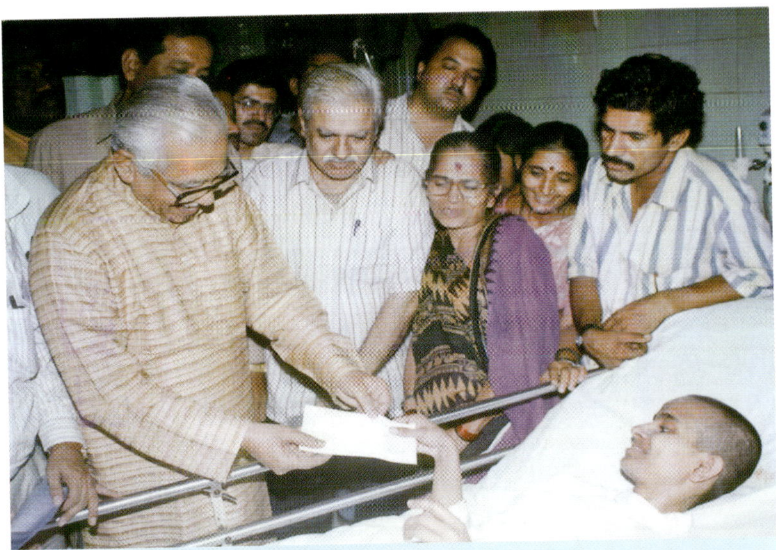

will be fully endorsed by women suburban train commuters in Mumbai, who are compelled to enter overcrowded trains to reach to their offices in time and commute in inhuman conditions for over an hour on the average. Some even hang out of trains due to the overcrowding.

In one such tragic instance, twenty-six women commuters died in a train mishap in Mumbai. This prompted me to press for insurance cover for victims of railway accidents. The genesis of this demand was a tragic accident that happened on the night of October 13, 1993. The reason for the accident was the smoke billowing from the pantograph of a suburban train nearing Borivali station and the panic caused by the fear of a fire. It is commonplace during monsoons that pantographs atop train compartments begin emitting smoke since rainwater comes in contact with the electrical wiring. It was raining heavily that fatal evening and the women returning home saw the clouds of smoke. The pouring rain made it impossible for them to see exactly what was happening, neither could they see the fast approaching train coming from the opposite direction of the adjoining track. Scared and amidst shouts of 'fire, fire', many women jumped out of the train and were instantly crushed beneath the oncoming train. Their death affected me deeply, more so since they were residents of my constituency.

When I visited the victims' families to console, I was faced with another bitter reality that hit me hard. While it is true that no house is a home unless a woman administers it, an additional factor common to these middle-class bereaved families was that the deceased were earning members, too. This sudden tragedy had posed a financial emergency before them. Mere words, nor some token financial assistance, would have been adequate to provide them any succour. The horrible truth dawned on me; like air passengers, no insurance cover was available for train passengers. I raised this issue in the Lok Sabha and very soon this cover was granted to rail passengers as well.

Compassionate Appointments

As a Minister of State for Railways, I remember the case of Jaybala Ashar, a young girl, who lost her legs after she was thrown out of a running train while resisting some pickpocketeers in Mumbai on October 26, 1998. It was evident that the insurance compensation would not reach her in time and in view of the urgency of medical treatment, I arranged for free surgery on her. Jaybala was later felicitated for showing exemplary bravery and presented with a purse for ₹ 50,000. There was another case of a girl called Soni Joseph, who had lost an eye when she was hit by a stone thrown by some miscreant at the train in which she was travelling. I accommodated both these women in the railway service as exceptional cases. In fact, there was no provision for such recruitments in the rulebooks of the railways. I had to face bouquets and brickbats for doing this. I remained silent and did not react to either. But I experience joy and satisfaction when I receive a letter of gratitude from Jaybala on each Diwali. I feel happy that I had succeeded in highlighting the issue of women rail passengers' safety. To crown it all, I inaugurated the first-ever Women's Railway Police Battalion as a Minister of State for Railways.

Encouragement to Breastfeeding

As an MP, I have had another novel feat to my credit.

It may be regarded as an important step for women, but in reality, what I did was in the national interest. It was during the last decade of the past century. Newspapers and magazines were spilling over with baby food advertisements, which were misleading not only illiterate women, but even educated young mothers. These advertisements sought to create an illusion that readymade baby foods provided babies with better nutrition than did mother's milk. To complement that statement, mothers were given to believe that their 'beauty' would remain unaffected if they were to feed babies with such foods, rather than breastfeed them. Such misinformation would very likely affect the health of our new generation.

Around this time, the World Health Organisation (WHO) had begun propagating that breastfeeding for babies was advisable and the entrenched concepts in the West about the alleged unwanted after-effects of breastfeeding were a misconception. Though it had been conclusively established that a baby's immunity is enhanced due to mother's milk and babies are protected from various diseases and infections during and even after they are weaned off mother's milk, the advertisement onslaught continued in India. Disturbed by this, respected medical practitioners like Dr. Narasimha Kumtha, Dr. Shyam Agrawal and Dr. Pawan Sureka came to meet me. During our discussions, we all agreed that the government must take the initiative to stop this deception. Spurred by this support from the medical community, I decided to make use of a Parliamentary device.

In the Lok Sabha, I moved a Private Member's Bill seeking promotion of breastfeeding and a ban on baby food advertising. It was discussed in great detail in the

House. HRD Minister of State, Mamata Banerjee, assured the House in her reply that the government itself would move this Bill. This assurance was later implemented. Ever since, baby food advertisements have been banned in India. Moreover, baby food containers are compulsorily labelled with the advisory that 'mother's milk is the best for babies'. It is the only instance in our Parliamentary history that a private member's Bill had been converted into an official Bill. Following this, the Vajpayee government started granting breastfeeding leave to new mothers. I am happy that I could contribute towards the protection of the health of our future generations.

Women Rule at Home

I have no hesitation in saying that 'Mahila Raj' exists in my home. I have two daughters. Owing to my preoccupation with politics and social work, my wife took care of our household singlehandedly, while holding a job outside the home. Besides, she lent a helping hand to my social and political work as well. Before my every election, she would apply for leave and devote herself to helping me from home for my electioneering. During the early days of my membership of the Assembly, Kunda was my typist too. My daughters have grown under her influence and training. My elder daughter, Dr. Nishigandha, is a scientist. We call her our Rani of Jhansi – a fighter, since she plunges right into challenging any irregularity or injustice she encounters. While she was a student, she came to me one day with a petition signed by her and several students. Their grievance was that the government was not paying their scholarship money on time. She persisted with me till I promised to take up the matter. When I raised it in the Legislative Assembly, the funds were released forthwith and the students affected by this inconvenience throughout the State heaved a collective sigh of relief. Though I was given credit for this, I have to admit that my daughters and wife were instrumental in bringing such everyday problems they encountered to my attention, which I would then try to redress. As my own home had three representatives of working women who were also railway train commuters, I was never short of updates and feedback about the difficulties working women faced.

I sincerely believe in women's empowerment and I am among the first lot of political workers who rose in support of 33 percent reservation for women in Parliament and State Legislatures. When Parliament set up a committee under Chairmanship of Communist MP Smt. Geeta Mukherjee to consider the issue of reservations, I was nominated as a member. According to a generally acceptable formula suggested by me, even the States having just one or two Lok Sabha seats could implement this reservation. Regrettably, the legislation couldn't come up for discussion during my stint as an MP.

For this reason, I am incensed when I read about cases of female foeticide. When we brought up our two daughters, the thought that "they are girls" never even remotely touched our minds. Our love for them was complete in every way. I had relatively more free time when Nishigandha was growing up and I taught her many skills, including replacing a burnt-out fuse, or a worn-out washer in a water tap. I had been elected to the Assembly when Vishakha, our younger daughter, was in school. This put a great demand on my time. But she liked to hover around me. At the time, my office was in my tiny two-room flat in Goregaon. To keep her busy, I would entrust her with some trivial errands. Over the past two decades, Vishakha has been looking after my office. This Women's Brigade within my own household has prodded me into constantly championing the cause of women in every sphere.

Smoke-free Kitchens

The only domestic chore they could not handle on their own was the replacement or lifting of an empty cooking-gas cylinder. I have had first-hand experience of the problems faced by a working housewife if a refilled gas cylinder is not delivered by the supply agency on time. Witnessing these everyday inconveniences faced by working women became a motif of sorts when I became the Petroleum Minister.

My childhood had been spent in a village and I had seen the torture endured by my mother and other women as well due to the traditional coal or wood stoves which would envelop the kitchen in a blanket of smoke while cooking. I envisioned that every household in India should be free of this menace. With this objective, I sanctioned cooking-gas connections like never before. When I took over the reins as Minister of Petroleum, India had a waiting list of over eleven million households for gas connections. During my tenure, this list was down to zero and, besides, the number of newly sanctioned connections by the end of my tenure was more than thirty-five million.

The weight of a cylinder till then was fourteen kg. and it was difficult to carry such cylinders in urban slums or hilly regions. To resolve this issue, I introduced smaller five-kg. cylinders designed for easy transport and handling. The

Ram Naik presenting cooking gas agency allotment letter to wife of a Kargil martyr

successful commissioning of a piped-gas supply network in Mumbai is another accomplishment that brought much ease and convenience to the city women.

Gratitude Towards Martyrs

I am reminded of another touching incident during this tenure; the Kargil War with Pakistan had just taken place and many of our brave soldiers had lost their lives fighting for the country. The sentiment that something concrete should be done for their families was felt by the common man. I, too, wished to transform these altruistic sentiments into reality.

It seemed a good idea to me that the wives, or families, of these martyrs could be made self-reliant by either allotting them a petrol pump, or a cooking-gas agency. Prime Minister Atal Bihari Vajpayee too, was in favour of it. Accordingly, I proposed this at a cabinet meeting and it was passed unanimously. I began implementing it forthwith.

While the construction of a petrol pump would entail an investment of up to ₹ 4.5 million, the capital investment for a gas agency was around ₹ 2.5 million. When the wives of these bravehearts received the allotment letters, they were overcome with feelings of grief and gratitude. Watching their reaction and relief left me with a sense of gratification and satisfaction. I was happy for giving these 439 families life-long economic security.

Another incident at the time of the Kargil War that I can never forget, also needs a mention. People throughout the country had been contributing to the Armed Forces Welfare Fund. I received a telephone call from Vasai to inform me that Vasudeo Pai, a veteran freedom fighter, was no more. Both his sons were working with me in the Party. So, I reached their residence to offer my condolences. Putting aside her grief, Pai's aged wife handed me a box. She had filled it up with her entire jewellery – the 'Stree Dhan' (a woman's expensive belongings). She requested me to take it to the Prime Minister as her contribution to the war effort. I was unable to hide my tears. She had proved that Indian women are unique personalities. Such manifestations of women's power have enriched my life journey.

(May 17, 2015)

❒

Ram Naik addressing a group of agitators outside the Vidhan Bhavan, Mumbai, to support their demand for renaming of Marathwada University after Dr B.R. Ambedkar

IN THE LEGISLATIVE ASSEMBLY - PART I

I was elected to the Legislative Assembly thrice consecutively, with record margins in Mumbai each time. This record was not unique in Mumbai alone but was unprecedented in the legislative history of Maharashtra. It seems to me that the time I spent as an MLA between 1978 and 1989 was a pleasant, though stormy, phase of my life. For some time during this period, I was also President of the Mumbai BJP, which meant that I had to look after both – the legislative and organisational responsibilities. The BJP had just been formed in 1980 and it was a formidable task to spread its message and work among the masses. On the other hand, given our meager strength in the

Assembly, we needed to make the Party's presence felt on the assembly floor.

Between 1978 and 1980, Maharashtra had a coalition government, of which the Janata Party was the main partner. The number of Janata Party MLAs in the House was quite large. Veteran parliamentarians like Rambhau Mhalgi, G.P. Pradhan and Dattajee Tamhane would coach us about how to function in the House and how our interaction with the electorate should be. In the Assembly itself, seniors like Uttamrao Patil, Hashu Advani and G.B. Kanitkar gave us hands-on training.

Due to political upheavals in the country, there was a split in the Janata Party and our leaders established the Bharatiya Janata Party (BJP). This newly born Party had barely fifteen members in the 288-member Maharashtra Assembly between 1980 and 1985. Mumbai had elected just two BJP candidates from two geographical ends – Prem Kumar Sharma from South Mumbai, elected by a slender margin of thirty-two votes, and myself from the northern extreme at Borivali, with a record margin. The other BJP MLAs had been elected from outside Mumbai. Due to this challenging political situation, Prof. Ram Kapse and I were required to lead the Party in the House, although we had a mere two years of legislative experience. When I was elected for a third term in 1985, I had created a niche position for myself on the basis of sheer hard work and performance. The media was accustomed to getting some ground breaking news whenever I spoke in the House. All this happened with breathtaking speed and had become possible only due to the strong support from my party colleagues.

Friendly Environment

Annual winter sessions at Nagpur, which is the second capital of Maharashtra, was a much sought-after opportunity for Legislature members belonging to different political parties. Arguments, debates and discussions often took place among us, shedding party affiliations. Such occasions were interspersed with some lighter moments too. One of my senior Party colleagues, Madhu Deolekar was accomplished in English oratory and enjoyed at poking fun at others. Naturally, we all looked for the slightest chance to retaliate in the same coin. Due to Mumbai's coastal climate, we Mumbaikars were averse to Nagpur's severe cold and Deolekar was rather more susceptible to it. He was literally draped with all sorts of woolen apparels – sweater, scarf and any other piece of warm clothing he could lay his hands on. When there was no subject left to pull his leg, his Eskimo-like attire sufficed. This jovial atmosphere enlivened our stay during the session.

Ram Naik having lunch at residence of a party colleague Dhirubhai Shah. Also seen are Dr. Vasudev Shringi and Harishchandra Paliwal

Mumbai BJP President Ram Naik leading a protest march alongwith leaders Jayawantiben Mehta, Ramdas Nayak, G.B.Kanitkar, Premkumar Sharma, Nanubhai Patel, Hashu Advnai and others.

One of our routine practices was to meet in somebody's room in the MLAs' Hostel after dinner and chat late into the night, after which we would return to our respective rooms. On one occasion, our senior Prof. G.B. Kanitkar became the object of our humour, due to his absent-mindedness. One night after our daily post-dinner discussions, each left to return to his own quarters as usual. Kanitkar too, started to walking out. Prof. Pradhan asked him, "Where are you going?" to which Kanitkar countered, "to my room... do you want me to sleep in yours?" There was an eruption of laughter, since we were sitting in Kanitkar's room that night. This happened since our usual meeting place used to be Prof. Pradhan's room. When the confusion was cleared, Kanitkar's laughter was the loudest! It is said that professors are known for their absent-mindedness and Kanitkar had certainly lived up to that reputation!

Hashu jee – My Idol

Besides Kanitkar, another person in the Legislature whom I considered to be my guru was Hashu Advani. He trained me in the minute details of legislative working. Hashu jee was among those RSS activists who had lived in Pakistan after the 1947 Partition and had come to India only after ensuring that the thousands of Hindus fleeing that country were safely transported to India. He was a much revered leader, who remained unmarried to serve the motherland in a better way. All BJP workers and colleagues were like family to him.

In the 1980 Assembly elections, we contested as BJP candidates. The counting of the votes was a manual affair in those days and in many constituencies, suspense lasted until the final round was counted. When I was declared elected, I came out of the counting centre and was mobbed by cheering crowds. Naturally, I was elated, but was shocked to see Hashu jee in the procession. Since he himself was a candidate from Chembur constituency, there was no apparent reason for him to be present in Borivali.

I suddenly had a sense of foreboding as he greeted me with a hug and I asked him the reason he had come all this way to meet and greet me. We had presumed that Hashu jee would be victorious, given his stints in the past as a Municipal Corporator from Chembur and later as Urban Development Minister of Maharashtra in the 1978-80 coalition government. Given this history, his presence at Borivali disturbed me.

Beaming, he replied, "All the results have been declared. Counting continues in Prem Kumar's constituency, as a recount has been demanded by his opponent, since the margin with which Prem is declared victorious is very small. So far you are the only one from among us who has won from Mumbai. That's why I have come to celebrate your win." Such large-heartedness and affection are rare. That moment taught me so much. Those who feel that I accepted the defeats in the Lok Sabha elections in 2004 and 2009 with equanimity may not have seen or known Hashu jee. Otherwise, they would not have shown surprise at my acceptance of defeats with such coolness.

Cement Scam

For eleven years in the Assembly, I worked like a person possessed. An incident that took place during this time illustrates how miracles can be made to happen when a challenge is accepted collectively. It concerned the then infamous cement scam. A BJP team that took up the cudgels against the scam and exposed it, comprised Madhu Deolekar in the Legislative Council, myself in the Assembly and Ramdas Nayak in the Mumbai High Court. At the same time, veteran Socialist leaders, P.B. (Baburao) Samant and

Ram Naik inaugurating a hand-pump drilled through his MLA Fund at the Sanjay Gandhi National Park

Ram Naik inaugurating the first BEST bus service inside the Sanjay Gandhi National Park

Mrinal Gore had also risen against the corrupt practices in the cement scam. We laid threadbare the arbitrary control on cement, the corruption involved in its allocation and the compulsion to contribute donations to the Indira Gandhi Pratibha Pratishthan (Foundation), later rechristened Indira Pratishthan, set up by the then Chief Minister, A.R. Antulay, who was the fountainhead of this scam. Antulay had misused the name of the then Prime Minister, Smt. Indira Gandhi to collect funds. Collectively and consistently, we pursued this battle and finally, Antulay was forced to step down. This was a major jolt to his political prospects and for over a decade, he was left reeling at the sidelines of the corridors of power. However, our personal relations with Antulay remained unaffected, it being a political and social altercation.

I clashed with Antulay on several occasions in the Assembly during his term as Chief Minister. One such occasion

Ram Naik with Father D'Souza and others at Manori Church

was the deteriorating law and order situation. In Mumbai's western suburbs, all police stations were to the west of the railway line between Goregaon and Borivali. Given the peculiar topography of Mumbai, the western side of these suburbs had more public amenities, while on the eastern side, the people were somewhat neglected. I argued in the Assembly that the eastern parts of the suburbs were in dire need of police stations due to their swelling population. To bolster my claim, I cited several cases, thus convincing him about the urgency of my demand. Soon, the Kasturba police station was inaugurated at Borivali East, followed by the police stations at Samata Nagar in Kandivali, Kurar in Malad and Goregaon in the east. It was a chain reaction. The need had become so pressing that an Additional Commissioner of Police now looks after the suburbs. I am happy that this began due to my initiative.

MLA Fund

Several novel schemes were born through my constant endeavour to do something different and useful for the constituency. A year after Antulay's ignominious exit, Vasantdada Patil became the Chief Minister. The MP (or MLA/MLC) Local Area Development (LAD) Fund had its genesis here. Till then, every district was given ₹ 4 million for taking up minor development works through the District Planning and Development Committee (DPDC), an entity set up by the government to accord priority to the developmental demands which came through elected representatives. The DPDC would then take a final decision to spend this amount. Guardian Ministers were appointed chairmen of the respective DPDCs. Those outside Mumbai were in a position to get certain works done through this Fund, since the number of MLAs was low in proportion with the Fund. However, Mumbai was treated as one district and it had 34 MLAs, besides some MLCs. Notwithstanding this, the amount for them was the same – ₹ 4 million.

We took up our demand to change this formula and Vasantdada was convinced that it was a just and necessary demand. After several rounds of discussion, the concept of the MLA Fund was born in 1984. In later years, when I became an MP, I pursued this demand in the Lok Sabha and Prime Minister P.V. Narasimha Rao granted it to create the MP Fund of ₹ 10 million per year per MP. It was raised to ₹ 20 million when I was Minister of State for Planning & Programme Implementation. Presently, it is ₹ 50 million per year.

Problem of SGNP

Though I was fairly successful in tackling a slew of

public causes, certain issues could not be resolved despite my persistent efforts. Of course, there is satisfaction that I did try my best. One such matter is that of the Sanjay Gandhi National Park (SGNP) at Borivali, in my assembly constituency. My heart aches even today when this subject is broached. At the time, I was elected as MLA in 1978, it was known as 'Krishnagiri Udyan' and was quite famous for its flora and fauna. Sanjay Gandhi died in a tragic air crash in 1980 and the park was named after him. Before that renaming and soon after my election, various problems faced by the people in the park were being brought to my attention. Even before I was able to do anything about it, the park had been renamed. Although it is called a national park, the reality is rather different.

Generally, a national park is miles away from a big city, whereas SGNP is partly within the Mumbai limits, on the outskirts of Mumbai and Thane city. Therefore, no one imagined that it was soon to become a national park. This declaration created many difficulties. Among them was the major problem of rehabilitation of the tribal population living within the park.

As motorised vehicles were banned inside the park, horse-carts were the preferred mode of transport. For the convenience of the visitors, food and cold drink stalls were set up years ago. Both these activities were conducted with licenses issued by the authorities. But with one order, the horse-carts were banned, without making any alternative employment available to the operators. Even today, this injustice rankles with me. Similar unjust treatment was meted out to the stall owners, even though they had valid licenses. They were hounded out by force and without a thought for their livelihood, or the future of their families. As an MLA and also as an MP, I continued to fight for both. A glimmer of hope has now emerged, as Maharashtra Chief Minister, Devendra Fadnavis recently heard me out as I recounted to him the stall owners' plight. His reaction was positive!

Peace Pact

Although I was unable to redress such instances and achieve a positive conclusion, there were some problems that I was able to end permanently. I find solace in successfully ending the social tension between Hindus and Christians in the Manori-Gorai fishing villages in my Constituency and in Uttan village a little beyond. Clashes between the two communities had been a chronic problem for generations. The situation was somewhat aggravated when the work of developing 'Keshav Srishti', a socio-cultural complex, began at Uttan. This project was initiated by the Rashtriya Swayamsevak Sangh (RSS) and the foray of the 'Sangh Parivar' in this predominantly Christian belt created unease in certain quarters. A serious violent incident took place as a consequence of this tension. I proposed to Father D'Souza of the Manori Church and to Vasai MLA, Dominic Gonsalves, who belonged to the Janata Party, that we should and could find a solution through a dialogue. They accepted my proposal and convened a joint meeting in the church. A series of meetings followed and peace was soon reigning along this belt. I forged a lasting friendship with well-known author and thinker, Father Francis D'Britto through this effort. As the project progressed, Keshav Srishti and the Rambhau Mhalgi Prabodhini (academy of excellence) came up at Uttan. The performance of the Prabodhini, which has been acknowledged by UNICEF, can be emulated by those who wish to develop model institutions of study and knowledge for political and social workers.

Slip of Tongue

The only time I found myself in a tight spot in the Assembly was when I uttered a rather objectionable remark. I was extricated from this sticky situation by my fast friend and colleague, Prof. Ram Kapse. It is a common occurrence in all Legislatures that the government is castigated by Opposition members for some reason or the other. In the heat of one argument, I said, "This House seems like a fool's paradise." Pandemonium erupted because of this

Ram-Ram: Prof. Ram Kapse began his legislative career in tandem with Ram Naik. Both rose politically very rapidly and soon became known as 'Two Rams' of the BJP

comment. While some members demanded that I withdraw my remark, others began threatening me with a breach of privilege motion. I am a temperate speaker, but had temporarily lost my sense of decorum while uttering that particular remark. Nonetheless, I had never imagined that passions would ignite so violently with this remark. I was speechless and at a loss as to how to react. Speaker Sharad Dighe, too, was taken aback by the reaction of the House.

During this clamour, Kapse rose to speak. He said, "I am a professor of Marathi and, hence, in a position to explain what Ram Naik meant. He has not shown contempt towards any member, nor called any member a fool. He was just using an English turn of phrase, but has not directed it at any one particular member. This is a common idiom and should not be taken as a personal affront..." As Kapse went on elaborating on what he felt, reason and calm returned to the House and Speaker Dighe finally quipped, "Kapse, don't hold a grammar period here. I concede that Ram Naik has not said anything objectionable, but stop your lecture, please." I had narrowly escaped a disastrous situation and decided at that moment that, I would never again say anything thoughtlessly. I followed this vow so sincerely that in later years, it used to be said that Ram Naik will not say anything wrong or improper. In fact, the Speaker of the Lok Sabha once expressed this sentiment in so many words, leaving me with a sense of gratification.

(May 31, 2015)

❒

Inauguration of the first mobile toilet stationed at Shanti Nagar in Dahisar through Ram Naik's MLA Fund, attended by Nana Chudasama, Vinod Ghedia, Girish Gokhale and Wamanrao Parab

IN THE LEGISLATIVE ASSEMBLY - PART 2

I had to face a stormy protest in the Maharashtra Legislative Assembly due to a remark I had made, using a common English figure of speech. But, this happened once, and only once. I have narrated this incident in the previous chapter. However, this embarrassment was more than compensated when with another remark, my comments hit the headlines the next day.

While speaking on Supplementary Demands of the 1983-84 Annual Budget in the House, I highlighted how urgent it was for the government's urban development department to provide basic amenities in slums to achieve the overall development of Mumbai.

I had said, "Once a beautiful city, Mumbai has now become a Toilet City." This was highlighted by all the newspapers. My remark was based on the fact that out of an estimated population of 5.9 million in Mumbai at that time, nearly 2.8 million were living in slums, without the basic amenity of toilets. Out of compulsion, they had to defecate in the open. I was arguing that the government needed to provide one toilet seat per twenty slum-dwellers and hence must construct at least one lakh toilets forthwith. It was during this exchange that the remark on Mumbai being a toilet city was picked up by the alert media and flashed across the front pages the next morning. There were no private TV channels in those days. Many members were scandalised when they heard the remark, but had to acknowledge the bitter truth. Readers at large were confronted with this harsh reality, seen by them daily. Urban researcher Rashmi Mayoor, who had originally used this phrase in one of his reports on Mumbai, would never have dreamed that it would become a permanent feature in describing one of the major problems faced by the metropolis. The unfortunate reality is that even today, there are not enough toilets for Mumbai's slum population.

Nonetheless, there is a silver lining to every cloud and the struggle I waged on behalf of the slum-dwellers had its own positive impact. The government conceded that providing basic amenities like water, power and sanitation was its responsibility. Millions of people live in slums out of sheer necessity. In many cases, the land on which slums come up is privately owned. My insistence was that irrespective of the land ownership, the government must accept this responsibility, and I pursued it tirelessly. The

Keshav Nagar cooperative housing society coming up at Ram Naik's initiative for rehabilitating affected slumdwellers staying at stone quarries

result is that it has now become a part of official policy. I am truly satisfied at this achievement.

Keshav Nagar and Stone Quarries

One is unable to truly comprehend the gravity of the problems faced by slum-dwellers by just reading about them or seeing them on television. One has to witness it firsthand by visiting these informal housing clusters. People who reside here are forced to live under almost inhumane conditions as they cannot afford to buy formal housing, given Mumbai's high real estate costs.

I remember one such case of Ketkipada in my Borivali Constituency. The residents were always threatened by unexpected showers of stone on their homes caused by explosives being used for stone quarrying in nearby hillocks. They had no option but to live under this imminent threat.

Lorries carrying stones brushed by their hutments. The explosions and stone-breaking made the air around thick with dust, so much so that residents found it a problem even to take a fresh breath. Moved by their plight, I launched a campaign against the quarrying. My mission was that the slum-dwellers be rehoused a safe distance away from the quarry work and dust.

The 'Keshav Nagar' housing society emerged from this struggle and its memory gives me a sense of satisfaction even today. Many of my colleagues were apprehensive about my physical safety since they feared that this struggle could take some undesirable twist. Local BJP workers like Rambrij Yadav, Advocate Jayprakash Mishra and Karunashankar Oza became my constant companions. I never dreamt of asking for any police protection since my battle was not against any individual, its only objective being safe rehabilitation

RSS Chief Balasaheb Deoras, Mumbai Mayor Ramesh Prabhu, music legend Sudhir Phadke and BJP leader Ramdas Nayak at the unveiling of Swami Vivekananda's lifesize statue installed at Ram Naik's initiative

of the slum-dwellers. When you take up any cause with a positive approach, that sentiment does not need any verbal expression but is conveyed to the people by its very motive. This was illustrated many years down the line when the son of one of the quarry owners, K.N. Shaikh, called up to request me to intervene on behalf of his father, who wanted to be admitted into Hinduja Hospital following a serious accident that night. Responding to this, I arranged for his admission after midnight. Shaikh received timely treatment and recovered well.

Sculptor in Hutment

The difficulties encountered by slum-dwellers are beyond the imagination of home dwellers and so some have

Ram Naik unveiling murals created by famous sculptor Uttam Pacharane at Lucknow depicting India's brave soldiers honoured with 'Param Veer Chakra'.

had strange arguments while criticising them. Some people pose questions such as "Why do they sleep on roadsides in the first place?" A few years ago, a film star's car allegedly crushed some people while they were sleeping on a footpath in Bandra, Mumbai. In the wake of that tragedy, such naive questions were posed.

This brings to mind my introduction to famous sculptor Uttam Pacharane over three decades ago. Around the mid-eighties, a pregnant woman was killed under a lorry in a similar accident on Borivali's Gorai Road. It was such a gruesome accident, that even the unborn child in her womb was crushed to death on that unfortunate night. As a local MLA, I visited the spot. As I listened to the crowd narrating the details of the accident, my attention was distracted by some stone chips scattered a little distance ahead. My curiosity got the better of me and I enquired about them being there. A member from the crowd asked me to accompany him to a hutment where a sculptor had been shaping his work of art. I was amazed to learn that the occupant of the hutment was Uttam, a young graduate from the renowned J.J. School of Arts, whose father was a construction labourer. Uttam was articulating his talents through his sculptures. It seemed right to me that this exceptional talent found among the slums, be given an opportunity to showcase such excellent work and have an opportunity to become successful. Sometime later, it was decided to install a life-size statue of Swami Vivekananda in Borivali, at the end of the main arterial road, named after Swami jee. A fund for this project was raised with a contribution of ₹ 5 each from the people. We entrusted this assignment to Uttam. His life-size creation proved to be captivating, exhibiting his excellent workmanship in every detail.

RSS Chief, Balasaheb Deoras was invited to inaugurate this statue. He gracefully agreed. I met the then Chief Minister, Shankarrao Chavan to request his presence as well. He candidly admitted that it would be politically inconvenient for him to share a dais with Deoras. I appreciated his quandary, given the fact that Chavan was a Congress Chief Minister and attending a public function with the RSS Chief would have been fatal for his political prospects. However, he surprised me when he said, "I won't attend, but can be of help in any other way if you so require." Help from the government would normally denote financial help, but we had already collected sufficient funds and had no need of any monetary assistance. Then, an idea struck me; I thought of Uttam's hutment and said to Chavan, "Such an accomplished artist has to live in a pavement dwelling. Please sanction him a flat from the Chief Minister's discretionary quota." Chavan immediately sanctioned one and issued directions to allot a three-bedroom flat to Uttam at Raheja Complex at Malad. "Give me a formal application later," Chavan added to my amazement. When I narrated this to my colleagues and Uttam, they could hardly believe this turn of events.

Uttam has been living in this flat for the past twenty eight years, creating one beautiful sculpture after another. He was also elected president of the prestigious Bombay Art Society. Some of his memorable creations include, the Swantrya Jyot (Eternal Flame of Independence) installed in Andaman, the life-size statue of Chhatrapati Shahu Maharaj at Mumbai's Vidhan Bhavan (Legislature complex) premises, the statue of Swatantryaveer (freedom-fighter) Savarkar at Borivali and the imposing equestrian statue of Chhatrapati

Shivaji at Dahisar at Mumbai's north entrance. Uttam also sculpted beautiful columns to commemorate the freedom struggle in the then Hyderabad princely state soon after India's Independence. The columns he created have been erected in every district of Marathwada region.

Uttam wished to sculpt a huge mural of the martyred soldiers who were decorated with the Param Veer Chakra (PVC), the highest Indian honour for valour by a soldier and he showed me its outline. He had planned that it by a soldier cast in bronze and I was confident of its potential impact. However, the project would entail a substantial cost and the mural would need constant upkeep. Still, I was keen that it materialises because of the unique theme and its importance.

As Governor of UP, I receive many distinguished visitors. One of them was the GOC-in-C of the Central Command of the Indian Army, having its headquarters at Lucknow. At one of our meetings, I explained the mural project to him. He and his staff officers were charmed with the idea. The State Government also readily accepted the responsibility of funding the project. The Central Command has gifted three PVC laureates of Uttar Pradesh to the nation. The first, Jadunath Singh, was from this part of the country. Abdul Hamid, revered throughout India for his incredible feat of destroying many Pakistani battle tanks in the 1965 war and Captain Manoj Kumar Pandey, who laid down his life at Kargil, also hailed from UP. Their murals were sculpted by Uttam and were installed ceremoniously at the 'Smritika' (War Memorial) of the Central Command on 22 December, 2014. The Memorial is among the prominent military attractions in India and is scrupulously maintained by the

Command. Uttam has now gained international recognition for his work. I am indeed happy to record my contribution to his ascent to fame.

Challenge to Governor

A State Governor's word has tremendous respect and is always obeyed. When I requested the GOC-in-C, I was aware of this fact. In an altogether different context, I remember former Maharashtra Governor, Kona Prabhakar Rao, who had issued a malafide directive, so that a Chief Minister's daughter could benefit in a medical examination held by Mumbai University. Rao had to resign when some of us MLAs not only criticised this action, but called on the President of India and submitted evidence to this effect.

Ram Naik and wife Kunda laying foundation stone of Swami Vivekanand Education Centre which now runs school in four mediums for lower income group of Dahisar, Mumbai

The official reason for Rao's resignation was stated to be his indifferent health.

As an MLA, I had to take on many influential persons for varied reasons. I held Shiv Sena Chief Bal Thackeray in high esteem. Still, I had to take a stand against him when he was shielding some erring forest officials from the Sanjay Gandhi National Park at Borivali. But, I took care that my opposition would be issue-based and not personal. This is the reason why Mrinal Tai Gore and I took a united stand regarding some public interest issues, though we were political opponents. We were both in the Assembly between 1985 and 1989. She strongly supported a Private Member's Bill, which I had moved against unscrupulous builders. Every person dreams of owning a home. However, it came to light that flat-owners in several cooperative housing societies had to suffer since dishonest builders didn't hand over possession of the society to them. My bill aimed at eliminating these lacunae. Mrinal Tai's speech in my support created ripples in political circles and the media blew it up.

Bill Against Roadside Romeos

Another Private Member's Bill I moved received support from all sides of the House. It was to roadside romeos who indulged in eve teasing. Prior to moving this bill, the victims of eve teasing would mostly stay silent since even if a complaint was filed, the police would simply admonish the offenders and let them go. After my Bill, the Minister of State for Home, J.T. Mahajan assured the House that provisions would be made to imprison such offenders up to seven days and that other stringent sections would be added to the law. This decision made eve-teasing an offence

Ram Naik raised voice against unprecedented hike in State Transport Buses fares. He led Mumbaites in several such issues as a dynamic MLA

by law. Many such instances come to mind while recalling those days.

As an MLA, I could initiate several projects in the interest of my constituency. Similarly, many could be started for the entire state of Maharashtra, by making adept use of different legislative devices. This experience proved very helpful when I was elected to the Lok Sabha.

(June 14, 2015)

❒

Union Housing Minister Sikandar Bakht (in suit) listening intently to Ram Naik at a conference of Maharashtra Housing Board residents alongwith MPs Vasantkumar Pandit and Mrinal Gore and MLAs Baburao Samant and Sadanand Varde in Mumbai

JANATA PARTY DAYS

It was indeed a black day for India when over three decades ago, on June 26, 1975, Prime Minister Indira Gandhi declared an internal Emergency. When political parties with differing ideologies fought the Emergency together and later amalgamated under the Janata Party banner, it was the harbinger of a new era in Indian polity. The erstwhile Jana Sangh workers such as myself, remained members of the Janata Party for barely three years, but even this brief interlude gave my political career a different turn.

After the formation of the Janata Party, veteran Socialist, S.M. Joshi, was nominated to head its Maharashtra unit, while my guru in politics, Prof. G.B.

Ram Naik as President, Janata Party, Mumbai addressed numerous corner meetings demanding action against Smt. Indira Gandhi as per Justice Shah Commission's Report

Kanitkar, was appointed President of the Mumbai unit. Although we had gathered under one Party banner, workers of some of the parties lacked team spirit. These elements began covert machinations of political victimisation and were successful in replacing Prof. Kanitkar with Dr. Shanti Patel, a Congress (O) leader with socialist leanings. This was the first spark of dissent in the Mumbai Janata Party. Former Jana Sangh workers were expectedly irate, but many others who cared for values in public life too, were averse to this sudden development. This dissent culminated in a 'Remove Shanti Patel' campaign. As a result, the Party announced an election for the post.

Crown of Thorns

We, the former Jana Sangh workers, resolved to teach these disruptive elements a lesson for their divisive politics of groupism and factionalism. I had liaised with workers of all constituent parties during the Emergency. Added to this fact was the belief that my elective merit was quite substantial and that some workers of the constituent parties were also likely to vote for me due to my personal networking, an analysis also shared by Kanitkar. All things considered, I filed my nomination for the post of Mumbai Janata Party President.

In a counter-move, Dr. Patel and his supporters fielded another Congress (O) leader, Mukundrao Bhujbal Patil, who enjoyed considerable goodwill. This election was an altogether new experience for me, since in the Jana Sangh, such important posts were filled through consultations and consensus, not by ballot. But, the situation was such that there was no looking back now. We were fuelled with the determination to win and I was finally declared elected. This brought home the realisation as to why politics is referred to as a bed of thorns.

During the Janata Party days, most of our energy and time were uselessly consumed in pleading, persuading and infighting, even when the object was common. This became a daily regimen. Conversely, in the Jana Sangh, we were trained to work unitedly once a decision was reached. Working in the Janata Party was a volatile experience. I had never imagined that one such clash would be against the then Prime Minister, Shri Morarjee Desai. But, I had to undergo that harrowing experience too.

Rift with Morarajee Desai

It is customary in political parties, that whenever a top leader is to visit a city, the party prepares the V.I.P.'s itinerary with his consent, while the local unit President is responsible for implementing it. This applies to all top leaders, including the Prime Minister, when invitations for non-official functions are accepted. Accordingly, when Prime Minister

Ram Naik welcoming Prime Minister Morarjee Desai at Mumbai airport alongwith (R-L) Pradyumna Badheka, Ishaq Jamkhanwala, Shanti Patel, Mayor A.U.Memon, Vasantrao Bhagwat, Subramanian Swamy and others

Morarjee Desai's visit to Mumbai was confirmed, we drew up a schedule which included a public meeting at Shivaji Park, a sprawling ground at Dadar, in the heart of Mumbai. Jayaprakash Narayan (called JP), who had spearheaded the crusade against the Emergency, was at the time undergoing treatment at the Jaslok Hospital. Since the Janata Party owed its formation to JP, we planned that Desai will visit JP on his way to Shivaji Park. Accordingly, this itinerary was sent to the PM's office and it was duly endorsed.

Desai was given a huge reception at the Mumbai airport, since it was his maiden visit as Prime Minister. He was senior to us all in age and was respected for his strong views against social evils such as alcohol and tobacco. He was also a former Chief Minister of the erstwhile Bombay State.

I was under a lot of pressure, as I had to accompany him and was responsible for ensuring that his visit was a success. A mixed feeling of joy and pride pervaded me. As customary, Desai asked me to sit in his car. He was to first go to his residence from the airport. We began discussing the day's schedule. Without any indication, Desai suddenly declared that he was not visiting the Jaslok Hospital, but would go directly to the venue of the public meeting from his residence. This was a rude shock to me. We had publicised his itinerary in advance. Given JP's sacrifice and his failing health, the PM's visit to him in the hospital was bound to make major news and media persons and Janata Party workers were expected to throng the Jaslok Hospital to witness his arrival. If Desai did not turn up as expected, speculation would be rife that the PM had insulted JP, or that the Janata Party had forgotten its mentor. I was visualising the headlines in the next day's newspapers. I indicated to Desai that this would not be advisable. But he was adamant. I surmised that his son, Kantilal, could have possibly been behind this skullduggery.

I was seething with anger that such a top leader could behave in such an impolite manner. Finally, unable to control my anguish, I simply said, "If the hospital visit is cancelled, so is the public meeting." I thought that as the Mumbai unit President and organiser of the public meeting, I had the authority to call it off as well.

A seasoned leader, Desai instantly weighed the situation and realised that his adamancy was going to cause the party workforce much embarrassment. To his credit, he gallantly agreed that he would do both; the hospital visit and the rally and both events went through smoothly.

I grew accustomed to encountering such tricky situations in the Janata Party on a daily basis. When the elections to the Mumbai Municipal Corporation were declared in November 1978, selecting candidates had become an ordeal, since each constituent party wanted a larger slice of the total number of 184 seats.

Allocating seats is not an easy task, even under normal conditions. In this case, workers of differing ideologies had gathered under the Janata Party banner. In the past, each constituent party had contested almost all the seats. It was evident now that they would all have to make some sacrifice in terms of the seats to be contested. Clashes on seat-sharing were going to be inevitable. I had to shoulder the thorny responsibility of talking individually with each group and convincing its leaders about adjustments. I held talks with each constituent separately and then with all of them collectively. I studied the total electoral scenario minutely and identified the seats the Jana Sangh faction should demand. I compiled the statistics of previous elections to decide which faction had better prospects for which seat. It was a learning experience for me and I understood then the arithmetic of elections.

As the Mumbai unit President, my presence was compulsory for each round of negotiations. This was a demanding period. I held a series of meetings at the party's Mumbai headquarters through three days and nights without a break. The Jana Sangh faction was allotted forty-five seats. It was a challenge to resolve the disputes for each seat. The last candidature so decided, was that of Chandrakanta Goyal, the mother of present Union Power Minister Piyush Goyal from Sion. Despite the shortage of time, we made all

L.K.Advani addressing first election campaign meeting for Ram Naik. On the dais are G.B.Kanitkar, Jhamatmal Wadhvani, Mohanlal Parikh and others

the preparations and the Jana Sangh faction won twenty seven seats. Promising young men like Madhu Chavan were elected to the Corporation in this election. Although the situation was favourable for the Janata Party, I was rather uneasy, because unnecessary wrangling was constantly taking place, even on such joyous occasions.

Dirty Politics

Friendship was forged with former Socialists, like Prabhubhai Sanghavi, Narayan Tawade, former Congress (O) leaders, like Pranlal Vohra, Natubhai Shah, Pradyumna Badheka and many in the Janata Party. They didn't have a soft corner for the Jana Sangh, but, this did not hinder our relations, which were based on mutual respect and affection. On the other hand, certain elements in the Janata Party continued to indulge in needless bickering.

In my capacity as Mumbai unit President of the party, I was invited on one occasion for the Eid prayer held at Azad Maidan, which entails offering the Namaz. I was offered a cap by the organisers, which I dutifully donned out of the same reverence I observe while removing my footwear at a Pooja performed by Hindus, or covering the head while entering a Gurudwara. All the party workers accompanying me did likewise. Some elements in the Janata Party launched a whispering campaign against me over this act of normal courtesy. A canard was started that the Jana Sangh was trying to appease the Muslims. Photographs of this event were sent to the 'Organiser', the Sangh Parivar's English weekly, to create misunderstanding about me.

But, by now, I was accustomed to these pranks and had grown habituated to ignoring such malicious acts on the grounds that the Janata Party had been given a mandate by the general public and hence it was our duty to respect popular sentiments, irrespective of one's religious affiliation. However, such petty squabbles had begun plaguing the leadership of the Janata Party at the Centre as well. While some were against Prime Minister Morarjee Desai's economic policies, some were objecting to our commitment to the RSS. Certain leaders were hungry for power, while others wished to create political instability. Firebrand Socialist leaders like George Fernandes and Mrinal Gore began opposing the Desai government, disregarding the people's mandate. Due to these internal differences, the Janata Government went into a tailspin. The average workers in the constituent parties were hurt due to this

Ram Naik speaking at a felicitation held at Borivali on his election as Mumbai Janata Party President

raw and unconcealed hunger for power among top leaders. Finally, a mid-term election was declared and the Janata Party rule came to an ignominious end.

Mumbai Seats Retained

The after-effects of this break-up hit Mumbai unit very hard. Party workers were in a quandary. But the common line of thought was that the leaders who had walked out of the party should not be pardoned at any cost. At the same time, it was a major challenge to find formidable candidates to field against influential leaders like Mrinal Gore and Ahilya Rangnekar. A person inexperienced in national politics such as me, was holding on to the reins of the Mumbai Janata Party. Despite such obstacles, we decided to teach these divisive elements a lesson.

We fielded Pramila Dandavate, a respected Socialist crusader, against Ahilya Ranganekar. It was a challenge to take on Mrinal Tai. We requested Congress (O) leader from Kerala, Ravindra Verma, to contest against her. Some former Socialists had stayed on with the Janata Party. Among them were Prof. Madhu Dandavate, a towering figure, and his wife Pramila. The task before us looked all the more formidable, with the media being partial towards Mrinal Gore and Ahilya Rangnekar.

But amidst that tense milieu, we received an unexpected suggestion; we were asked to support these two women fighters. This meant that we would not be able to enter the fray and hence it was not welcomed by us, as our firm resolve was to trounce them both because of their treachery with the Janata Party. This advice was therefore ignored and we began preparations for a pitched battle.

Though we girded up for the fight, it was obvious that I would have to accept the responsibility of the outcome, whatever it may be. And there was no dearth of 'well-wishers' who reminded me of this, time and again. Notwithstanding such covert warnings, we began our electioneering in the right earnest. The one factor which motivated us was that we were fighting for a just cause. As the results were declared, the nation witnessed a miracle! While the Janata Party was able to win just thirty one Lok Sabha seats across the nation, we had won five of the six seats in Mumbai. Many veterans across the country had to eat humble pie, but we were successful in getting an unknown candidate like Ravindra Verma elected, and that too, by defeating Mrinal Tai. The other astounding win was that of Pramila Dandavate, who defeated Ahilya Tai. Those re-elected were Ratan Singh Rajda, Ram Jethmalani and Dr. Subramanian Swamy. We had declared our support to Republican Party candidate, B.C. Kamble, but he lost. Still, we were consoled by the fact that the Congress candidate also lost from this constituency, which returned militant trade union leader Dr. Datta Samant. I was complimented for this sterling performance.

I did not claim the sole credit for this all-round victory, but the experience gained during this period was another extremely valuable lesson for my future political career. Also, my presence was noticed in the national polity for the first time. The dispute which had arisen over our loyalty to the RSS resurfaced after the 1980 Parliamentary elections. The matter reached such a point, that an ultimatum was given – "either stay within the Janata Party, or snap ties with the RSS". A meeting of the top former Jana Sangh leaders was therefore convened in Delhi to consider this issue. I was one of the invitees. I did not in the least imagine that these developments would give another turn to my future.

The new chapter in my political life was to be the birth of the Bharatiya Janata Party – the BJP.

(June 28, 2015)

❐

Ram Naik at the unveiling ceremony of Savarkar's portrait at Parliament House on 26 February, 2003

INSPIRED BY SWATANTRYAVEER SAVARKAR

The Eternal Flame of Independence dedicated to the legendary Swatantryaveer (the heroic freedom fighter) Vinayak Damodar Savarkar, at the Cellular Jail on the Andaman Islands, is a sacred spot which inspires every patriotic Indian, but petty political thinking had mired it in a controversy for a while. Finally, that horrible chapter in India's history came to an end, as the reinstallation of Savarkar's immortal words on that memorial began at my hands, on July 4, 2015.

The deep wound inflicted on my psyche by that unseemly wrangling began healing that day. As Petroleum Minister, I had discovered that supplying

LPG cylinders to some remote corners of the country was an expensive proposition, due to the cost of transportation and the government had to highly subsidise the price. I found a solution to this problem by erecting gas bottling plants in some of these remote areas, so that the supply of cylinders from the plants to the nearby consumers would cut costs.

One such area was the Andaman Islands, which can be accessed from the mainland only after a long air travel, or an even longer one by sea, either from Chennai or Kolkata. This transport caused an additional burden of ₹ 250 for each cylinder, almost doubling the cost to be borne by consumers. The solution was to erect a bottling plant at Andaman. On April 20, 2003, this became a welcome reality when I visited the islands to inaugurate the plant.

Patriots' Piligrimage

This was my maiden visit to Andaman, an island regarded by every patriotic Indian as a place of pilgrimage, where Savarkar and countless other freedom fighters were incarcerated. The Cellular Jail in which they were confined, is considered as a temple by people like me. The moment I alighted at the Andaman airport, my very first destination was the Cellular Jail. It is so called, because it has rows of tiny cells in which the freedom fighters were shackled for years. Savarkar is the only freedom fighter in the world who was awarded two consecutive life terms of twenty five years each. His sacrifice is unprecedented.

We approached the corner cell where Savarkar had been kept. I am not an emotional person generally, but, that moment moved me beyond words. I was overwhelmed by the emotion that engulfed me as I stood in the very cell to which he was confined. It was situated just above the 'Phansi Kothari' – the hanging block. I could only imagine the stressful circumstances under which Savarkar must have preserved his sanity, even feeling inspired to write a long poem on the stone wall of his cell, using only a broken iron nail as a pen.

I was accompanied by a large entourage that included a media team from Delhi. This was the only time during my ministerial tenure that my entire family was with me. I had especially invited a media corps from Mumbai as well, in view of the solemnity of the occasion. My intention was that as many people as possible, should have the opportunity to witness the torture Savarkar must have endured in that environment.

While on the Bristol coast in England, Savarkar had written an epic poem, "Ne Majsee Ne, Parat Matrubhoomila" (take me back to my motherland), as an ode to the ocean. It has become a glittering gem of Marathi literature. As we gazed at his portrait displayed before us, I requested that everybody observe a moment's silence, while I played the poem on a cassette player, sung soulfully by Melody Queen, Lata Mangeshkar. We may have been in the cell for barely five minutes before we were dripping with sweat owing to the sweltering heat.

Savarkar's cell had a tiny hole and legend has it that a little chirping sparrow would make an appearance through this aperture. Savarkar's feathered visitor would have certainly been a welcome diversion in harsh surrounding. While narrating these historical incidents some among us became very uncomfortable and one of them quipped, "Come on, let's go. No need to suffocate and perish here." It made me more aware of Savarkar's plight in his cell for

Petroleum Minister Mani Shankar Aiyar inaugurating the Eternal Flame at Andaman. At his right are Andaman Lt Governor Ram Kapse and Ram Naik. Removal of Savarkar's poem from the plaque of this memorial created a furore (9 August, 2004)

eleven long years and I was visibly moved. We toured the rest of the jail under the spell of by those haunting memories. Savarkar was not alone, of course, in that jail. Numerous unnamed freedom fighters had languished there. We saluted them as well.

I felt that an imposing memorial needed to be erected at Andaman. 'India Gate' in Delhi has been built to honour the soldiers who fought in World War I. The Andaman memorial should be as awe-inspiring, I felt. Indian Oil Corporation, which was erecting the bottling plant, welcomed my suggestion that an Eternal Flame of Independence should be lit at Andaman.

The management of IOC Foundation, the trust which was registered when I was the Petroleum Minister got down to work. It was thought that the sculpture on top of which the Flame was to be placed, should be adorned with quotations from three other equally imposing freedom fighters – the fourth being Savarkar, on its four faces. Renowned sculptor Uttam Pacharane was selected through a process of calling tenders and other formalities, to design and erect the memorial. By the time this whole regimen was completed, the 2004 Parliamentary election was announced and the model Code of Conduct was enforced. Under this Code, no new project can be inaugurated or launched by the government, till the election is over.

Mean-minded Mani Shankar

The BJP-led alliance lost the election, as did I and a coalition led by the Congress party came to power. The petroleum portfolio was entrusted to senior Congress leader, Mani Shankar Aiyar, a former Foreign Service Officer.

I urged the new government to inaugurate the memorial at the earliest and that I be invited for the opening ceremony, due to my emotional involvement with the project. Accordingly, the function took place on August 9, 2004 and I was one of the invitees. I was elated as I attended the event. However, I was deliberately humiliated by not being asked to grace the dais. The moment the curtain was removed to declare the memorial open, I was stunned and enraged to find that Aiyar had committed the cardinal sin of removing Savarkar's poem from the face of the memorial. This generated a wave of anger across the country. The matter was discussed in the Parliament too, but Prime Minister Manmohan Singh did not respond. In Maharashtra, the intensity of anger was palpable. In atonement for this outrage, I arranged for the installation of a Savarkar sculpture at Borivali on a recreation ground development project undertaken by my party colleague, Gopal Shetty, who is now the MP from that area. Shri Narendra Modi, then Chief Minister of Gujarat, honoured my request and inaugurated it. The ground is now used for holding various events, the main among them being a memorial lecture series on the birth anniversary of Savarkar.

Hououring People's Sentiments

When Modi became the Prime Minister of India after the 2014 election, I brought the aberration committed at Andaman to his attention and requested him to remove this national stigma. I pursued the matter with him, with the result that a decision was taken to erect the Flame anew, decorated with Savarkar's poem. I was invited as Chief Guest for the foundation function, which was held on July 4, 2015 in a jubilant and celebratory atmosphere. Words are not enough to express my sentiments at this turn of events.

This made me reminisce about my association with Savarkar's thoughts. I recalled my childhood, when it was not a practice to pamper children. My father too followed this. He was a double graduate and could have landed a comfortable government job very easily. However, he had chosen to become a school teacher in a Princely State and that too, in a small village. Naturally, there was no possibility of him being in a position to spend on any indulgences for his children. But instead he had opened up a treasure trove of knowledge for us, by building a library of select books, which he himself was fond of reading. To supplement his meagre income, he sold books bought from Pune and Mumbai at a commission, as there were no book shops around. He ensured that we developed the habit of reading. During my school going years, he gave me a book entitled, "The Freedom Struggle of 1857," written by Savarkar. I was so captivated by it, that I asked him for another of Savarkar's legendary books, "My Incarceration," which described his

Ram Naik laying foundation of the replica of 'Amar Jyoti', Eternal Flame, displaying Savarkar's poem, along with Andaman Lt Governor A.K. Singh, MP Vishnupad Ray and sculptor Uttam Paçharane (4 July, 2015)

eleven years inside the Cellular Jail. After reading these books, I grew obsessed with the thought of meeting Savarkar in person.

Savarkar in Person

Later, when I arrived in Pune for my college education, I joined an RSS training camp in May 1952. According to a strict regulation for such RSS camps, no one is permitted to leave the camp until the completion of the course. However, an exception was made that year for a special reason; Savarkar had decided to wind up the 'Abhinav Bharat Sanstha', which had been set up during the freedom struggle for organising protests against the British rule and had selected Pune to announce this decision. Many towering patriots were present for this epic event. One of

(L-R) Nitin Gadkari, Ram Naik, Narendra Modi, Datta Dalvi, Uttam Pacharane, Dada Idate and Gopal Shetty are seen at unveling Statue of Veer Savarkar at Borivali

them was the RSS Chief, M.S. Golwalkar, who was referred to as Guruji. A statement made by Savarkar at this function still echoes in my mind. He had said, "Although the present Congress regime has tortured me, I have no grievance, since this is our government. If we wish to bring about a change in India, we will have to do it through ballot and not bullet. We should all remember this." His commitment to democracy remained undiminished.

Savarkar spoke for three consecutive days – 10, 11 and 12 May, on the freedom struggle that began in 1857 and concluded on August 15, 1947 – India's Independence Day. He narrated the many sacrifices made by the freedom fighters. These lectures capsualised his great dissertation, 'The six Golden Pages of Indian History.' Knowing the potential impact of the speeches, we were made to attend the event. It would not be an exaggeration to mention here that the three speeches have since remained imprinted in my memory and were the catalysts that motivated my zeal to work to achieve something worthwhile for the nation.

I heard Savarkar for the first time when I was a mere youth of eighteen. But I vividly remember his words even today. He was an ardent rationalist, with an unshakeable commitment to life's mission. Undaunted by any challenge, he took it for granted that only adverse would ensue and was prepared to wage in an ardent struggle for his convictions, till victory was claimed.

Savarkar has left every Indian indebted. In my case, my association with him had another dimension; my wife Kunda is the daughter of a committed Hindu Mahasabha leader, the late K.N. Dharap, a renowned lawyer. The Hindu Mahasabha was the Party that had for years, been led by Savarkar. While our wedding was being finalised, I had heard that my father-in-law had extended legal assistance to Savarkar, who was falsely accused in the Gandhi assassination case. I envy Kunda, because she had the opportunity to welcome Savarkar when he visited Dharap's home in Girgaon after his acquittal.

Honouring Martyrs

I consider Savarkar the epitome of the nation's ethos. Like the Andaman Flame, I erected similar memorials at two other sites of national importance. In the first instance, I chose Jallianwalla Bagh in Amritsar, since the massacre there on April 13, 1919 had claimed three hundred and seventy-nine lives, when non-violent protesters were fired upon by troops under the command of Colonel Reginald Dyer. It is a national monument.

The second was the Hutatma Chowk, or Martyrs' Square, in downtown Mumbai. Popularly known as Flora Fountain, this is a sacred spot since a hundred and five protestors lost their lives, while demanding a separate Maharashtra state with Mumbai as its capital. Though the Flame has been erected, it is not as imposing as I had envisioned it to be. Nevertheless, I am satisfied that I was instrumental in its installation.

I fail to understand how and why some people can derive perverse pleasure by defaming freedom fighters such as Savarkar, or overlooking the great sacrifices made by them. As an MP, I took the initiative, along with the then Lok Sabha Speaker, Manohar Joshi, to install a life-size portrait of Savarkar in Sansad Bhavan, the Parliament House. Eventually, it was installed in the Central Hall of Parliament, though not a single Congress MP attended that unveiling ceremony. Congress President, Sonia Gandhi had issued a whip to that effect. Such callous disregard for Savarkar angers me. Savarkar's message was that we should work for the nation, but not forget the sacrifice of the martyrs.

I have already narrated how my appeal to the Central Command of the Army resulted in a beautiful mural being installed in Lucknow, dedicated to the bravehearts, who laid down their lives for the country. The inspiration within me that had been ignited by Savarkar so many years ago is the catalyst behind the motivation that drives me to take up and pursue such projects.

(July 12, 2015)

❐

I am indeed happy that during the course of publication of this book 'Veer Savarkar Jyot' was dedicated to the nation on Savarkar's birth anniversary on May 28, 2016 by Shri Amit Shah, President-BJP, Shri Dharmendra Pradhan, Petroleum Minister, Lt-Governor A.K. Singh and Shri Vishnupad Ray, MP at Cellulor Jail, Andman.

Atal Bihari Vajpayee declaring that 'The darkness will end, the sun will rise and the lotus will bloom' at the BJP's maiden session in Mumbai. On the dais are L.K.Advani, Sikandar Bakht, Ram Naik and Ram Jethmalani

BIRTH OF THE BJP

"The darkness will end, the sun will shine and the lotus will bloom!" Shri Atal Bihari Vajpayee's voice thundered across the vast expanse of Mumbai's Shivaji Park in Dadar.

It was the evening of December 30, 1980 and masses of the public had assembled to witness the birth of the Bharatiya Janata Party. Atal jee's declaration surcharged the eager crowd and was met with a deafening applause. All the erstwhile Jana Sangh workers, who had walked out of the Janata Party, welcomed the announcement made against the backdrop of the Arabian Sea, at the conclusion of the first plenary of the newly-formed Party. This was a turning point, not only in my life, but in that of India's too. The rest is history!

As mentioned earlier, the Janata Party was defeated conclusively in the 1980 Parliamentary elections and internal squabbles had become its common occurrence. The RSS activists were caught in a cleft stick – either snap ties with the RSS, or leave the Janata Party.

A meeting of select leaders and workers of the erstwhile Jana Sangh was convened in Delhi on April 6, 1980, to take stock of the situation and decide on the plan for the future. The agenda for the meeting was to ruminate on various issues, such as the sentiments of the rank and file at local levels, retaining our self-respect by ensuring that the trust reposed in us by the people was not betrayed and to discuss possible ramifications in the emerging situation. I was one of the invitees to this meeting. The reason for my attendance was obvious. I was President of the Mumbai Janata Party at the time and had been part of the vanguard in the fight against the Emergency between 1975 and 1977. Besides, I had also worked as Organising Secretary of the Mumbai Jana Sangh before the Emergency was imposed. A decision was taken at this meeting to establish a separate party – the Bharatiya Janata Party. The birth of the BJP extricated us from this quandary and we were free once again to function according to our ideology.

Challenge of Plenary

One of the crucial issues discussed was whether we should rejoin the Jana Sangh. But there was a catch; several workers from other constituents of the Janata Party were known to be willing to join us, although they would not want to join the Jana Sangh. Therefore, to resolve this conundrum, it was decided to form an entirely new party, so that anyone believing in its ideology, would be free to join without any stipulations. The meeting mandated that each of us explore the possibilities of bringing such workers on board.

Following this, a review meeting was held in September 1980 at Hyderabad, attended by senior leaders. It was resolved that a convention of the workers from all over the country be held in December to formulate the policies and objectives of the new Party and, thereafter, formally declare its launch. The next question: Where were we to hold this national-level convention?

It was estimated that at least 15-20 thousand delegates would attend. How were we to arrange for their stay, food and safety in such a short span of time? This was a big challenge indeed! Would the people of India be amenable to our decision? Would the administration at our chosen venue cooperate with us? And how were we to manage such a mass of people and the galaxy of leaders? There was much brainstorming to resolve the various issues that would impact the nature of the convention.

My brain was now ticking. "If we could fight the evil Emergency, why can't we face this challenge," I asked myself. I began to feel a sense of confidence and submitted to the leadership that I, meaning the Mumbai unit, would be ready to take on the responsibility. I was a junior functionary then and a newcomer in that gathering of giants. Even today, I can't explain what motivated me to make this offer in front of such top leaders. But, all were in agreement that holding the convention in a mega-capital like Mumbai would be very effective. Still, doubts persisted about the availability of space in the city for such a large gathering and the total expenditure, given Mumbai's costly standards. However, I assured them that we, the workers in Mumbai, would shoulder this responsibility. My assurance sealed the decision in favour of Mumbai and I was appointed convener of the convention.

On my way home, the enormity of the project began to sink in and I began to feel the tension that this mammoth task would entail. I was besieged with numerous possible scenarios, such as the response of my co-workers, or our capability of undertaking such a colossal task. But then, Maharashtra Organising Secretary, Vasantrao Bhagwat revived my ebbing confidence, commenting, "Very good! You have given us an opportunity to show our capabilities to the entire nation. Let's all start working together to make it a success." Bhagwat continued to inspire the workers at every level. We toiled round the clock, possessed with a single objective – to organise a successful convention!

Building up Samata Nagar

The foremost challenge was to obtain a venue in the crowded city, where space was at a premium, even in 1980. There were no grounds large enough to accommodate the stay of about 15-20 thousand delegates and our top leaders. Besides, a big enough space was required for holding the deliberation of the convention.

Finally, we zeroed in on the Bandra Reclamation, which was a sprawling open space by the sea. While the land had been prepared by reclaiming the creek, there was not much construction on it. Though the plot was a little away from

Ram Naik addressing the BJP's maiden session in Mumbai. On the dais are (L-R) Murli Manohar Joshi, Sikandar Bakht, Kailaspati Mishra, Atal Bihari Vajpayee and Ram Jethmalani

the main thoroughfare, it was adequately large for the purpose. We decided to erect tents for the delegates.

An army of college students, who had associated themselves with us in the fight against the Emergency, was eager to extend a helping hand in whatever way it was needed. Famous cinema art director, Shanti Deo, decided to take up the job of preparing an imposing dais befitting the occasion. In this, he was assisted by these youngsters and within no time, a huge lotus was installed at the entrance to the convention ground. The dais was erected soon after. Even children from our families participated in physical work. Today's senior leaders, like Kirit Somaiya, Arun Deo, Ramesh Medhekar and Madhu Chavan were at the forefront of this young brigade. Renowned architect, Ramesh Sheth and his young associate – Arvind Nanadapurkar put the finishing touches to the construction of the rostrum. Present Central

Ram Naik with Atal Bihari Vajpayee leading a grand procession in Mumbai on the occasion of the maiden BJP session

Power Minister, Piyush Goyal, who was then in his early teens and was fondly called 'Happy' by all, was another enthusiast who toiled alongside us.

In a short while, a mini-township had mushroomed in this sprawling open space. It was decided to name it 'Samata Nagar' – the City of Equality, to propagate the message of the common thread of equality and fraternity. The *bhoomi pooja*, the consecration of the site, was performed by former Congress (O) leader, Sikandar Bakht, who had decided to come with us. While it was obvious that workers from the four corners of the country would stay at Samata Nagar, a fiat was received from Delhi that our topmost leaders like Atal jee and Lal Krishna Advani too, would camp there as well. To this daunting list was added the name of Vijaya Raje Scindia, a queen in every respect.

We were under tremendous pressure. The intent of these leaders was clear that they wanted to be near the common workers, but making suitable arrangements was a major challenge for us. This was made all the more formidable with the task of feeding these delegates with simple, but wholesome food, that would satisfy every palate.

Unprecedented Response

Every worker strove to make the convention successful, as if it were some personal festive occasion to be celebrated within their own family. We made preparations to cater to about twenty thousand delegates, presuming that the turnout would be more than expected. The D-day, December 27, 1980, literally descended upon us. The pressure in the atmosphere on us was tangible and we were ready to galvanise the workers arriving from beyond Mumbai and Maharashtra as well, so that they would devote themselves to the newly formed party.

But our guess estimate excelled our preconceived numbers, that we were out of our wits! On the first day itself, more than 54,000 delegates had arrived. Anybody familiar with Mumbai would know that one can manage just about anything in the city. But not space. We were overwhelmed by this onslaught of numbers, but could not lose heart at this crucial juncture. The atmosphere and sentiments were so charged that not a single delegate complained about the inadequate arrangements. Many of them had no qualms about sleeping out in the open, seeing that there were not enough tents. Still the challenge to feed these constantly increasing numbers loomed ominously ahead of us.

Volunteers in the kitchen were working round the clock, without a moment's respite. So large were the numbers that lunch hours often extended beyond tea time. On one of those days, Atal jee himself waited until 5 pm to have lunch, just to raise our morale. Many workers were touched by the humility of Raj Mata Scindia, when she herself went up to dispose her used plate, after her meal. The presence of newcomers like Sikandar Bakht proved to be a morale-booster.

Justice M.C. Chagla's Prophecy

Driven by the determination to make the convention successful, we had arranged interactions with some special invitees who had no connection with the Jana Sangh in the past. This was a bonus for the rank and file, which was already captivated by the speeches of top leaders like Atal jee and Jagannathrao Joshi. One such tall personality was Justice M.C. Chagla, who was known internationally for his brilliant stint as the Chief Justice of the Bombay High Court and later as a Union Minister in the Cabinet of Indira Gandhi. One of his statements grabbed the headlines. Chagla told the audience of thousands, "I can see a miniature India here and by my side sits a future Prime Minister of India – Atal Bihari Vajpayee." This prophecy was received with a thundering applause. No doubt, there were sceptics who ridiculed this statement, but their ilk was mortified when Atal jee did actually take over as Prime Minister within less than two decades. Chagla's prophecy lifted our spirits considerably.

Atal jee was elected the President of the new Party – the BJP and we took him out in a huge procession to Shivaji Park from the convention venue – Samata Nagar for the public rally. When Atal jee reached the venue, the tail end of the procession was still five km away at Samata Nagar. Mumbai had never witnessed such a spectacle till then.

The birth of the BJP was not just an addition to the already crowded polity of various parties. It was an epochal event, where builders of the future India had vowed to change the national mindset and create history. The convention was widely covered by Indian and foreign news media. The one mantra for every BJP worker from that day on, was that Atal jee take over as the Prime Minister as soon as possible. The popular slogan 'Agli Bari, Atal Bihari (next time, Atal Bihari), was born at this convention, sixteen years before it came to fruition.

Beginning of New Era

A new era had dawned in India and it was the common workers who began this avalanche.

Ram Naik and Madhu Deolekar (in sweater) welcoming BJP leaders Atal Bihari Vajpayee and L.K.Advani at Mumbai airport on their arrival for the maiden plenary of the party

Ram Naik escorting Atal Bihari Vajpayee who is marching to hoist flag of BJP

Atal jee spared no words in complimenting the workforce for the success of the convention. It was a collective effort, led by luminaries, like Jhamatmal Wadhvani, Wamanrao Parab, Balasaheb Kanitkar, Bal Dharap, Swaroop Chand Goyal, Shanti Deo, Ved Prakash Goyal, Ramdas Nayak, Madhav Marathe, Jayawantiben Mehta, Malatibai Narawane, Madhu Deolekar, Mukundrao Kulkarni, Padmanabh Acharya and Madhukar Desai, just to mention a few. Under their guidance, thousands of workers had toiled relentlessly, day and night. It was their collective achievement. As I was the President of the Mumbai BJP, the

delegates from around the country, as well as the media gave me credit for this success, which created my image as a meticulous organiser.

As the BJP's Mumbai Unit Chief, I vowed to work more determinedly to build up the Party.

(July 26, 2015)

❒

Ram Naik flanked by Madhu Deolekar, Jayawantiben Mehta and Nanubhai Patel at a protest march taken to Reserve Bank of India to condemn the Stock Market Scam

SURCHARGED DAYS

The period between 1980 and 1994 was a period of much activity and achievement in my life. Those two years in particular are more significant, since the BJP was formed in 1980 and I was afflicted by cancer in 1994. The intervening fourteen years were spent in consistent working for the BJP and my constituency.

Every BJP worker around the country was engaged in a sort of constructive competition – that of spreading the Party's message. Innovative campaigns and agitations were being launched to make the BJP's presence felt in every ward and constituency. The Maharashtra Legislative Assembly elections were declared amidst this excitement. Being the Mumbai

BJP President I was also responsible for the selection of candidates. However, seniors like Hashu Advani, Ved Prakash Goyal and Balasaheb Kanitkar were there to guide me. We contested the Assembly elections to the best of our abilities. The result was that the new House had fourteen BJP MLAs from Maharashtra, which included five from Mumbai. I was one among the very few who had been elected for the second term and so came to be regarded a veteran in BJP. However, I had decided as the Mumbai BJP President to give the Party work more priority. Following this decision, I showed little interest in taking up any post in the Legislative Wing of the Party, nor was I inclined to work on any of the Legislative Committees. Hashu jee, our Group Leader in the Assembly, asked me to work diligently in the House and the constituency and reassured me, much to my relief, that it would be alright if I did not take up any legislative responsibilities.

Programmes & Publicity

As the Mumbai BJP President, I became more active and began Organising one programme after another successfully. The Youth Wing, the Zopadpatti Janata Parishad (the People's Slum Council) and the Mahila Morcha – the Women's Front, were among the activities in which I participated proactively. I had made it a point to ensure that the news of every event we organised, especially the agitational ones, reached newspaper offices, along with relevant photographs, within the deadline. I was assisted in this work by Madhu Deolekar and Santosh Vaidya. Fax machines and computers were nowhere on the horizon in those days. Even arranging for a typist was a problem on many occasions. At times like this, my neat handwriting stood us in good stead as I wrote the entire news item neatly in black ink – so that the ready-to-print press notes would get to the newspaper offices in time for printing.

Our mission of spreading the Party philosophy was successful, thanks to much hard work. Though many media persons poked fun at me for this promptness, most were helpful, since every press note had news value. After a while, the same journalists began to advise leaders of other political parties to emulate my practice and learn to prepare a press release like I had been doing.

But times have changed and even greenhorns in politics have begun employing media professionals to ensure publicity for themselves, something I avoided doing. My resolve was to master the three main languages: Marathi, Hindi and English. In this, I succeeded and was soon preparing press releases in all the three languages. In those days, it was a rarity in Mumbai to issue press notes in the three languages simultaneously. I had uncovered the trade secret – a ready-to-use press note was more likely to be published by the newspapers. My skill proved immensely useful. As the Party continued to expand, many talented workers were attracted to it and took up the responsibility of media relations.

We had organised several events which had great news potential. The Mumbai BJP raised its voice of protest on many issues of public interest. These ranged from the increasing price of cooking gas cylinders to the worsening law and order situation. I concentrated more on Mumbai's suburban railway network, since it was and still is the lifeline of the metropolis.

It was during my tenure as President that Vasantrao Bhagwat, BJP State Organising Secretary decided to induct full-time women workers into the Party. He selected Shaila Patange and entrusted me with the responsibility of training her. We were working hard and had become rather complacent, presuming that the BJP had entrenched itself in Mumbai. But the 1984 Parliamentary elections jolted us out of this illusion, for just two BJP candidates were elected to the Lok Sabha from all over the country. Our Prime Ministerial candidate, Atal Bihari Vajpayee, was among those defeated. Still, our resolve to rise from the ashes like the proverbial phoenix remained unshaken. Taking this defeat in stride, we got down to working for the Maharashtra Assembly elections due in 1985. It was decided to showcase our determination by Organising a rally to be addressed by Atal jee at Shivaji Park. The overwhelming response from the people of Mumbai was evident in the large crowds that spilled over this huge ground.

Beginning his speech in his unique style, Atal jee commented with dry humour, "This ocean of heads has turned up to see how the trounced Atal Bihari looks." His frank and open submission won over the audience and he sailed through the rest of his address. At that rally, Atal jee taught us how to accept defeat with dignity and poise.

Decreased Strength

We were able to increase our strength in the Assembly by two, but Mumbai had rejected us. While five BJP MLAs had been elected in 1980, only Prem Kumar Sharma and I were elected this time from the city. But we continued working, not allowing psychological depression to set in. The twenty-four-hour day was proving insufficient for us.

Ram Naik accompanying L.K.Advani who came to Mumbai to meet the victims of the 1993 bomb blasts

According to the BJP's constitution, an individual can be the president of a unit for only two consecutive terms. After the expiry of my second tenure in 1985, Hashu Advani was elected President of the Mumbai unit. Our work continued, complementing each other's efforts. Differences among political workers are inevitable, but our rare disagreements remained confined to just the two of us. No third person would ever hear about them. The many things I learnt from Hashu jee included simple tasks, such as maintaining a record of each telephone call and returning the calls wherever needed. He died in 1995 after a brief illness. I had spoken with him on the telephone just a day before he fell ill. He was the Finance Minister of Maharashtra at the time and had not returned home until late that night. I had left a message for him to call me, however late it was. Hashu jee returned my call at 12.30 am, anxious that I may have something urgent to discuss with him. That was to be our last conversation, for he was hospitalised the next morning. I was always impressed by his devotion to work and I continue to follow his promptness.

Ram Naik addressing a conference organised to oppose the Postal Department's fiat not to deliver mail to each household. On the dais are (L-R) Ratnakar Kamat, Nanubhai Patel and journalist Rahul Deo

Effective MP

Let me digress a bit at this juncture: The 1989 Parliamentary elections were declared when Hashu jee was at the helm in Mumbai. I have already narrated how I was forced to contest and had won. As an MP, I spent half of the year in Delhi and it became necessary to change my work priorities. I felt that as an MP, I should use the platform of the Lok Sabha effectively, so that the larger social good be achieved, my work thereby also benefitting the Mumbai BJP. My efforts received the nod of approval from Mumbaites when I took up the renaming of 'Bombay' to 'Mumbai' and to launch a mission to improve the suburban rail system in the city.

Sensing this overall satisfaction from the people, I felt that I would be able to do much more in this direction. Therefore, I expressed my desire to shed my organisational responsibility in Mumbai and my seniors in the Party acquiesced to this request. It was, however, suggested that I should concentrate more on the organisational work in my

North Mumbai Parliamentary constituency, something I was already doing. The result was that North Mumbai became renowned as a constituency with the best organisational set-up.

Presidentship Once More

After Hashu jee's two terms, the search for a new incumbent began. Emerging leaders like Ramdas Nayak, Kirit Somaiya, Madhu Chavan and Prakash Mehta still needed more experience and greater acceptability. The quest returned to Party seniors and the need was felt to find a worker who would be acceptable all around and take everybody along. As a political party grows, such consensus becomes difficult since the number of aspirants also increase. Seniors thought that I should don the mantle again, since the Party was heading for a brighter future and internal bickering should be strictly avoided. As a disciplined party worker, it was unthinkable for me to defy such a directive from seniors and to accord more importance to my own career promotion. I accepted the responsibility once more.

Friends in Delhi would tease me, saying, "You are physically present in Delhi, but your heart remains in Mumbai." I was finding it very taxing to handle both. I would fly to Mumbai almost every Friday evening, the moment the Lok Sabha sitting had concluded, and return to Delhi on Monday mornings for the week's sessions. Even Atal jee had teased me once, saying, "Why do you air-dash to your constituency in Mumbai at the drop of a hat? Do we not have our constituencies to look after?" This riposte from a leader looking after the organisational responsibility of the

Ram Naik felicitated by L.K. Advani during Ramdas Nayak's tenure as Mumbai BJP President

entire country left me with just one choice of response – a sheepish grin.

Obsession of Work

I remained the Mumbai BJP President for the next three years, till 1993. Looking back at my career, I feel that these three years were the busiest of my life. I was obsessed with work, work and more work. It was during this time that the infamous serial bomb blasts shook Mumbai on March 12, 1993, claiming over two hundred and sixty lives and seriously injuring more than seven hundred innocent people. I took the initiative to restore peace. This was just one public cause among the many I championed in my dual responsibility as an MP and the Mumbai BJP President.

Opposition parties launch a variety of agitations for many reasons. But some issues were crucial enough for us to take up cudgels and fight tooth and nail till we forced the authorities to yield.

One of these was the diktat of the postal authorities to install letter boxes at the ground floor of each multi-storeyed building. It was decreed that the postmen would not climb up floors to deliver mail at individual dwellings, if such boxes were not fixed. This order was issued by those postal bosses sitting in ivory towers. Though it was true that the postmen had a harrowing time climbing many floors in every building without letter boxes, our contention was that this rule should be applied to the newly constructed buildings and not to the existing ones, since the paucity of space in a large number of old buildings made it impossible to install letter boxes. This order would have caused much inconvenience in thousands of such buildings and to numerous families living in them. How could the postal department deprive them of receiving their mail?

We triggered an agitation which was supported by all sections of the population, since the sufferers would be both, those living in upscale areas like Cuffe Parade and those in the textile workers' chawls alike. The agitation was successful beyond our imagination.

Similar success was achieved when we agitated in connection with the Stock Scam, masterminded by notorious share-broker – Harshad Mehta. Our demand was a ban on Mehta from trading stocks. We sat outside the Reserve Bank of India to press our protest and the scam was thoroughly exposed. This unseemly episode became a milestone in our history and only strengthened our determination for launching more such struggles.

One incident during this period keeps coming to mind; my involvement in this was unintentional, but proved the talk of the town at the time. The Mumbai Municipal Corporation elections were declared in 1992 and I was constantly surrounded by visitors who were trying to get a BJP nomination to contest. I would meet them only by appointment at the Mumbai BJP's Kaththak Bhavan office, now named 'Vasant Smriti' after the late Vasantrao Bhagwat, at Dadar.

As the interviews were going on, an expensive visiting card was placed before me. I had not granted the person an appointment, nor did his name seem familiar. I asked our usher to find out why he wished to meet me. I was told by our office-in-charge, Santosh Vaidya, who seemed somewhat uneasy, that I should ask the visitor about this myself. I responded that the visitor be asked to wait, or take an appointment for later. Santosh reluctantly conveyed my message, returning with the visitor's reply that he was prepared to wait.

The interviews in my cabin continued, but soon I heard some commotion outside. Santosh returned to my cabin insisting that I should meet this visitor immediately, since the disturbance was caused by his presence. I agreed and asked that the visitor be sent in.

No sooner had the visitor stepped into my cabin, I realised the cause of the melee outside! He was Amar Naik, a dreaded gangster. His name was a terror. He was here to see me, seeking the BJP's nomination for his wife. I responded gently that it was not in accordance with our Party policy and would therefore not be possible. There was no emotion on his face as he heard my response. He simply walked out. In an instant after his departure, the atmosphere in and around my cabin returned to normal. I was to learn a few days later that his wife had been nominated to contest by another Party.

Nonetheless, there were many incidents that did disturb me and I would lose my temper when some Party colleague behaved irrationally. Some of them did test the boundaries of my tolerance.

Ramdas and Me

My young associate, Ramdas Nayak, was in the limelight due to the Antulay episode, which culminated in the dismissal of the Chief Minister. Ramdas was a favourite of mine. He was a lovable character due to his audacity and rebellious nature, though he could occasionally behave like a spoilt child, at which time we had no choice, but to concede to his demands, however unwillingly. Ramdas was rather impulsive by nature and would threaten us with his resignation from the Party if something was decided against his wishes. This would lead to some tension, but we would persuade him otherwise, since we could not afford losing such a dedicated worker. Such ardent workers are found in every political party and sometimes their egos need to be cosseted in the interests of the organisation.

But on one occasion, I had to take a firm stand. Ramdas had put in his resignation in a fit of anger, when some decision was taken against his wishes in regard to the mayoral election. I promptly accepted it after consulting Vasantrao Bhagwat. This alacrity on my part created a crisis in the Party and confounded Ramdas, as he had never imagined that I would call his bluff. Though Ramdas was dedicated to the BJP and unable to remain away, his options were closed. Eventually, he apologised and both of us decided to forgive, forget and move on. Ramdas succeeded me as the Mumbai BJP President. This incident, however, sent a strong message to party members that none should take the extreme step of walking out of the Party. Later, Ramdas felicitated me at

BJP Celebrated Golden Jubilee of August Kranti Day, when Ram Naik was heading Mumbai BJP. Alog with Atal Bihari Vajpayee (L tp R) Anna Dange, N.S. Pharande, Hashu Advani, Ram Naik and Gopinath Munde reiterating pledge of 'Swadeshi' on the day

the hands of L.K. Advani, who was the National President of the BJP.

Our association was fraught with many amazing coincidences. While I was down with cancer in 1994, Ramdas was assassinated. Due to the similarity of our names, several newspapers outside Mumbai and Maharashtra used my picture and name as that of the deceased. Many expressed the sentiment that Ramdas had donated many years of his life to me and that is how I recovered and conquered the cancer.

Resignation from BJP

In 1993, I decided to take up Parliamentary responsibilities in place of organisational work. History repeated when I was asked to take up some organisational responsibility after my unexpected defeat in the 2004 Lok Sabha elections. I accepted since it seemed appropriate to me at the time. I was appointed National Chairman of the BJP's Disciplinary Committee in late 2004.

People are wont to see only the crown, not the thorns. In this new capacity, I had to take disciplinary action against leaders like Madanlal Khurana, who had once remained Delhi's Chief Minister, and Uma Bharti, now a Union Minister. Both have been longstanding colleagues of mine. This stringent action on my part projected me as a stern and unbiased disciplinarian.

This responsibility was followed by the charge of the MLA-MP Training and Development Cell. I organised workshops for the newly elected MPs and MLAs in several states. At the time of my appointment as the Governor of UP, I was the National Convener of the newly created Good Governance Cell. I have resigned all my posts before taking over as the Governor.

My life in the BJP, however, remains a cherished memory.

(August 9, 2015)

❒

Ram Naik flanked by Viren Shah, Subhash Desai and Hashu Advani while filing nomination for his first Lok Sabha election in 1989. Those standing behind include Ratnakar Kamat, Nandkumar Kale, Gajanan Kirtikar, Murarilal Chaturvedi, Jayprakash Thakur, Vikas Agvekar and Nana Pawar

DAYS IN THE PARLIAMENT - I

I had earned some fame in Mumbai's socio-political circles, but on entering the much wider platform of the Lok Sabha in 1989, I felt more like a fledging. Curiousity about me had arisen ever since I had defeated a stalwart like Mrinal Gore, who was famous as 'Paniwali Bai' – the water woman. She had achieved this sobriquet since she had organised a series of agitations for demanding water supply for the people in Goregaon, a developing suburb of Mumbai.

Delhi correspondents of Mumbai-based newspapers were also eager to meet me for the same reason. One of them, Ashok Jain of the 'Maharashtra

Ram Naik inaugurating a computer lab developed out of his MP Fund at well-known Patkar-Varde College, Goregaon, Mumbai

Times' had earlier offered me some 'friendly' advice, which was not to contest against Mrinal Tai. "You are doing so well in Maharashtra, why invite the ignominy of a defeat?" Jain had advised me. In that exchange, we both decided to stake a wager on the outcome of the contest between Mrinal Gore and me. I had even written in Jain's diary that I would win the election against her with a margin of at least a hundred thousand votes. I proved more than correct, given that my margin was of 130,000 votes. Since then, I was especially interested in accosting Jain. Of course, it was a casual banter. My objective was to obtain as much consultation from those steeped in Delhi's politics, so as to easily adapt myself in the national capital. Besides Jain, 'Sakal' correspondent – Vijay Naik, 'Tarun Bharat' representative – Bapurao Lele and The Times of India's Rajdeep Sardesai were on my priority list of the people to meet.

I had learned on the floor of the Assembly that one's performance in the House plays a great role in his or her success as a people's representative. Based on this, I began my stint in the Lok Sabha with great enthusiasm. I became the focus of attention after taking the oath as I was among those twenty-six members who had taken the oath in Sanskrit. This was following a campaign by Mumbai-based scholar Shripad Dhundiraj Kavishwar, who had been urging members to take the oath in Sanskrit – the ancient language, which is the mother of all Indian regional languages. Until then, members would recite the oath in Hindi, English or in their mother-tongue. My entry in Parliament coincided with many members taking the oath in Sanskrit and this became a major news item the next day. This tradition, which we had begun, continues.

Well begun is half done, it is said. But this did not apply in my case. I delivered my maiden speech in the Lok Sabha on December 26, 1989. Rather than elation, it gave me a feeling of mortification due to my lack of fluency.

I had given a notice for speaking on the Supplementary Demands of the Union Budget and was permitted accordingly. Not many members speak on these demands. I began my speech with confidence. Usually, those elected to the Lok Sabha from Maharashtra find it difficult to speak fluently in Hindi or English. However, having conducted Jana Sangh and BJP meetings in Mumbai in Hindi, it did not occur to me that I would have any trouble in addressing the House in Hindi. In Maharashtra, the Speaker of the Assembly is addressed as 'Adhyaksha Maharaj' (Honourable Speaker Sir). I now used the same honorific in the Lok Sabha and immediately saw the House erupting. While most members burst out with gales of laughter, some rose to object. I was soon to learn about my faux pas. While the term 'Maharaj' is a respectful mode of address in Marathi, in Hindi, it is used for a cook.

My lapse was an opportune occasion for several members to ridicule a newcomer. Finance Minister Madhu Dandavate, a fellow Maharashtrian, came to my rescue. He admonished those laughing at me. Dandavate said, "Rather than deriding a new member for such an unintended mistake, you should compliment a Marathi-speaking member for trying to address the House in Hindi. How many of us, whose mother-tongue is not Hindi, speak in the national language here? We should encourage members like Naik." Dandavate's intervention gave my first speech in the Lok Sabha its moment in the spotlight and, to be sure, it was not for speaking on supplementary demands.

Not demoralised by my initial setback, I managed to learn the ropes within a short time. My priority remained highlighting the problems in my constituency, but I gave attention to other major matters and political developments to making use. I soon began using various parliamentary devices like Question Hour, Zero Hour and calling-attention motions and was able to initiate and accelerate a number of works in the interest of the public due to my proactive role. Later, as a Union Minister, I initiated and accomplished path-breaking schemes and programmes. I am happy with my achievements, though I shall limit this reminiscence to just four topics I dwelt with as an MP and have given me a feeling of fulfillment.

I raised them in the Lok Sabha and I became instrumental in their implementation too. Each of these

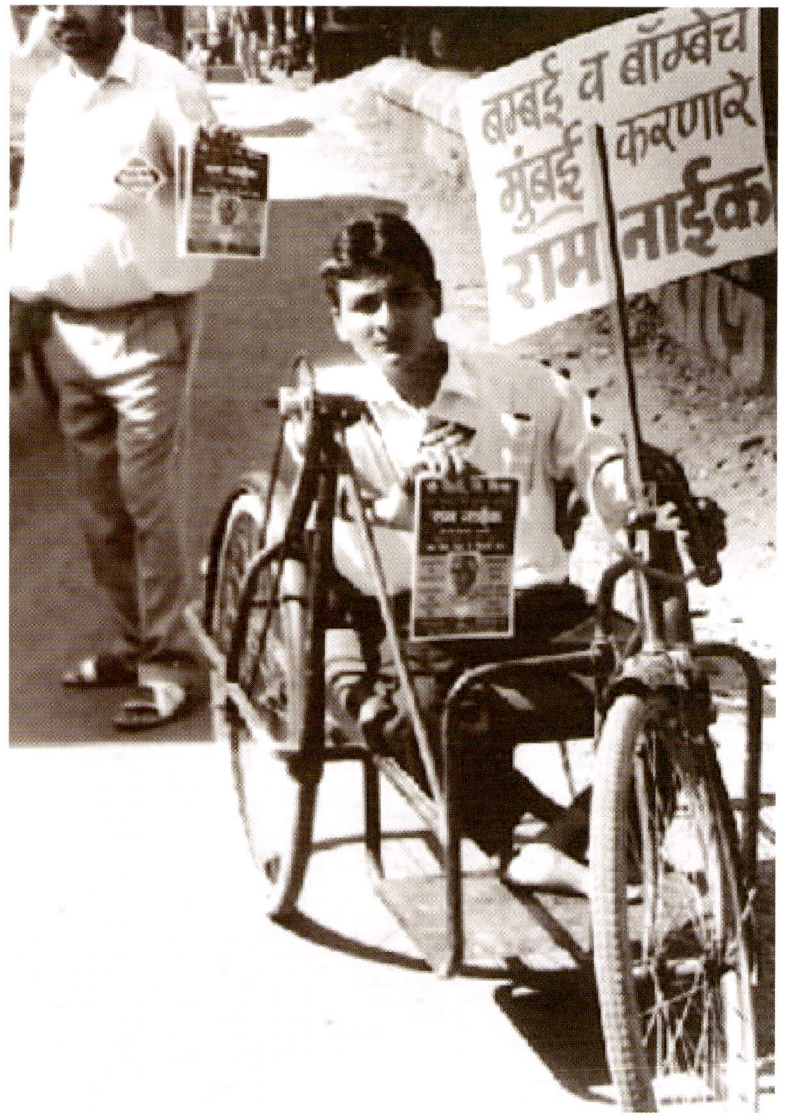

A physically challenged activist voluntarily joined Ram Naik's election campaign exhibiting a playcard of renaming 'Bombay' as 'Mumbai'

issues was unique. I succeeded in highlighting them while in the Opposition. This proves that a member can work splendidly even when in the Opposition.

'Mumbai', not 'Bombay' or 'Bambai'

It is a universally accepted dictum that proper nouns remain unchanged, irrespective of the language in which they are used. A proper noun cannot be translated or modified. According to this rule, I felt that Mumbai should be the only name for my city and must be used in all languages everywhere. This was felt when I received a draft of my participation in the Lok Sabha. This dichotomy or trichotomy about Mumbai's name disturbed me greatly. The draft speeches are circulated in both Hindi and English. In the speech dealt with my oath taking, it was written as 'Ram Nayak, Uttar Bambai' in Hindi and as 'Ram Naik, North Bombay' in English. I immediately dashed off a letter to the Lok Sabha Speaker, Rabi Ray and lodged my objection, demanding that my name be written only as 'Ram Naik, Uttar Mumbai'.

I discussed the matter with him and Ray conceded my contention in principle. He took the decision that, henceforth, my name would be written only as Ram Naik. As far as Mumbai was concerned, Ray decreed that only the name Mumbai would be used in the working of the Lok Sabha from then on. This fuelled my campaign for the use of the name 'Mumbai', in place of 'Bombay' or 'Bambai'. I wrote to all the authorities concerned and raised the matter in the Lok Sabha, but the stumbling block was a technicality. Renaming a town or city is the prerogative of a State Government under the revenue code. As per the procedure, a State has to adopt a motion for renaming a city or town and send the proposal to the Union government for its approval. When the Shiv Sena-BJP alliance government was formed in Maharashtra, the Cabinet under Chief

Minister Manohar Joshi adopted this resolution and sent it to the Centre. But there was yet another hurdle; the then Congress government at the Centre kept the matter on the backburner. Once more I pursued the matter with the Centre and, finally, the Union Government issued a notification on December 15, 1995 to the effect that henceforth, Mumbai will be known only by that single name in all languages. 'Bombay' or 'Bambai' be renamed 'Mumbai'. It was with a sense of achievement that I recall my success in this matter after such a prolonged battle.

Soon thereafter, Madras was renamed Chennai, Calcutta as Kolkata, Bangalore became Bengaluru, while Trivandrum was renamed Thiruvananthpuram.

Vande Mararam and Jana Gana Mana in Parliament

While the renaming of Mumbai needed a struggle about half a decade, the cause of 'Vande Mataram', which occurred to me out of the blue a while later, was embraced throughout the country with lightning speed; its implementation beginning immediately. I am most satisfied on a personal level about this accomplishment.

Vande Mataram, translated means, "I pray thee, Mother." It is a poem from Bankim Chandra Chatterjee's 1882 novel, 'Anandmath', written in Bengali. It played an inspiring role in the Indian freedom struggle and has since been associated with patriotism and an ardent love for the motherland. Post-independence, in 1950, the song's first two couplets were given the status of the 'national song' of India, while the national anthem is 'Jana Gana Mana' written by Rabindranath Tagore.

The genesis of my demand that the recital of Vande

Ram Naik inaugurating a light house at Satpati port from his MP Fund

Mataram and Jana Gana Mana at the start and conclusion of Parliament sessions dates back to 1991. The government had replied to a query from two Lok Sabha members that the recital of these two epic songs was not taking place in certain schools due to disregard. I was extremely chagrined at this unfortunate official response and raised half-an-hour discussion on this issue in the Lok Sabha on December 9, 1991. While speaking on the motion, I suggested that Parliament take the initiative in reciting the songs, it being the highest democratic forum in the country. Removal of this disregard was the prime duty of Parliament, I argued.

Leaders of all major political parties supported me. I pursued the demand with the General Purposes Committee of Parliament, since the procedure is that it must approve the demand first.

This Committee frames the rules and regulations for the working of the House. I discussed the demand, eventually deciding that each session of Parliament should begin with Jana Gana Mana and conclude with Vande Mataram. Sadly, a few members of the Committee disagreed, questioning the need for such a recital. Some others contended that it would amount to compulsion for some specific sections of the population. Few others detected a shade of Hinduism or retrograde tendencies. The media highlighted the issue by discussing its pros and cons, but I continued to fight on all fronts. Finally, the decision was endorsed and forty-five years after India became independent, Jana Gana Mana was sung for the first time in Parliament on November 24, 1992 and Vande Mataram on December 23, 1992. I feel proud to claim that these songs embodying our national ethos have become a permanent feature of our Parliamentary tradition. Many visitors from around the world recall this contribution even now. Several seniors greet me with Vande Mataram, rather than using the customary Namaskar. Veteran journalist and now an MP, Tarun Vijay's salutation for writing about me is 'Vande Mataram Ram Naik' instead of the usual 'Shri' (Mr). Such acknowledgements have strengthened my fervour to keep on with my work.

Promoting Breastfeeding, Banning Baby Food Advertisements

December 1992 was perhaps the most glorious month of my tenure as an MP. I have narrated in detail how I spearheaded a campaign to ban advertisements of baby foods and moved a Private Member's Bill to this effect. This was in 1991. About a year elapsed before the Constitutional formalities were completed, including the Official Bill moved by the government, its endorsement by both Houses of Parliament and ultimately getting the assent of the President of India, who signed it as an Act on December 29, 1992.

MP Fund

It is extremely rare in Parliament that members belonging to all parties in the House support a motion moved by an opposition member. I was fortunate to enjoy such an honour. An MP occupied a much higher position in the democratic structure than a city corporator, but did not have any say in sanctioning works of general interest within his or her constituency. Though he could participate in finalising the nation's annual budget and plan, he was unable to contribute directly in any developmental work within his own area. I felt that like the MLA Fund in Maharashtra, which had become a reality due to my initiative, a fund for the MPs should also be created. Accordingly, I put forward this proposal before the then Finance Minister, Madhu Dandavate, on January 14, 1990 and began pursuing it at various forums.

I presented a petition to the Prime Minister, signed by over a hundred MPs belonging to Ruling and Opposition Parties. I also campaigned through the media and approached the Planning Commission. On July 26, 1991, I asked a starred question in this regard in the Lok Sabha, remarking, "Even a village council member is able to get certain works done, but an MP, who is involved in sanctioning the country's national budget running into billions of rupees, is not authorised to get any work of his choice done in his own constituency. This is like water, water, everywhere, but not a drop to drink." Several members supported my argument.

Meanwhile, a new government had taken over under Prime Minister P.V. Narasimha Rao. The then Finance Minister, Dr. Manmohan Singh, who later became the Prime Minister, agreed to discuss the proposal with an all-party delegation. Several rounds of discussions took place. Finally, the Prime Minister made an announcement in the House on December 23, 1993 that the government had decided to launch the MP Fund. Accordingly, each MP was sanctioned ₹ 10 million annually for taking up developmental works in his or her constituency. Norms were formulated to implement such works. It was decided that an MP would recommend such works to the District Collector, who is the topmost revenue authority in a district, to the tune of ₹ 10 million a year and the authority should implement them within the norms.

This was an epochal decision in our Parliamentary history. While many MPs felt that this would invest some power in them, the reality was that they were now entrusted with the responsibility of ensuring that these works were completed. This was very inconvenient for inactive MPs since they found it impossible to face the electorate in the absence of any performance. But those truly interested in the constituency were able to transform their areas. I was now convinced of the usefulness of the MP Fund, which I raised to ₹ 20 million when I became the Minister of State for Programme Implementation in the Vajpayee government. It has now been enhanced to ₹ 50 million. I like to cite this achievement as a landmark step.

The satisfaction I have derived on these four counts is boundless.

(August 30, 2015)

❒

This original print of the Constitution in Hindi is now displayed in Parliament Library due to the efforts of Ram Naik

DAYS IN THE PARLIAMENT - 2

When I was elected for the first time to the Lok Sabha in 1989, every BJP worker was upbeat and positive. Though a BJP government has been installed in India in 2014, the victory of 1989 was really special.

Just two BJP members had been elected to the Lok Sabha in 1984 – one from Gujarat and the other from Andhra Pradesh. Against this dismal performance, we had eighty five MPs in 1989. Our performance had shown remarkable improvement. Statistically, it was 42 times. We were, of course, far from becoming complacent with this windfall. But the victory had assured us that the BJP can form its government in

Railway Consultative Committee members Basudev Acharya, S.S. Ahuwalia, etc. took a suburban train ride in Mumbai since Ram Naik wanted them to witness firsthand sufferings of commuters

India within the next few years and accordingly a strategy was structured.

Shadow Railway Minister

The concept of a shadow cabinet was implemented by Atal jee. Considering the interests, experience and Constituency of every MP, we were assigned specific ministries and were nominated by the Party on the Parliamentary Consultative Committees of these respective ministries. The MPs concerned were also given an opportunity to speak on these subjects in the House. I was entrusted with the railway ministry, a subject close to my heart.

My friend Ram Kapse and I began to take up matters concerning the railways in the House. Both of us, had been elected from the metropolis with the largest suburban rail network in India. We were both rail commuters, Kapse on the Central Railway and I on the Western Railway in Mumbai. We would study the subject on which we were slated to speak thoroughly and compliment each other's work. When both of us were MLAs in 1978, we had presented a Petition to the Parliament to air the grievances of the rail commuters of Mumbai and its environs through BJP MP – Rambhau Mhalgi. In the first year after our election to the Lok Sabha, we were given an opportunity to work on the various committees connected with the Railway Ministry. They included the Parliamentary Consultative Committee and the Convention Committee of the railways. We realised that something concrete could be achieved by working on such committees.

As an MLA, my priority was the organisational work, but as an MP, I began to participate in the proceedings of various committees. I was also appointed Chief Whip of the BJP Parliamentary Group.

My colleagues called me a workaholic, who seemed to be disinterested in everything else. During parliamentary sessions, I was required to stay in Delhi and at the conclusion of the day's sitting; I often found free time on my hands. I utilised that time to study a variety of subjects in order to pursue various issues. Occasionally, I would come across something strange, or issues that had gone unnoticed by others.

As a law graduate, I had studied the Constitution of India. So, I was astonished when a member used the word 'Hind' while taking oath in Urdu. In the Constitution, our country is "India, that is Bharat." Therefore, I felt that using the word 'Hind' would not be proper, although it has a sentimental connotation. I argued this point in the House. Since then, care is taken that only India or Bharat is used in every oath-taking.

भारत का संविधान

हम भारत के लोग, भारत को एक सम्पूर्ण
प्रभुत्व-सम्पन्न लोकतंत्रात्मक गणराज्य
के लिये तथा उस के समस्त नागरिकों को :
सामाजिक आर्थिक और राजनैतिक न्याय,
विचार, अभिव्यक्ति, विश्वास धर्म
और उपासना की स्वतंत्रता,
प्रतिष्ठा और अवसर की समता
प्राप्त कराने के लिये,
तथा उन सब में
व्यक्ति की गरिमा और राष्ट्र की
एकता सुनिश्चित करने वाली बन्धुता
बढ़ाने के लिये
दृढ संकल्प हो कर अपनी इस संविधान सभा में
आज तारीख २६ नवम्बर १९४९ ई० (मिति मार्गशीर्ष
शुक्ला सप्तमी, संवत् दो हजार छ विक्रमी) को
एतद्द्वारा इस संविधान को अङ्गीकृत अधि-
नियमित और आत्मार्पित करते हैं।

The original print of the Constitution manifests artistic excellence

Original Copy of Constitution

Anyone now has access to the original Hindi edition of the Constitution, which was made possible owing to my efforts. But, the chain of events that led it is quite interesting. It so happened that one day, while I was reading in the Parliament Library, I came across the original English edition of the Constitution. Curious, I asked to see the original Hindi edition of the Constitution. Quite an amusing tale unfolded from this simple query. The original Hindi edition was written down by Vasant Vaidya, a Maharashtra calligraphist. Gold-plated pages were imported from Germany and a special kind of ink, used for writing this edition, was bought from a reputed firm in China. The writing instrument, was a special pen, crafted by the famous Watkins Company, made in Washington State, USA. It had taken Vaidya a full year to complete the writing of the Constitution on the gold plated pages. The Hindi edition is decorated with sketches of Lord Shri Ram, Shri Krishna, Gautam Buddha, the Rani of Jhansi and several personalities from our cultural and historical past. Conceding my demand, this original manuscript is now available in Parliament Library for viewing, while replicas of this edition are for sale.

I had to spend considerable time in protracted correspondence to press my demand for publishing postage stamps bearing images of the great saints of Maharashtra, like Dnyaneshwar, Tukaram and Eknath. This is a time consuming process, for one has to spend hours in studying various complex pieces of legislation. But, I rarely had any social engagements between Parliamentary sittings. Moreover, my family was in Mumbai, so I was able to find much free time while in Delhi. My Mumbai office assistants stayed with me in Delhi by rotation, helping me late into the night. To save time, we avoided going out for dinner, instead ordering food at my residence, while we took lunches in the Parliament canteen.

Parliamentary Committees

When I read some news items criticizing the perquisites available to MPs, especially the nominal prices for the canteen food, I could not help laughing. Many MPs are away from their homes and families for long durations, occasionally even for six months a year. How are they to manage without this canteen? I am no food connoisseur, but I do understand management. When I complained about the unsatisfactory quality of food in the canteen during a meeting of the General Purposes Committee,

Speaker – Shivraj Patil immediately decided to form a Canteen Committee and I was appointed its Chairman by consensus. A longstanding problem was solved during my tenure and problems faced by the canteen personnel were also resolved.

I enjoyed working on the Consultative Committee for the Railway Ministry. I also enjoyed my stint on the Murari Committee, which was constituted to study the impact of the permission granted to foreign trawlers for fishing near the Indian coastline and the resultant inconvenience to the Indian fishermen.

Thanks to the terms of reference for the Murari Committee, we visited several major ports around the country. Such tours tend to forge friendships with MPs from other parties. Communist MPs – Basudeb Acharia and Geeta Mukherjee and Congress MPs – Madhavrao Scindia and Priyaranjan Dasmunshi – became good friends during such tours.

Fishermen's leader – Thomas Kocheri was a member of the Committee, though he was not an MP. I had raised the matter in the Lok Sabha regarding his indefinite hunger strike, which culminated into the formation of the Murari Committee. I was regarded proxy spokesman for the fishermen throughout India and working on this Committee had made it possible for me to speak with authority. Our thought process had synced to such a degree, that we were later able to work together seamlessly on various issues concerning the fishermen. Bhai Bandarkar, a firebrand leader of the fishermen in Maharashtra, often spoke publicly, about my contribution, giving me a sense of satisfaction.

I was also nominated a member of the Stocks Scam Parliamentary Inquiry Committee. The scam masterminded by Big Bull, Harshad Mehta was of massive proportions and had been the most serious untill then. Over ₹ 4,000 crore (one crore being ten million) belonging to the general public had been misappropriated in this scam. The situation was so critical that the people's faith in the banking system was on the brink of collapse. The Committee did pioneering work in this case. So immersed was I in the frequent tours and meetings of the Committee, that I did not notice the insidious spread of cancer inside my body. The point that I want to make is that the Committee members dealt with this sensitive subject seriously, proving that such a legislative body's contribution can be a force to reckon with.

Ram Naik welcoming Dr. Narendra Jadhav at Lucknow Raj Bhavan

We had taken out a morcha (protest march) to the Reserve Bank of India, on behalf of the BJP and our delegation was invited by the Governor of the Bank to discuss the matter. A top officer of the Bank, Narendra Jadhav, brought his message to us and took the delegation for the meeting. Subsequently, Jadhav earned fame as an accomplished writer after publishing a biographical account. Later, he was appointed Vice Chancellor of Pune University and a member of the Planning Commission. He and I became friends and, to date, we still meet occasionally.

Public Accounts Committee

In 1995, in acknowledgement of my effective participation in the working of various important Committees, I was appointed Chairman of the most prestigious of them; the Public Accounts Committee or PAC. Giants like P.V. Narasimha Rao, former President of India – R. Venkataraman, Atal Bihari Vajpayee had earlier graced this office. I was the first MP from Maharashtra to be bestowed with this honour. One of the major assignments of the PAC is to investigate in case of any dubious transactions made by various government agencies after they are recorded by the Comptroller and Auditor General of India (CAG). In a way, the PAC functions as a check on governmental expenditure. I created a record by submitting eight reports of PAC in one year.

The most sensational of these reports was about the misuse of the official aircraft belonging to the Railway Ministry by the then Railway Minister, C.K. Jaffer Sharief. We both shared an excellent personal relationship. While I was down with cancer, he had come down to meet me in Mumbai.

Ram Naik is welcomed aboard 'INS Vikrant' by Commander V.S.Patil and Rear Admiral Anand Kalaskar

But this consideration could not impede my working – since I was inculcated with the training imparted by my father: duty first, all else secondary. I have lived by this credo and it has proved very effective in my career. This report put the government in a bind. The railway aircraft is to be used in emergencies, such as rail mishaps and natural calamities. However, it was established that Sharief had utilised it on many occasions with his family and friends for private visits. Some other ministers, too, had to face difficulties, since it transpired that Sharief had dispatched an empty plane to fetch them from Tirupati, a famous temple in South India.

In another report, I pointed out that the then Urban Development Minister, Sheila Kaul had misused her office for the reservation of government quarters. Subsequently, she had to face judicial proceedings. However, I ensured that I did not lose my self-control and sense of decorum while preparing these reports, or speaking on them. Therefore, none of these leaders harboured any personal animosity towards me. On the other hand, I was able to make many friends since I had exposed culpable malpractices impartially, with no malice towards anyone.

Friendly Help

As an MP, I was required to handle a plethora of diverse matters. One of them was prohibiting sweetmeat makers from using edible colours in their products. Union Health Minister, A.R. Antulay was among my acquaintances. The makers argued that it would be more reasonable to order them to use only permitted food colours of specified quality. However, if the ban was implemented in toto, there would only be white sweets. Imagine eating white *jalebis* and *pedhas*.

The other was the imposition of a cess on Indian savouries like *sev*, *chivda* and potato *wada*. These decisions created a difficult situation for small-scale makers. On both occasions, my friend Rajabhau Chitale led delegations to me. Although it appeared to be a simple problem, much running around was needed to resolve it. Most of the difficulties were eliminated after a discussion with Finance Minister Dr. Manmohan Singh. With the handling of such issues too, my circle of friends increased.

Many matters came to my attention through my personal networking and resolving some of them has created a history of sorts. Renowned museum expert Sadashiv Gorakshkar has been my friend for decades as we had worked together since the formative years of the Jana Sangh. He earned an enviable reputation as the Director of the Prince of Wales Museum (now named after Chhatrapati Shivaji) in Mumbai. I had been to his bungalow within the Museum premises on several occasions.

The Union Government had taken over the Museum in 1993. I felt that its imperialistic name should be changed and moved a motion in the House on May 5, 1993 to name it after the great warrior, Chhatrapati Shivaji Maharaj. Although there was no apparent hurdle in its renaming, the procedure took its time and came to a successful conclusion only in 2001. I am very happy that I could contribute to the perpetuation of the memory of the founder of Hindavi Swaraj, Shivaji Maharaj.

The warship that helped India to win the 1971 war against Pakistan, INS Vikrant was a symbol of national pride. I demanded in the Lok Sabha on March 21, 1997 that this aircraft carrier, the Indian Navy's first, should be preserved as a national monument. This was done and thousands of visitors could tour the historic ship and relish the memories of that glorious victory. However, my own first visit to INS Vikrant was as late as in 2008, when I was neither an MP nor holding any post. Still, Naval officers and ratings gave me a grand welcome, in honour of my initiative.

Sadly, the matter of its preservation was bandied about between the Union and Maharashtra governments and eventually resulted in INS Vikrant's tragical disposal as scrap.

(September 13, 2015)

❒

Ram Naik was delighted during his cancer affliction when a towering leader like Atal Bihari Vajpayee came to enquire after his health without giving any prior intimation

BATTLING THE DREADED CANCER

As soon as the ten-day Ganesh Festival is over, people begin planning for the great celebration of Diwali, known as the festival of lights, while the working classes eagerly look forward to their annual bonus.

I, too, have received a great bonus and it came directly from the Almighty, in the form of my life after cancer. On September 25, 1994, I was given a new lease on life, when my doctors declared me cured. I have since been enjoying this bonus, working as tirelessly as before, even after completing eighty-one years of an eventful life.

Many people candidly say that they envy my robust health. This was a sentiment I heard of even in 1994. Nobody believed then that I was nearing sixty years of age. I was appointed on the Stocks Scam Inquiry Committee of Parliament and had been doing much travelling as part of its visits. A lot of my time had been consumed by the ongoing budget session of Parliament as well. Notwithstanding all this, I arrived in Mumbai around March 12, after a gap of a month. On my arrival home, my wife commented that I had lost weight, a remark I casually dismissed, putting it down to my erratic meal timings.

Cancer Suspected

The next day I returned to Delhi to attend the ongoing budget session at the Lok Sabha, taking my seat next to Pune MP, Anna Joshi, who was known for his humorous nature. As soon as I was seated, he said, "Rambhau, do you have jaundice? Your skin is looking yellowish." I reprimanded him for cracking jokes while the House was in the midst of a serious discussion. But he was relentless. During the lunch break, he persisted with his queries, calling our Party MP, Dr. Gunwant Sarode to take a look at me. Dr. Sarode asked me to accompany him out into the open where he could examine my complexion in natural light. He barely glanced at me before immediately insisting that we go straight to the Parliament dispensary. My blood and urine were examined, which the doctors declared to be free from jaundice. But they did ask me to undergo a sonography test. When that report was received, the lady doctor in the dispensary enquired if there were any family members with me in Delhi. But I was not worried by her questions since

I was confident that there was nothing wrong with me, given my history of good health and strong physique. There is a streak of obstinacy in me! All the same, I pressed her to explain why she had asked such a question. "You may as well tell me, as no family member is here," I persisted. She cautiously replied, "I feel you should go to Mumbai and undergo some tests at the Tata Hospital." I was taken aback by her words. The Tata Hospital is synonymous with cancer and I was not expecting this to be happening to me in the least. Recovering my composure, I requested her to write down the tests that were needed to be conducted. While leaving the Parliament House with that note in my pocket, the only thought that kept swirling in my mind was, 'How long before did I return here?'

Blessings and Optimism

The Almighty has blessed me with an abundance sense of optimism. That I would not return to Parliament was not the issue my mind contended with. The only question for me was: How long shall I remain away? This happened even though the doctor had hinted at the possibility of cancer in my body. This optimism was reiterated by Atal jee the next day, when I called on him to resign as Chairman of the Canteen Committee, pleading my impending long absence. After listening intently, Atal jee responded, "Get yourself cured quickly and return. I don't want your resignation." This affirmative response instilled in me a huge dose of energy. Workers like me can't think of disregarding Atal jee's orders, but he gallantly yielded to my entreaty. He nominated Sushma Swaraj, who is now the External Affairs Minister, to the chairmanship.

She, too, honoured my sentiments and accepted the responsibility. I need to mention this since she immediately relinquished the chairmanship in my favour when I returned after my recovery.

As I was leaving for the airport on the night of March 19 to fly to Mumbai, Ram Kapse arrived at my doorstep. He said, "I feel that you should not travel alone. Advani jee, too, asked me to accompany you. So here I am!" Though Kapse spoke in a rather seemingly casual manner, I understood his underlying concern for me. We travelled to Mumbai together that night.

The affection and concern of seniors and colleagues was comforting and enabled me to overcome the dreaded cancer. As I look back, I feel that those harrowing days went by like a film sequence on fast forward. I find three reasons for the cure and recovery: First, the excellent medical treatment at my disposal. Second, my will power and the indomitable support and courage of my family members. And, finally, the prayers of my numerous well-wishers.

The day I was admitted for an examination at the Tata Hospital a telephone call was received from the Prime Minister's Office. Prime Minister P.V. Narasimha Rao had called to enquire after my health. This gesture boosted my morale by several degrees. It also stimulated the staff around me to take better care of me. Dr. Shanti Swaroop, who had come to inform me that my affliction was called 'lymphoma', had to navigate his way through the crowd of my colleagues and followers. Members from the crowd also included coolies from the Borivali railway station, their concern for me evident for having championed their cause some years ago. Senior colleagues like Wamanrao Parab and Hashu Advani were present too. Doctors treating me were a bit flustered with the situation. It was going to be a challenge for them to maintain my immunity, to prevent any sort of infection caused on account of the visitors. My wife was somewhat reassured when she saw the surge of well-wishers around me. The doctors, expectedly, ordered strict control on visitors. At the same time, Hashu jee's words echoed through my mind all the while. He had said, "We are men of the masses. People meeting us are our real tonic." Among the visitors was Wamanrao, a burly colleague, who broke down, making everyone around to become emotional. The overall concern was my ability to cope with the grief of my dear and near ones and how to hold them without hurting sentiments. This was worrying me too. But, finally, a compromise was reached!

Fight Against the 'Big C'

When I returned home three days later, following the first chemotherapy, I found it completely transformed. The tiny single-bedroom flat had the drawing room and

A chemotherapy and a visit by L.K. Advani happened unfailingly every month. Ramesh Medhekar looking on during one such visit

the bedroom adjacent to each other. One of my co-workers, Ram Moorat Vishvakarma, had replaced the connecting door within two days. The wooden door had been redesigned with its top half now fitted with glass, and a curtain in place to afford me privacy when required. With this novel idea, I was able to see my visitors and they could also see me, without any risk of infection as they would be away from me. This proved to be very convenient. I was glad to have the good wishes of my visitors. This arrangement kept my morale and optimism afloat. While some conveyed their wishes through gestures, others wrote their wishes and sentiments in a notebook. Many of them were unknown to me. Some of them even wept at the sight of my bald head and emaciated body. An auto-rickshaw driver, Jayaprakash Chettiar, on the verge of tears, confided in my daughter that even though he was illiterate, he was keen on sending me a written message. Touched by his concern, Vishakha took it down verbatim. It read "Sir, we feel your pain even if a mosquito bites you. Please recover fast." The simplicity and sincerity of his words were a balm to my soul. Such wishes proved more potent than the medicine.

Ram Naik went for casting his ballot for the Legislative Council election inspite of his cancer affliction

Everybody who knew me was helping out in some way or the other. Jaiprakash Thakur would accompany me to the Tata Hospital. Party MLA, Madhavrao Marathe was always present to welcome any prominent leader who came to visit me. Yashwant Patil, a well-wisher from Vasai, regularly sent tender coconuts from his garden, as coconut water was known to be effective in reducing body heat. Omprakash Mishra, a leader of fruit vendors from Borivali, selected choice fruits for me and delivered them to my home himself.

As soon as it became known that I would need a couple of bottles of blood, voluntary donors mobbed the hospital in compliance. Some occasional visitors to the Party office included well-wishers like Madhav Prabhu and Tulsidas Deshmukh. But now they camped out at the hospital to look after me. The stream of visitors included local workers and old friends and leaders from outside Mumbai. Socialist leaders like Mrinal Gore and Baburao Samant came to lift my spirits and boost my morale, while veteran Communist

Twenty years after conquering cancer Ram Naik being awarded 'Cancer Survivor Award' of Nurgis Dutt Foundation by Sunil Dutt's daughter Priya Dutt, M.P.

ideologue Somnath Chatterjee in Delhi sought regular updates about my condition.

By some quirk of fate, actor Sanjay Dutt once came to visit me. It so happened that his father, thespian Sunil Dutt, had been elected to the Lok Sabha from Mumbai North-West along with me. We had interacted quite frequently. I myself did not like cinema and was not among his fans. Still his affection for me was quite touching. Sunil was not in Mumbai when he heard of my illness. Feeling a sense of urgency to enquire about my health, he had asked his son Sanjay to meet me. Sanjay's arrival in our middle-class locality created a huge sensation. The irony was that Sanjay was arrested the next day in connection with the Mumbai bomb blasts of 1993 and speculation was rife about the timing of his visit. Poor Sunil Dutt could never have imagined that his son's visit would be interpreted in this manner.

All the workers and leaders of the BJP visited me; but mentioning everybody by name will prove impossible. Still I wish to mention three of them: Atal jee was to halt at the Mumbai airport for a few hours, on his way to Geneva. He came to meet me without alerting anyone. His arrival was so sudden and unannounced that my family members, so busy in the midst of this crisis, could serve him only with the fruits that were available in the house. My wife was mortified that she was unable to welcome him in a manner befitting his stature.

During the six months of my compulsory confinement, Advani jee came to meet me almost every month and enquired regularly about my progress. Pramod Mahajan stood by my family like a younger brother. My elder daughter, Nishigandha was studying abroad as a cancer research scientist. Once I had casually remarked my regret that she was not near me. Mahajan heard this and made arrangements within the week to bring her to Mumbai, without anyone making aware in the slightest of his plan, giving no financial burden on my family in this regard. He had told my family to ask for financial help without any hesitation, in case it was needed.

The BJP rank and file in North Mumbai cared for me during this period as if I were one of their own. Even the Almighty would have found it a difficult task to count their prayers for me. Every deity in every temple was in a way ordered by its devotees to ensure my cure. My constituency had a sizeable Christian population in Vasai, where prayers were held for me in several churches. Father Francis D'Britto, the famous author, reported to me that he had prayed for me while he was at the Vatican. Such affection from all quarters was filling me with so much positive energy.

While my well-wishers were offering prayers, my family members had no time even for that. All their time was claimed by my treatment, keeping my medicines ready and looking after the visitors. Prasanna Kudtalkar, who works in my office, was omnipresent. So were my relatives, who were always available. The food sent to the hospital by my sister-in-law Swati was far better than any fare served in a five-star hotel. I still remember that fantastic cuisine! Anyone undergoing chemotherapy will find that the treatment causes food to taste like rubber. But not so with Swati's tiffin! The sight of that food tickled my palate, arousing my appetite.

My well-wishers' blessings were bolstered by a team of doctors at the hospital. Dr. Shanti Swaroop and Dr. R. Gopal, both medical oncologists, and radiologist Dr. N.H. Merchant were among those caring for me. Their efforts were supplemented by Dr. Sulabha Ranade, Dr. Rajeev Tungare and Dr. Mukund Phadke, who were just a telephone call away and who arranged most of my treatment to be made possible at home.

Soon my body began responding positively to this collective care. The prescribed cycle of chemotherapy was followed. Initially, until the third chemo cycle, the doctors were reticent about commenting on my condition, except to say that it was serious. Within a couple of months, however, the very same doctors were reassuring everyone that I would soon be cured.

Blow Worse than the Cancer

But suddenly out of the blue, another blow! I was hit below the belt. The pain of this particular injury would have shammed the suffering caused by the cancer. A news

Renowned Cancer Care Oraganization of Mumbai 'V Care' felicitated Ram Naik with 'Cancer Survivor Award 2013'

item had been published by The Times of India, based on a confidential report by the Lok Ayukta (Government Ombudsman) of Maharashtra. The report was about an issue that had taken place six years ago. It had some adverse remarks against me. I had earlier issued a challenge that the charges against me in this report should be proven in a court of law. My surmise was that this sudden resurrection of an old matter must have been caused by a tiff between the then Municipal Commissioner, S.S. Tinaikar and Additional Commissioner, S. Ramamurthi.

For no earthly reason at all, Tinaikar began castigating me. It was impossible for me to tolerate this mud-slinging as it was creating doubts about my integrity. I remembered a saying in the Bhagwat Geeta: "For a gentleman, defamation is more torturous than death." I girded up my physical and emotional strength to rebut the charges, even in my weakened condition. I shall share the saga of this struggle in next article.

(September 27, 2015)

❐

Atal Bihari Vajpayee leading Ram Naik to the dais after his victory over cancer. Others present included (L-R) Jayprakash Thakur, Ved Prakash Goyal, Prakash Javadekar, Gopinath Munde and Ramesh Medhekar

BACK TO THE GRINDSTONE

Bouquets and brickbats are part and parcel of a politician's life and accepting them with equanimity is the only sensible way to move ahead. Though I am aware of this, I am unable to tolerate any allegation of misbehaviour or misappropriation made against me. As I was then fighting cancer, my body and mind had become quite frail. The news mentioned in the previous chapter hit me hard. Although the news item was published in 1994, the matter dated back to 1988 when I was an MLA.

The Mumbai Municipal Corporation had decided to demolish the huts of three agricultural workers who had been holding ration cards issued in 1966. Their huts were erected on agricultural land. The government had decided to protect all pre-1980 hutments–legal or otherwise. Not only were these three huts legal, but according to the revenue code of the time, they did not require any permission, as they stood on agricultural land. I pointed out these facts and asked Additional Municipal Commissioner, S. Ramamurthi not to demolish them. He conceded my request.

However, Municipal Commissioner, S.S. Tinaikar, who was on a higher ladder than Ramamurthi in bureaucracy had filed a complaint against Ramamurthi with the Lok Ayukta (The Government Ombudsman), without verifying the facts. This may have happened due to their personal differences. At the time, in 1988, I had challenged Tinaikar that he could file a court case against me if the Lok Ayukta had recorded any objections in his report. And since Tinaikar could not face my challenge, he had dumped the report in cold storage. Now six years later, in 1994, while I was battling the odds against cancer, this issue resurfaced and had been published in The Times of India. I sent my clarification which was duly published and the Times ended the matter then and there.

Days of Anguish

But perhaps destiny had wished otherwise. Tinaikar had retired by that time and became a hobby writer. He began writing in various newspapers on the issue. He went to the extent of alleging that the huts, in fact, did not ever exist. As I was in the clear, I was not afraid to submit my version to the newspapers concerned. But in my fragile state, this was torture for my mind and body. I was so weak that I could not eat properly, or even talk. In spite of this, I managed to write down the facts of the matter and got it typed. Normally, under healthy circumstances, such an activity would not have taken me more than an hour – but due to illness, it required more than three hours to finish. I was so tired by the end of it that I writhed with pain and the mental trauma caused me to toss and turn in my bed during the nights. Whole nights would pass in this manner. My wife, daughters and workers berated me for taking undue cognizance of these defamatory statements. Initially, Kunda would not allow me to read newspapers, but eventually she had to yield at my insistence.

Journalist Kapil Patil calling on Ram Naik at Lucknow Raj Bhavan to renew their 20-year-old friendship

This self-torture had a negative effect on my already feeble health. My haemoglobin level dipped to such an alarming level that it was felt that I would have to be re-admitted into hospital. But medication and a noble deed by journalist Kapil Patil, who is now a Member of Legislative Council in Maharashtra, provided me some relief.

Patil is a Socialist and thus my ideological opponent. He was then running a popular evening newspaper, 'Aaj Dinank' (Today). Whether due to my unblemished reputation, which had also gained the trust of my opponents, or perhaps because of his investigative nature, Patil, unbeknownst to anyone, decided to visit that agricultural land in Borivali. Like any Mumbai resident, he may have found it difficult to believe that a piece of agricultural land did actually exist in a concrete jungle like Mumbai. In any case, he witnessed the three huts and the land on which they stood, as well as met the farmhands. Since he had seen the situation first-hand, the genuine journalist in Patil came to the fore.

Patil published a comprehensive news item, along with photographs of the huts, highlighting the truth of the situation. As a result, all newspapers ceased publishing Tinaikar's slanderous articles about this controversy. Moreover, the Assembly Speaker directed that proceedings be instituted against Tinaikar for leaking out a confidential report of the Lok Ayukta. Although he was well aware that I was afflicted with cancer and, therefore, bedridden, Tinaikar seemed to have no qualms about causing me this mental anguish. I could not understand what satisfaction he derived from this, but it caused me to gain an unexpected benefit; my image was now burnished and the number of friends and well-wishers continued to increase.

Concerned about my health due to such defamation, legendary musician and singer Sudhir Phadke, also known as Babujee, once came to meet me. I have written earlier about his affection for me. A visit by such an illustrious personality is a rarity and an honour. Phadke had taken the trouble to climb two storeys to my home, although he himself had very recently undergone a bypass surgery. "Ram," he implored me, "Don't be perturbed by such incidents. Everybody is aware of your clean character." He embraced me tightly and it seemed as if his embrace led to the loosening of the stranglehold of cancer on my body.

Fight for MP Fund

As if Tinaikar's slander was not enough, another development added to my woes! A writ petition had been filed in the Mumbai High Court seeking cancellation of the MP Fund. The writ was against the governments at the Centre and in the State. The petitioners were former Vice Chancellor of Mumbai University, Ram Joshi, veteran editor, Madhav Gadkari and former MLA and Socialist leader, Navanit Shah from Palghar. I understood that the intent behind the petition was issue-based and that it was not a personal affront to my character. Still it was I who had initiated the creation of this Fund. Although the writ had not brought me into the picture, it had deprived me of mental peace. Its main argument could be described as an apprehension that the Fund was likely to be misused by a few unscrupulous Parliamentarians sometime in the future.

I was worried that the Fund could be scrapped by the judiciary if the government did not file a satisfactory response. I contacted renowned legal expert, Balasaheb

Apte, a senior BJP leader. He was convinced of my stand and appreciated my concern. Apte said, "Rambhau, you are the best person to respond to the plea in the writ. I shall prepare an intervening application on your behalf. But first read the draft application." Even as I was replying in the affirmative, a worried Apte asked if I had the strength to go through it. He sent it to me the very next day.

In the midst of all this, I had been re-admitted into the hospital for a fresh blood transfusion. Despite this, I went through the application with a fine-tooth comb, the blood supply tube dangling from my arm while I read it. My law degree and deep knowledge of the subject proved most useful. I thought that making some important changes was inevitable. But how was I to do it?

As if by a Godsend, my old typist Bharavi Otavanekar came by to enquire after me and stayed that night. "You can dictate at your own speed," he said, "and I shall type it." As I was unable to sleep, we worked late into the night and by early next morning, Bharavi had finalised the draft. The nurse attending to me lodged a strong complaint against this. However, the doctors treating me knew well that whenever I was busy working, I tended to forget my pain.

Eventually, the matter reached the Supreme Court. All the petitions against the MP Fund from around the country were clubbed and heard by the Supreme Court, which endorsed the constitutionality of the MP Fund by its verdict announced on May 6, 2010.

Though such incidents generated pain in my mind and body, in hindsight, they seemed to have proved useful in getting through those agonising months, as I overcame the torment in my body, for that duration at least.

Ram Naik and wife Kunda relishing Atal Bihari Vajpayee's address

August 1994 arrived and fresh tests were conducted on me. The improvement in my health seemed very promising and the doctors soon declared that I was out of danger. Moreover, they confirmed that I could resume my routine, albeit gradually, once I got past the next two chemo procedures. My spirits soared at this prognosis.

As an elected representative, I had made it a practice to publish my annual performance report every year in March-April. As it had not been possible in 1994 due to my illness, I was left with a feeling of unfulfilled duty. I felt the need to publish it, even though it was well past the designated date. After September, the doctors gave me permission to step out of the house. I interpreted this permission as a green signal to begin working from home, a decision that upset my wife, who was displeased when I announced that I would resume my activities slowly. Nonetheless, my family members, friends, colleagues and workers were pleased that I was regaining my health.

Ram Naik with daughters Vishakha and Dr Nishigandha during his illness

Atal jee's Promise

While all this was happening, Atal jee once called up to find out about my progress. I shared the details and told him about the plan to publish my performance report. Welcoming the idea, he commented, "Very good, but take it easy. Take your own time. I shall come to release it for publication whenever you wish." This encouragement was a very welcome reinforcement to my improving health.

My last chemo procedure took place in the first week of September, immediately after which I invited my team in North Mumbai to my home for a meeting. As the after-effects of chemo procedure take 3-4 days to manifest, I had decided to make the best of that interval and had called the meeting. Everybody was delighted to see me back in action. They all agreed that I should certainly get back to work, but said that when I step out of the house, it should be for a public event, as many people were eager to see me after my illness.

I decided to start my bonus life afresh with the publication of my annual report. Everyone agreed that the function should be on the first convenient date after September 21. This particular date was decided in view of my treatment. We felt that September 25 was suitable in many respects and especially since it is the birth anniversary of Pandit Deen Dayal Upadhyaya, whom everyone in the BJP regards as an ideal political guru. It also happened to be a Sunday, which would make it easy for people to attend the function. After consulting all concerned, I called Atal jee to tell him of our proposed plan. His personal attendant, Shiv Kumar dampened my spirits, stating that it would not be possible, as it was customary for Atal jee to visit Deen Dayal jee's village on the later's birth anniversary every year. This news left me rather despondent. I seemed to be more susceptible to emotional fluctuations at the time, perhaps due to the cancer, or it could have been the effects of the medication. But as keen as I was to resume my public life on Deen Dayal jee's birth anniversary, I was not willing to do so without Atal jee's presence.

I expressed my sense of despair and disappointment to Ram Kapse, who relayed our conversation to Atal jee without my knowledge. Great leader that he is, Atal jee called back to say, "I shall be in Mumbai on September 25. Deen Dayal jee would never approve if I do not keep my word. I shall go to his village in the morning and reach

Mumbai in the evening." I could barely thank him enough, murmuring a few incoherent words into the phone he hung up. I was left emotional after Atal jee's call. I did mention that I had become rather sensitive since my illness – this was one of those moments.

That single telephone call from Atal jee changed the atmosphere in Mumbai. I was elated! My family members were delighted! Party workers felt that since Atal jee would be making an appearance for an otherwise ordinary event like the publication of a performance report just for Ram Naik, it was their duty to make the function a resounding success and they all got down to work.

Bonus Life for Society

Finally, September 25 arrived and I left for the venue. I was now determined to work just as before, or even more, if that was possible. It had always been my practice to be present at the venue in advance for any function. However, this was the first time I reached the venue after the auditorium was full, with the graceful presence of Atal jee. A giant television screen had been installed outside the hall, as there were more people outside than inside. When we alighted from the car, several workers stopped short in their tracks. They were unable to recognise me as I had lost my hair, my eyes were swollen and my skin had acquired a blackish hue. The moment they realised it was me, they rushed forward. Atal jee held me by arm as he led me inside. I had heard Atal jee's public speeches on numerous occasions in the past, but was especially eager to hear him on this one. He normally does not make any personal references in his speeches, but that day was an exception; the only subject on which he spoke was 'Ram Naik'.

My wife still carried the guilt at not having been able to welcome Atal jee in a befitting manner when he had suddenly arrived at my home to enquire after my health. As if sensing that sentiment, Atal jee said, "I had gone to Ram Naik's flat. It is a small dwelling, but a large home. Every house is built of bricks and stones, but a home is built with hearts. I met that small family and witnessed its large hospitability." Listening to him, my wife wept, the tears washing away her feelings of the perceived guilt.

The audience had included my family, colleagues and the doctors treating me. Normally, the medical clan stays away from political activities, but they had attended that day just for me. A large number of colleagues and friends had arrived from outside Mumbai. As I scanned the crowd, I was surprised to see an emaciated figure seated beside my daughter. It was Sudhir Phadke who had come to bless me. He, too, was shedding tears.

On any occasion, Atal jee's oratory remains unparalleled. The people had come for me, of course, but more so to listen to Atal jee. This towering leader's humility shone through when he commented, "Sometimes, one feels envious that a colleague (meaning me) receives so much affection and is flooded with so many blessings." Concluding his speech by wishing me a long and healthy life, Atal jee said, "Just consider why you have been brought back from the brink of death. We have dreamt of a glorious Bharat. You have been reborn to fulfill this task."

I promised Atal jee that I would spend my bonus life for and only for serving the society.

(October 11, 2015)

❐

MLAs Ram Naik (middle), Ram Kapse and others along with MP Rambhau Mhalgi at Parliament House after submitting a petition on behalf of Mumbai's suburban rail commuters

FROM SUBURBAN TRAIN TO A RED-BEACON CAR

Suburban trains are the lifeline of Mumbai city, since the city's activities are dependent on the punctuality of these local trains. On any average day, about 7.5 million commuters travel in these suburban trains in Mumbai. I, too, was once a part of this faceless crowd. As my residence was in the suburbs and office in city, I would commute there by getting into a local train at a particular time. This time-bound routine establishes friendships among railway commuters, since they are apt to meet on a daily basis while getting into the same train when commuting to work and back home. While a part of this milieu, I grew acquainted with the problems faced by the everyday commuters and sought to make their commuting as free of problems as was possible.

To coordinate all such efforts, we formed a body; 'the Goregaon Pravasi Sangh' – the commuters' organisation, on March 14, 1964, on the auspicious occasion of Gudi Padvaa, which is the first day of the Hindu new year. A gathering of around thirty was convened on my terrace. Because of this collective effort, improvements at the Goregaon railway station came up much faster than they did at other stations.

In those years, it was a very crowded station. As suburban services did not commence from Goregaon, commuters boarding trains at this station hardly ever got a seat to sit and were forced to commute standing. We realised that if some trains emanated from intermediate stations like Goregaon, those boarding at such stations would be able to travel seated.

We began working in this direction and the first Goregaon-Churchgate train was introduced in 1969, with the number of services increased later. Now, such services commence from several intermediate stations. When the Goregaon Pravasi Sangh was established, we charged just eight annas, which was half a rupee, for a life membership. The amount was kept nominal because we needed many more people to join. It was not an easy task to enrol five thousand life members in the 1960s. Owing to our vigorous efforts, our organisation was given a representation on the Railway Users' Consultative Committee.

Entry into the Parliament

Given my nature of devoting myself completely to every cause I choose to champion, my metamorphosis from an activist for the Goregaon commuters' problems to a spokesman for all suburban rail commuters in Mumbai happened without any deliberate effort. I soon realised that it was imperative to highlight their problems before the rail authorities in Delhi for effective redressal. While Prof. Ram Kapse and I were elected MLAs in 1978, our mentor Rambhau Mhalgi was already an MP from Thane, an important station on the Central Railway. In him, we found an able advocate, endowed with the capacity to move Delhi's mandarins. Kapse would speak for Central Railway commuters and I took up the cause of the Western Railway commuting masses. We began working in tandem and discovered a surefire method to attract the rail authorities' attention to the plight of Mumbai's commuters.

We decided to adopt the Petition to Parliament device, which is seldom used. Accordingly, we presented a Petition to Parliament in 1978-79 through Mhalgi. It listed the commuters' long-pending demands. In doing so, we had indirectly entered into the Parliament much before we were elected to its Lower House – Lok Sabha in 1989.

I began leading agitations of rail commuters on different issues, such as fare hike, demanding more suburban train services, or pressing the need to increase the height of the station platforms to reduce the inconvenience and danger to the commuters.

Self-Expectations

When I was elected to the Lok Sabha in 1989, like millions of commuters, I expected that it would be possible for me to initiate certain measures to make train-commuting in Mumbai easier and safer. The first job I undertook was to meet commuters at all the suburban stations from one end of my constituency to the other, namely from Jogeshwari to Palghar and a little beyond till Dahanu Road. I accepted their representations and prepared a Charter of Demands based on their various demands and suggestions which was then presented to the Railway Minister. Now that I was in Delhi, my speed and vigour to redress their grievances increased.

I could achieve much as an MP, but insofar as the railways are concerned, let me mention just two:

First Ladies Special

I was aware that the number of working women in Mumbai had been steadily increasing and the reservation of just two women's coaches in each train was woefully inadequate for them. I pursued the demand to start Women's Special Services during morning and evening rush hours. I was successful and the first of such a service was inaugurated on May 5, 1992, just three days before the International Women's Day between Churchgate and Borivali. This was the first such service anywhere in the world. It became immensely popular and the authorities were convinced of the need to introduce more services. After this such significant achievement, women commuters began approaching me with their various problems, beginning a chain reaction that resulted in most of them being redressed.

Ram Naik Shuttle

My North Mumbai constituency started from Jogeshwari in Mumbai's western suburbs with its other extreme at the Palghar-Boisar belt in the then Thane district. At the time,

Prof. Madhu Dandavate flagging off 'Ram Naik Shuttle' along with Ram Naik

the Mumbai suburban rail jurisdiction of Western Railway terminated at Virar, a station between these two points. But it was necessary to think about the thousands of people who commuted to Mumbai from Dahanu, which was even beyond the Palghar-Boisar area.

Industrialisation in Dahanu, Palghar and Boisar had accelerated, thereby increasing the number of commuters to these destinations from everywhere, even from Mumbai. Thus, though the commuters travelling to and fro along this stretch were in hundreds of thousands, they had to depend on long-distance trains to get to work, as there was no suburban service. A journey which would normally take a couple of hours took almost four hours because of this situation. In Mumbai, time is a precious commodity and wasting two hours either way on a daily basis was torturous.

As soon as I was elected to the Lok Sabha, I demanded that the Western Railway suburban services be extended up to Dahanu. Pending that, my demand was for launching a shuttle service between Virar and Dahanu for the benefit of this huge workforce. I persisted in this endeavour and got it sanctioned speedily. I was elected in December of

1989 and the first Virar-Dahanu Road shuttle service was inaugurated on September 2, 1990 – in less than a year. The duration of this journey is about an hour, but its usefulness is immeasurable. I felt that the presence of Railway Minister, George Fernandes for the inaugural would highlight the importance of this vital link, but at the eleventh hour, he was held up and conveyed his inability to attend. So, I requested Finance Minister Madhu Dandavate, who was a Mumbai resident and, hence, aware of the ordeal faced by the rail commuters daily. This service was welcomed by the commuters. they fondly started calling it the 'Ram Naik Shuttle'. This show of gratitude towards me is more valuable than a ministership. The number of services on this link continued to increase. Initially, it ran on a diesel engine and was later upgraded to operate on electricity. It is now a vital link between Mumbai and the outlying areas.

Minister of State

Atal jee inducted me as a Minister of State in his first cabinet of 1998. I was the only junior Minister in his Council of Ministers handling five portfolios simultaneously. Along with the Railways, I was appointed a Minister of State for Parliamentary Affairs, Planning and Programme Implementation. Later, Atal jee, in a way acknowledging my contribution, entrusted independent charge of Railways. There is a general misconception that a Minister of State is in reality a junior Minister who has limited authority and cannot show an impressive performance. I was determined to dispel this myth through my work.

As part of my responsibility, I was able to pay attention to the MP Fund, which had been created due to my

Ram Naik accompanied by Dr. R. Chidambaram, Chairman, Atomic Energy Commission at the time of laying foundation of TAPP

demand. Its cabinet charge was with the Prime Minister. Atal jee was preoccupied with too much work as head of the government. His vision was to change the complexion of the nation. So, every moment of his time was precious. His method was to repose full confidence in his colleagues and, accordingly, he gave me complete freedom. I raised the MP Fund to ₹ 20 million a year due to its proven usefulness across the country. My other milestone achievement was the completion of the 1080 mw Tarapur Atomic Power Station (TAPS) before its deadline, by persuading the people affected by the project to cooperate unitedly in its completion. It was completed at an expenditure of ₹ 6100 crore, against the sanctioned amount of ₹ 6500 crore. The chronic evil of cost and time overrun for every government project did not plague TAPS. This was a historic exception.

For a brief while, I was asked to look after the Non-conventional Energy portfolio. I was able to install solar power-based traffic signals for the first time in Delhi. This was done in view of the need to produce clean energy. This was a small beginning, but had limitless potential.

Another achievement gave me much satisfaction, because I felt that I could repay, at least to some extent, the debt of those who fought for the freedom of our country.

The 1999 mid-term Parliamentary elections had been announced. All ministers and MPs feel the need to return to their constituencies for campaigning – an understandable sentiment. Some ministers do make themselves scarce from Delhi and camp in their areas. I could not do so. Deputy PM and Home Minister L.K. Advani was required to tour the country for electioneering for the BJP and the National Democratic Alliance (NDA). However, it was not possible for Atal jee and Advani jee to reduce their priority towards the sensitive Home Ministry. To overcome this difficulty, I was asked to look after the Ministry as Minister of State, even as hectic campaigning had already begun. When I pleaded with Atal jee that I, too, had to contest the election, his reply was prompt: "North Mumbai voters will take care of your victory."

Dadra and Nagar Haveli Freedom Movement

One of my regrets needs to be mentioned here, since I failed dismally on this front in spite of my persistent efforts as an MP. Every patriotic Indian will understand my emotion. After India became independent in 1947, hundreds of freedom fighters were conferred scrolls of honour and given several facilities. There was an important criterion to endorse a person as a freedom fighter; such an individual had to have been either jailed or declared absconding, or recorded as a 'Satyagrahee' (peaceful protestor) by the then British regime. Those not fulfilling the criterion were not considered, notwithstanding their sacrifice, for any recognition or benefit. This had made grave injustice to a group of bravehearts, who had liberated Dadra and Nagar Haveli, a Union Territory now, on the night of July 31, 1954 from Portuguese rule. They had attacked this area and were successful in the very first operation to throw out the Portuguese occupiers. As the authorities had run away themselves, no arrests had taken place. Since this was an armed attack, there was no Satyagrahee. This band of a few fighters had liberated the territory, something the Indian government had been unable to do. But they were denied the status of freedom fighters on the basis of these flimsy technicalities. These attackers owed their allegiance to the RSS. They felt that they had been deprived of this honour due to the Congress party's ideological antipathy towards the RSS. They had not mounted this attack to get any monetary benefit from the government nor had they an eye on the future gains – such a contemptible idea had not crossed their minds. They were fighting for the freedom of an Indian territory. These people were ready to make the supreme sacrifice for the motherland and their deeds need to be viewed from this angle.

Several of these fighters were from Maharashtra. Melody Queen Lata Mangeshkar had raised funds for them by organising a music concert. This army of a hundred and twenty-five included Maharashtra Bhooshan (icon), Babasaheb Purandare, Sudhir Phadke, sports guru Rajabhau Wakankar, multi-lingual encyclopedia creator Vishwanath Narawane, Nana Kajarekar and consumer activist Bindumadhav Joshi. Each was a giant in his own field and was

Ram Naik along with (L-R) Shri Babasaheb Purandare, Ms Lata Mangeshkar, Shri N.S. Farande in Golden Jubilee Function of Dadra Nagar Haveli Freedom Day

well respected. I had been unable to do anything for them as an MP, but perhaps it was destiny that had decreed that I should have privilege to honour them. When Atal jee took over as the PM, I revived the issue. Advani jee was aware of this brave attack even at the time it was being planned.. So he also had issued directions to take some concrete decisions to honour them. I am happy that I completed this task as a Minister of State for Home. Some of these fighters had already passed away due to old age. Those surviving were mostly from Pune and its environs. Therefore, a gala function was organised in Pune to hand over the scrolls of honour to them. All of them had already received severall laurels, though this scroll had its own special place for them.. I witnessed the expressions on their faces as they accepted the honour. This was an unforgettable day in my life.

My tenure as a Minister of State for Railways (MOSR) was only nineteen months, but it is dotted with such memorable incidents. As a Minister, an official car with a red beacon atop was allotted to me. It is true that going around in such a vehicle makes one feel special. But even today, as I look back at my train travel days, I can candidly say that I still prefer travelling by a local train, which saves much time as it roars towards its destination.

The Railway Ministry will always remain a soft spot in my heart. My experiences as Minister of State for Railways are worth sharing separately.

(October 25, 2015)

❒

Ram Naik finds a few moments to have a hasty snack in a suburban train in motorman's cabin at the behest of his colleague Vikas Agvekar

RAILWAY: MOST PREFERRED VEHICLE

I was elected to the Lok Sabha in March 1998 for a fourth consecutive term. The BJP did not have a clear majority in the Lower House of Parliament. It had, however, emerged as the single largest party. Hence, our leader, Atal jee was invited by the President to form a government at the Centre. I had arrived in Delhi a day prior to the formation of the government and had received a message from Atal jee the same day. He was keen to induct me as a Minister of State for Railways in his Council of Ministers. His wish was command for me and I conveyed my consent.

At the time, I was caught up in a whirlwind of emotions. My mind went back to my father, who had followed the noble profession of a school teacher. Rather than preaching to others, he had set an example through his chosen path by moving home and hearth to a village to teach, ignoring the lure of a potential high-profile city career. He believed that one should try to give back to society as much as possible. He had certainly lived true to his motto! Another memory triggered thoughts of my childhood – frolicking in the RSS Shakha with my friends. Then to my college days. I had saved every rupee that I had earned delivering daily newspapers at early mornings so that I was able to fund my studies for my Bachelor's Degree in Commerce. It was during these formative years of my life that the spirit of serving the nation was inculcated into me by the RSS.

After my father's demise, I had searched for shelter in the crowded, bustling city of Mumbai and had to move from one accommodation to another. When I settled down

President K.R. Narayanan administering oath as a Minister of State to Ram Naik

and married, rather than enjoying the comfort of home and family, I plunged into full-time work for the Jana Sangh in 1969. The memory of quitting my stable job is still etched sharply in my mind. At that time, I could only dream that our party, the Jana Sangh, would come to power one day. I could never even have envisioned that the future held for me the possibility of becoming a Minister and at the Centre, no less. However, during the 1990s, this extremely distant possibility seemed to be emerging as a distinct one. It was during this decade that the BJP began growing from strength to strength.

Atal jee's message to me that day came as a complete surprise, for it had caught me off guard. But once reconciled to the idea and what it entailed for me, I began making plans for the future, envisioning my future role to assist people by making judicious use of power that was to be vested in me as a Minister of State at the Centre.

Red Becon Car

There were rather mixed reactions from colleagues and workers who had gathered at my Delhi residence. A few were disappointed that I had been asked to become a Minister of State and not a Cabinet Minister. One of them suggested that I should not accept the invite. But I would have considered such a refusal sacrilegious when the invite had come from Atal jee. I was keenly aware that Atal jee was walking a very fine line while trying to collate nearly two dozen constituent parties to form his coalition government. I understood fully well that the responsibility of distributing portfolios was not entirely his domain.

The first telephone call I made to convey this good news was to my closest friend, Ram Kapse. Though we had been together since our first assembly election in 1978, Kapse had not contested the 1998 Parliament election as the Thane seat, which had been returning him all these years, had been allotted to our alliance partner, the Shiv Sena. An astute politician, Kapse understood my sentiments at being offered a junior ministership. Complimenting me profusely, he said, "Fantastic that you will be appointed a Minister of State for Railways. We have been fighting for the commuters for such a long time. So, what more do we need? You now have the opportunity to do something concrete for them. Don't feel disappointed about being a junior minister, but go forward, for you are capable of making the most of this god-sent opportunity." As he spoke, I felt as if he was sitting right next to me and not in Kalyan, so many hundreds of miles away. Kapse's words were an elixir to my spirit for they had much truth in them.

The newspapers covered in detail my induction the next day. Expectedly, some expressed dismay that I was to be a junior minister. But, by and large, I received much encouragement and compliments for accepting the assignment without expressing any resentment.

Next day I was required to reach Rashtrapati Bhavan, the official residence of the President of India, for the oath-taking ceremony. As usual, I was about to call a taxi. But an official car flaunting a red beacon atop arrived at my doorstep just then.

Present Bihar Chief Minister, Nitish Kumar, who had also won the Lok Sabha election, was appointed the Minister of Railways, which meant that I would be working under him. One can only imagine the experience of working with someone from an altogether different background.

The next morning, I called him saying, "I am now your junior minister. When can I pay you a courtesy visit?" To this he replied, "I know your mastery of the railways. Never think of me as your Cabinet Minister, never consider yourself a junior Minister. Be assured that I will not impede your work in any way, but we will work hand in hand. We will run the Railway ministry together." His response was not mere words. He meant it! Setting protocol aside, Nitish Kumar came to my house to meet me. Such magnanimous gestures are very rare in Delhi's corridors of power, as snobbery and vain attempts to throw one's weight around are all too common in this political scene.

Mumbai Rail Vikas Corporation

Nitish Kumar's accommodating nature enabled me to take the decision to form an autonomous corporation for Mumbai's suburban rail section. It was a first of its kind in the history of Indian Railways. I was allowed to make this major decision, even though I was a junior Minister. Lady

Railway Minister Mamata Banerjee launching Mumbai Rail Vikas Corporation in presence of (L-R) Digvijay Singh, Manohar Joshi, Vilasrao Deshmukh, Ram Naik, Bangaru Laxman and Chhagan Bhujbal

BJP Maharashtra State President Devendra Fadnavis travelling in a suburban train with Ram Naik on their way to Palghar for publication of a booklet on Borivali-Dahanu shuttle services (10 May, 2013)

Luck seemed to be smiling on me, for adding to these favourable factors was the fact that the BJP-Shiv Sena alliance was in power in Maharashtra at the time. This meant that all necessary cooperation was forthcoming from the State government. My old friend Manohar Joshi was the Chief Minister of Maharashtra. A full-blooded Mumbaikar, he was aware of the ordeals faced by rail commuters. Therefore, there was an unwritten understanding that no delay would be brooked in the formation of the corporation. Joshi's commitment to this project was complete. With all preparations completed to set up the Mumbai Rail Vikas (Development) Corporation (MRVC) and a memorandum of understanding to be signed between the Central and State governments in this regard, Joshi arrived as scheduled for the ceremony, although he had undergone an eye surgery just two days earlier.

The mid-term Lok Sabha election was declared soon after the signing. However, as the MoU had already come into force, we wasted no time in implementing it. Atal jee returned as the PM in 1999. Firebrand leader, Mamta Banerjee was appointed as the Railway Minister and I was able to pursue the matter with her, making the MRVC files to move. At the inauguration of the MRVC, Banerjee requested my presence as a Special Invitee. It was a tremendous feeling of satisfaction to know that I provided the much-needed relief to the commuters by undertaking various projects worth ₹ 3,450 crore through MRVC.

But bear with me as I digress a little.

Developments on Fast Track

As a junior Minister, I had concentrated on improving various rail amenities. Until then, it was customary that each Railway Minister of the time had catered only to his constituency and State, neglecting the all-India operations. I, on the other hand, adopted a comprehensive approach. Naturally, my constituency benefited too. I initiated crash programmes to install computerised reservation centres and ticket-vending machines, sparing people from the ordeal of standing in long queues and wasting precious time.

Other landmark projects included the construction of broader pedestrian bridges at all major suburban stations, repair of old dilapidated railway bridges, extending suburban platforms to cater to twelve-coach trains in place of the standard nine-coach trains and subsequently the introduction of twelve-coach suburban services throughout the day.

One of the more outstanding feats of my tenure is the station constructed at Umroli. Umroli, which is a hamlet between Palghar and Boisar stations along the western line in my constituency. Although it is situated close to the rail tracks, until then it had no railway station. I was aware that sanctioning a station at the village would not be possible in the near future. Still, necessity is the mother of invention. I learned from the authorities that it would be administratively possible to halt trains at Umroli. So, taking its residents into confidence, we had a railway station constructed through their '*shram daan*' (voluntary labour) and trains could now halt at this station. The villagers had been clamouring for this project for three decades and now they had their wish fulfilled through this innovative initiative.

The demand for starting a suburban service up to Dahanu Road station had also been long pending. It was a just demand and I included the work in the new projects. But it would take a long time to materialise. Though the work began soon enough, it was inordinately delayed after 2004, finally being completed in 2014, after repeated agitations. Though I had been instrumental to this project, I was not invited for the inaugural function. Not heeding this, I did attend the function. Coincidentally, it was my birthday that day, April 16. Though the government had ignored me and my role, the commuters greeted the service and me at every station.

Prime Minister Atal Bihari Vajpayee dedicating Konkan Railway to the nation in presence of (L-R) Ram Naik, Sushma Swaraj, George Fernandes, P.C.Alexander, Nitish Kumar and Manohar Joshi

I made conscious efforts to forge an emotional bond between the passengers and the railway administration. The Konkan Railway (KR) project was completed soon after my tenure as the junior Railway Minister began and was inaugurated in the presence of Prime Minister Atal jee. KR was to launch a new train service between Mumbai and Mangalore. Officials approached me to finalise a name for this service. It occurred to me that a contest for suggesting an appropriate name be declared amongst passengers themselves and the winner should be given a free pass to travel first class on the train with his or her family any time during the first year of its run. When this contest was announced, we were inundated with suggestions. As the train was to travel through a coastal belt, the name 'Matsyagandha Express' was selected. 'Matsya' is the Sanskrit word for fish and 'Gandha' being the word for smell. The name proved most appropriate. The overwhelming response was a pleasant surprise and thereafter several services were similarly named.

It is a thrilling experience when a train service is launched that fulfills a long-pending popular demand and sentiment. It becomes one of the highlights of one's life.

One such demand was for a connecting service between Kolhapur in Maharashtra and Tirupati in Andhra Pradesh. The temples at both these pilgrimage towns are considered most sacred. There is an apocryphal story that Lord Balaji at Tirupati and Goddess Amba had a tiff, following which an angry Amba came to Kolhapur. Her temple faces the south, where Tirupati is located. The devotees believe that they can garner more divine blessings if they visit both these temples. Hence the demand for a connecting train service. One passenger suggested befitting name for this service – the 'Hari Priya Express'. Balaji is one of Lord Hari's incarnations. His beloved (Priya) is Amba. I did not just flag off the inaugural run of this service, but even travelled on it from Kolhapur to Tirupati. The service received a thunderous welcome at every station. While some trains were named thus, some stations were renamed to perpetuate nationalist sentiments. The Kurla terminus in Mumbai was named after legendary freedom fighter, Lokmanya Bal Gangadhar Tilak and has now become a household name.

Mean Mindedness

As a junior Minister, I had introduced another convenient service: I knew that in several countries, season tickets for train journeys are issued for brief durations. India, however, had no such facility. Especially in Mumbai, where people often visit for a week's stay or even more brief, but they had to buy a monthly season ticket, which was an unnecessary expense. Since the suburban train is the most economic and most dependable mode of transport in Mumbai, commuters had no choice but to buy monthly tickets even though their requirement was not for this such a long duration. Besides, long queues to buy tickets prove cumbersome and waste of time. To overcome this difficulty, I suggested a weekly season ticket. Some officials were not in favour of this scheme. They obeyed me reluctantly, but scrapped it after few days, claiming that the scheme had received poor response. It has since been revived and is now running well. I have recorded this episode to show how officers tend to create obstacles to nullify useful schemes suggested by ministers, who know the pulse and needs of the people. But these minor setbacks have actually enriched my life, making me more conscious of bureaucratic hurdles.

Though most journalists cooperated with me in a constructive fashion, there were some disgruntled element in the media who tried to hurt me by playing up trivial incidents. At times, their criticism was more hurtful than that of my political opponents.

All railway platforms and bridges in Mumbai are swamped by unauthorised hawkers and beggars who harass the commuters. I launched a campaign against this menace, which resulted in strong protest marches by hawkers. Some of the newspapers deliberately started publishing a picture of a lone beggar or hawker or even a dog on a platform. Another menace to commuters was stones and dirt hurled at suburban trains by pervert elements. I decided that the solution to this avert menace was to install wire nets on the windows of trains to reduce the risk of injury to commuters. But given Mumbai's overcrowding, several commuters are forced to travel balancing on the footboards of trains. These unfortunate commuters become victims of such hooligans.

In one such unfortunate incident, Sony Joseph, a young lady travelling on a train, had lost her eye due to a stone flung at her. I made it a point to enquire after her and ensured that she was given a job in the railways as a special case. This case made me realise that despite such regular mishaps taking place on a daily basis, the unlucky victims of such attacks were not even receiving any ex-gratia assistance. I got busy compiling the daily statistics of this menace and implemented stern measures such as patrolling along the tracks, which reduced the menace considerably. However, if any incidence of this sort took place, it was immediately highlighted by the media and they would castigate me without a qualm. This perturbed some top rail officials whose advice was that I should ignore such incidents as media's barbs are directed at me due to the fact that I was taking cognizance. But this was not acceptable to me. I continued to work in may own way.

It was my firm belief that selling cigarettes must be banned at all railway stations in the interest of public health. Though this was a popular demand, I also faced some opposition, mainly due to some people's addiction and others' selfish interests. But I remained firm and implemented it. Gradually, it has been accepted in toto, to the extent that the present generation is unaware that at one time, cigarettes were sold on railway platforms.

Railway: Best Mode of Travel

In August of 1999, following a major rail mishap, Nitish Kumar resigned, accepting moral responsibility. Rather than appointing another Cabinet Minister, Atal jee entrusted the responsibility to me as a Minister of State (Independent Charge). I handled this portfolio for about two-and-a-half months – from August to October 1999. Nonetheless,

I remained convinced that a suburban train was the best means of commuting in Mumbai, rather than an official car with a red beacon light, which was at my service. Knowing this, many senior colleagues have travelled with me likewise. For many, my love for the railways was a topic of admiration and jest too. Once Gopinath Munde publicly quipped, “I am always punctual to attend Rambhau’s programmes as I fear that he would make me travel by train to reach on time.”

Though I am now Governor of Uttar Pradesh, I did not have an official car for ten years since 2004. Mumbai’s suburban train was my favourite mode of transport even during this decade. Not just commuters, but motormen and guards too would insist that I travel in their cabin. I can recall many an occasion when I have eaten my lunch in their cabins and shared their bottle of drinking water. If I entered a crowded compartment, people always made room for me to be seated so I could travel in comfort.

I consider this affection and warmth far superior to any official aggrandisement. That is why, railway is my most preferred vehicle.

(November 8, 2015)

❐

Iraq President Saddam Hussein reciprocating Ram Naik's greeting in traditional Indian style 'Namaskar'

AROUND THE WORLD

My performance as a Minister of State was acknowledged by voters in the 1999 mid-term parliamentary elections. I was re-elected with a thumping majority form North Mumbai, creating a record by winning five consecutive terms from Mumbai with the largest margin from Maharashtra. My joy knew no bounds.

Nationally, the BJP had achieved spectacular success and it was certain that Atal jee would take over as Prime Minister yet again. There was a general expectation that I would be inducted into his Ministry once more. There were several probabilities that went through my mind; perhaps a Cabinet Minister, though the railway portfolio might go to a constituent party of the coalition. If this were to happen, I would have no longer any direct connection with the railways. It seemed a better option to remain a junior Minister, thereby continuing to hold charge of the Railway Ministry which was so close to my heart.

Of course, the overriding sentiment was that the BJP's stable government would be formed and my individual gain or elevation as a Minister was inconsequential.

Consumed by these thoughts, I arrived at Delhi airport where an official car awaited me. No sooner had I reached my residence than a message arrived, conveying good news, that I was to be inducted as a Cabinet Minister. This was soon followed by a formal invitation to join the oath-taking ceremony the next day. It would not be honest to claim that I was not thrilled with this turn of events. Even when one works sincerely without seeking any reward, such recognition is always welcome. Those present at my residence were soon speculating on the ministry to be allotted to me. Every telephone call was received with bated breath, assuming it was the call to consult me about my choice of a portfolio. However, I felt that it would be taken for granted that I would accept whatever Atal jee wished to entrust me and it happened exactly like that, but turned out to be a most pleasant surprise. I was appointed as India's Petroleum Minister!

Inflammable Portfolio

The Petroleum Ministry is considered a major ministry since India's crude oil requirement is met mostly through imports. It also looks after natural gas. The ministry presides over twelve public-sector corporations, five of which are called 'Nav Ratna' (a precious jewel) companies, while six are described as Mini Ratna companies. Running this ministry is an enormous responsibility since the entire nation's economy is dependent upon oil imports, which fluctuate in tandem with international oil prices.

It was always whispered in the corridors of power that a Petroleum Minister is collectively chosen by giant oil conglomerates and not the Prime Minister. Interestingly enough, I had no contact with any such firm in the past. Still, curious journalists in Delhi tried to unearth even the remotest connection by questioning my staff and officers if there had been any calls from representatives of such multinationals. It was a surprise for the political grapevine in Delhi, that nothing of the sort had transpired. It had also exposed the petty minds of such gossip mongers about Atal jee's unimpeachable uprightness and selfless nature.

Once he handed over the responsibility of the portfolio to me, Atal jee never did interfere with my working. On the contrary, he stood firmly behind me whenever I took any major decision, because of which I was able to initiate and materialise many path-breaking measures. Allow me to mention here that this was another record I have created, for I handled the petroleum portfolio for a full five-year term. This had not happened earlier, nor has it happened since.

I was aware that I would have to learn the ins and outs of the petroleum sector to perform effectively. After I took over, a senior journalist at a press conference questioned me about my agenda and my priorities for the petroleum sector. I already knew what it was to be!

Ram Naik signing the Sakhalin Agreement with Russian Deputy Prime Minister Viktor Borisovich Khristenko

I had been driving around Mumbai on my scooter as the Jana Sangh Organising Secretary, requiring that I refill petrol every other day. I took great care to refill only at those petrol pumps where adulteration did not take place. My first priority was to put an end to this rampant practice. And I had another pressing priority, the cooking gas. Whenever I was at home and the gas cylinder ran out, being the only male member of the family, I had to replace it. Besides whenever the government hiked the charges, I would lead an agitation. I have seen people hankering after a simple necessity such as a gas connection. Therefore, my next urgent priority was to put an end to the shortage of cooking-gas connections. When I spoke this out in the Press Conference, my response was greeted with howls of laughter. But it only served to strengthen my resolve to study this ministry thoroughly and work for my priorities.

Foreign Investments

Atal jee's support was soon to be tested. It occurred when we were to enter into an agreement with Russia. India's

Ram Naik in a discussion with Sudan's Vice President Ali Osman Taha

crude oil imports were then to the tune of almost seventy percent of the nation's requirement. In view of this, I had decided that this dependence could be reduced by signing agreements with certain countries for crude production and profit-sharing. It meant that we would have to participate in the production process. Accordingly, a decision was taken that Oil & Natural Gas Corporation (ONGC), a Nav Ratna corporation, would bid for an investment of ₹ 8,000 crore in the Sakhalin (Russia) island oil production facility. This investment was for twenty percent share of its production.

Never before had India made such a big investment abroad for oil or for any other product. When I moved the proposal at a cabinet meeting, several colleagues found it too far-reaching and adventurous. They were apprehensive that the investment would only show returns after seven years after the facility begins its production. Hence, they thought it would not make a wise investment. Another misgiving they voiced was that it had not yet been decided which other countries would be party to this agreement. In the face of these apprehensions, Atal jee was firm in his support, saying, "If Rambhau is confident, let us proceed. No daring, no gaining." Gradually, he coaxed the cabinet members to see my point of view. In fact, he presented my argument better than I could have done. Fortunately, the agreement decided India's share at twenty percent, while the US's and Japan's share was thirty percent each. I reached in Moscow on February 10, 2001 to sign the agreement. Actual production began within four years. Soon India had recovered the entire investment and begun earning profit. This was a major supporting factor that helped stabilise our nation's economy.

A somewhat similar situation occurred and Atal jee backed me to the hilt once again. I had presented a proposal for final ratification by the cabinet which involved signing an agreement with Sudan with an investment of ₹ 3,200 crore. Unexpectedly, some colleagues opposed it. Even as I was trying to explain how we stood to gain, a senior colleague remarked, "Let me be blunt. Our opposition is based on a different reason altogether. It may be unfounded, but this is our feeling. Sudan is caught up in anarchy. We worry that if we make such a major investment with them, we may repent later." I tried my best to reason with them, but in vain. It is said that there is no intellect and answer to an emotional argument. This was exactly what I was encountering. Finally, Atal jee intervened, saying, "I have full faith in Rambhau's capability to make the right decision. Give this proposal your consent even if you are not convinced, just because I am saying so." This changed the atmosphere and the proposal was endorsed.

The project was a success and went on to produce twelve million tonnes of crude oil annually, the returns of which began coming in within four years. Colleagues who had initially opposed the initiative now showered praise upon me. Historically, for India, the first quantum step in foreign collaboration in the petroleum sector was my initiative. But it is without doubt that Atal jee's support had guided me forward. I am glad that I could prove that the trust he had reposed in me was justified.

Globetrotter

Before I took over as Petroleum Minister, I had travelled out of India only once as a member of a delegation of the Parliament. I am not enamoured of foreign travel. Therefore, I had never visited other countries just for the pleasure of sight-seeing. It is another matter that I could not afford it financially either. Deputy Prime Minister Advani jee would tease me, saying, "Rambhau does not travel out of India since he doesn't have a suit." It was true that after taking over the reins of the Petroleum Ministry, I got two suits stitched. I have since travelled around the world.

Crude oil is a global requirement. 'Petroleum road-shows' are held every year in several countries, including the US and most countries participate in them. Exchange of products, plans and trading takes place at such gatherings. I visited many countries for this purpose. I cannot use the term 'toured' because I returned home as soon as my business was done. As this happened a few times, my secretary said, "Sir, please allow the officers to stay over for a few extra days, as they may not get the opportunity to visit these countries again and unless you ask them to stay, they cannot. You have no interest in sight-seeing, but they have to suppress their urge because of you." Conceding this,

I began occasionally allowing them to prolong their visit by a few days.

Memorable Visit to Iraq

Though I had travelled extensively, the biggest impact on me was made by my visit to Iraq. After we arrived at the airport, we were escorted to its famous five-star hotel, Al Rashid, for our stay. At the entrance of the hotel, we froze in our tracks. Staring at us from the floor of the entrance was the face of a US President!

It is Indian culture to say 'namaskar' to someone, even if our foot inadvertently touches that person. Trampling upon someone's face, although just a painting, was unthinkable. But the face of former US President, George Bush Sr., had been painted conspicuously at the entrance of the hotel and it was impossible to enter without stepping on it. This was an international rendezvous and Iraq had made its anger and hatred clear by this depiction.

I hesitated for a moment trying to find another entrance. Then I noticed the posse of the paparazzi in the lobby with their cameras ready. It was quite a dilemma to say the least. If I walked over the face and my expression showed my unease, it would become international news. And if I tried to avoid walking on it, the media would, no doubt, have a field day. But I could not stand there forever. So sporting a nonchalant expression and a broad grin and pretending that I had not noticed the painted face, I stepped into the hotel. I had passed the test. The next morning a senior official accompanying me said, "Sir, congrats. You did well. We tried to jump over it but did not succeed. Late at midnight, I went back to the entrance just to find out if there was an alternative. There was none."

My Iraq visit proved memorable for many reasons. The first thing that amazed me was the main roads. Even today, we in India could not envisage such huge roads. I have seen roads in the US and other developed countries; but the roads in Iraq stand apart. Nowhere else have I seen a ten-or twelve-lane system of roads. Moreover, none of the roads was congested. Traffic was sparse. My economical mind felt that four-lane roads would have sufficed for this demographic scenario. The quality of the roads was exceptional. Even while travelling at 140 km an hour, the vehicle remained as steady as if I was working at my office table. There was not a single pothole in sight. When I enquired as to how the roads had been built, I was informed that it had been the work of an Indian firm. It made me very proud to see such sterling workmanship. Of course, oil-based affluence had made it possible for Iraq to create such top-heavy infrastructure, even though it was not required.

Iraq's petrol prices were the fodder for discussions throughout my official entourage. Petrol in Iraq costs about the same as water. We had travelled to Baghdad from Jordan by car. While returning, our driver not only filled up the tank, but also took an additional can full of petrol. The riches acquired by Iraq's natural resource of petrol proved to be her undoing. Iraqis were well aware of their wealth and they were in a hurry to shore it up, one way or the other.

Whenever a delegation goes abroad for business talks, negotiations are held at three levels: the Secretary, the Minister and the Head of the State. We were informed that if black money was deposited in a particular international bank, we could buy petrol even cheaper without signing any agreement. My officials were trying to explain to them that this was not possible under Indian systems. But they were not convinced. They read out to us a list of the countries indulging in such practices. Although it became clear to them that such a deal could not be struck with us, their hospitality was in no way diminished. I have attended many a banquet as a foreign dignitary, but the sumptuous spread in Baghdad remains unsurpassed. The menu was so extensive that even a spoonful of each course would have filled my plate to overflowing.

Meeting with Saddam Hussein

The most exciting part of the Iraq visit was a meeting with President Saddam Hussein. His practice was to meet only other Heads of State. Therefore, his meeting with me was a matter of international importance. I was told that only one official would be allowed to accompany me. My team included a Foreign Service Official, Rajendra Abhyankar, a fellow Maharashtrian, whom I requested to accompany me. Our vehicle took a series of complicated routes and turns so that it would be impossible to remember exactly where Saddam's residence was. It is my habit to greet any foreign VVIP first with a 'namaskar' and then shake their hands. Saddam surprised me pleasantly for he reciprocated in like manner. This historic moment was captured on camera and the picture went viral.

This visit was significant, for I was the last Indian to meet Saddam. None of us could have foreseen the impending disaster for Iraq. We signed an agreement to develop a refinery in Iraq, but it did not materialise since Iraq was devastated soon thereafter.

A shadow that lingered with this visit was the demise of Dhirubhai Ambani, who had ushered a new era in the Indian

Ram Naik receiving first Crude Oil Stock from Sudan at Manglore on May 15, 2003. Also seen (L-R) ONGC Chairman Subir Raha, representative of Sudan, Dy. Prime Minister L.K. Advani, Santosh Gangwar, Ananth Kumar, Yedurappa

petroleum sector. He passed away on July 6, 2002 while I was in Baghdad. I sent the family a condolence message on the loss of such a stalwart personality.

During my tenure as India's Petroleum Minister, I visited the US, Australia, Brazil, Canada, China, Indonesia, Iran, Iraq, UK, Japan, Sweden, France, Singapore, Switzerland, Saudi Arabia, Sri Lanka, Venezuela and Mauritius, signing a string of agreements to reduce India's dependence on crude oil imports. I am proud that I have been able to bring around a major transformation in our petroleum sector.

(November 22, 2015)

❒

Ram Naik handing over a cheque for ₹ 40 crore to Prime Minister Atal Bihari Vajpayee on behalf of Navratna Companies of Petroleum Ministry for the aid of Gujarat's earthquake affected people in presence of Minister of State Santosh Gangwar and Chairmen of Oil Companies

THE GOLDEN ERA OF THE PETROLEUM SECTOR

I have already described how perfunctory my connection was with the petroleum sector; refilling my scooter with petrol and replacing the cooking-gas cylinder in my house. But this is not entirely true. In 1989, within a month of my election as an MP, a serious malpractice rampant in this sector came to my notice.

One evening, an unknown, well-dressed and smooth-talking individual accosted me. He wanted to buy a gas coupon book from me. Each MP was issued with such books every quarter, with twenty-five special coupons meant to be distributed in the MP's constituency for needy people. These coupon holders were allotted gas connections out of turn.

In those days, a gas connection was considered a great privilege. The man offered to pay me ₹ 2,000 per coupon amounting to ₹ 50,000 for the entire book – a substantial amount. When I refused to sell the book, he tried to convince me as to how much I would lose, but I didn't budge. Over the next few days, I was approached by some others with similar offers. A couple of them actually showed me coupon books that they had bought from other MPs. I was astounded to see this blatant corrupt practice. This was the first shock to jolt me in Delhi.

When I returned to Mumbai, several requests for these coupons were already awaiting me in my office. Most of them were from people who had been on the waiting list for many years and their expectation that a connection should be sanctioned to them was just and fair. This problem was especially faced by working women and a gas connection was greeted like a godsend by such families. In Mumbai, a working woman has to commute to her place of work, spend time in the office and return home; the entire process consuming over twelve hours of her day. I understood their problems first hand.

As an MP, I was entitled to receive a hundred coupons a year, but the requests were in the thousands. To overcome this challenge, I structured certain norms for the distribution of these coupons. The physically challenged and the working women were to be given first priority, and even then, just a hundred coupons were like a drop in the ocean. Moreover, my Parliamentary constituency was spread over a hundred kilometres from end to end, consisting of semi-urban area like Vasai and the tribal belts like Palghar. Most households in the tribal area were still using wood-fired stoves as late as the 1990s.

40 Million LPG Connections

When I took over as Petroleum Minister a decade later, the situation had remained practically unaltered and I decided it was time to change this dismal picture at the earliest. To begin with, I reviewed the waiting list in India. To my utmost horror, I found it to be over thirteen million pending applications. I prepared a crash programme to end this long wait. Officials in my ministry were aghast, since my predecessor had sanctioned about ten thousand gas connections out of turn in his constituency, while ignoring the waiting list.

I was supported by a team of efficient officials who were eager to implement the Minister's orders. Within four years, my ministry granted thirty-three-and-a-half million

Ram Naik inaugurating a CNG centre by driving an autorickshaw run on CNG

connections, completely ending the waiting list and then over and above granting new connections. While millions of families were rejoicing at this windfall, racketeers supplying gas cylinders in the black market were furious. This was India's fifty-second year of Independence and, in all, about thirty-five million gas connections had been granted all over the country in half a century. With a complete divergence against this miniscule achievement in fifty years, my achievement of sanctioning of over forty million connections in just half a decade gave me immense satisfaction. People's joy on getting these basic necessities was my reward as a Minister. Soon gas connections became available on demand and if a double connection was sought, it was also available. For the poor slum-dwellers and those living in remote hilly areas, we made small five-kilo cylinders available.

Piped Natural Gas (PNG) Supply

My next project was to provide piped natural gas (PNG) to domestic consumers in major cities for ease of consumption and to prevent any potential mishap, since gas cylinders need constant attention and also needed to be supplied manually. Moreover, PNG is more safe and supply is available round the clock. I had witnessed piped gas supply for the first time in my life in Mumbai in 1954. The supplier, the Bombay Gas Company, later discontinued its operations. In 1995, Mahanagar Gas Company was established to undertake the responsibility of providing piped gas connections, but their performance was not up to the mark.

It is said that a skilled captain can inspire his team and I proved the legitimacy of this dictum. In no time, I brought about transformation in Mumbai. The first PNG connection was installed at the house of noted Marathi writer, Sada Karhade in Goregaon to mark the inaugural of this massive plan. When I laid down office, almost two hundred thousand households in Mumbai were enjoying this facility. At the last count, the number was nearing a million.

Pollution Control

To ensure that pollution is negligible, CNG (compressed natural gas) outlets were opened in Mumbai and Delhi for vehicles. Initially, there was some opposition to this switch-over. However, now most of the public transport vehicles and thousands of private cars in both these cities use CNG.

I was well aware that the presence of lead in fuel causes many ills. When petroleum company officials came out with a proposal to introduce lead-free petrol, I climbed on board and endorsed it immediately. Such fuel has been available in India since 2000. Besides reducing pollution, vehicular damage such as a malfunctioning ignition has also reduced. Earlier, vehicle users, particularly two-wheelers, had to clean the carbon deposited on the spark plug every now and then. They are no longer plagued with this problem. Gone are the days.

New Exploration Licensing Policy

The main challenge before our nation is our dependence on imported crude oil and natural gas. When I took over, it was almost seventy percent of the requirement, costing us billions of dollars in foreign exchange. Any fluctuation in international crude prices affects our economy one way or the other. It was the need of the hour to reduce

Sharad Pawar and Gopinath Munde flank Ram Naik at the inauguration of a pilot project of ethanol in Miraj, Maharashtra (15 April, 2001)

this dependence by initiating some concrete measures. In response to this urgency, I decided to reinstate the oil exploration and research activity that had taken place in only twenty-two blocks since the past ten years prior to my ministership. Domestic and global bids were invited for this. By the end of my five-year term, ninety blocks had been explored.

In the first year itself, work began in twenty-four blocks and the first sweet taste of success came within thirteen months. Cairn India struck gas in a field in the deep sea in the Krishna-Godavari basin. On July 5, 2001, I named the gas field 'Annapoorna'. Other companies that discovered gas included ONGC, Niko Resources and Reliance Industries. We were in high spirits since the Reliance find in 2002 was declared the largest gas field in the world. Another major oil find was at Barmer in the Rajasthan desert. In a short while,

Petroleum Minister Ram Naik inviting participation under new exploration licensing policy

production began in all these wells. Regrettably, this speed has not been maintained since the exit of the Vajpayee government in 2004. As a result, our dependence on imports is now over eighty percent of the nation's requirement.

Ethanol and Biodiesel

I initiated a slew of measures to reduce the nation's dependence on oil. One such step was the use of bio-diesel. But, more importantly, we were successful in introducing ethanol as a vehicular fuel. The use of ethanol had been discussed ad nauseam, but nothing was forthcoming about its actual use. As Petroleum Minister, I was seized with a compulsion to create a mission that would reduce our dependence on oil imports and also to reduce atmospheric pollution caused by vehicular traffic. Around that time, the media was awash with stories of the travails of Indian farmers due to crashing sugarcane prices. This prompted me to look at the use of ethanol in another light. Maharashtra is a major sugarcane-producing state and contributes to almost forty percent of the country's sugar production. This being so, it is bound to have a galaxy of experts on all aspects of this sector.

I had been told that ethanol was being used extensively in Brazil as vehicular fuel for a long time and I wanted to study this firsthand. I arranged to lead a delegation to Brazil that included Nitin Gadkari, who had evinced a keen interest in the subject, MP M.K. Anna Patil, who was chairman of a cooperative sugar mill, Anna Dange, who hailed from a sugarcane producing belt, and my officials. But some top officials of the oil companies were not ready to consider this option. Their argument was that it would be cheaper to import crude oil, rather than installing ethanol-producing plants.

By this time, I had begun to understand that the logistics some of these officials had in mind were based on a different motive, rather than that of protecting the national interest. In addition, the liquor lobby across the country activated its campaign against ethanol since the molasses, from which ethanol is produced, is used for distilling liquor. If the farmers began getting better price for molasses, the liquor production was bound to take a hit. It was in this lobby's interest to oppose the move. But I steamrolled this resistance and launched a few pilot projects, beginning in Uttar Pradesh and Maharashtra. My scheme was three-tier: use of five percent ethanol in fuel in eight states, covering some more states in the second phase and going upto ten percent ethanol in the final stage. The plan was a complete success. I was labelled as 'the ethanol pioneer' of the

After inaugurating the longest 1,270 km CNG pipeline of Loni (U.P.), Prime Minister Vajpayee viewing exhibits alongwith U.P. Governor Vishnukant Shastri and Ram Naik

country. Senior leader Sharad Pawar complimented me, saying, "Ram Naik has administered a life-saving drug for sugarcane farmers."

Unfortunately, the Manmohan Singh government reversed this decision. It ignored the reality that the use of ethanol had reduced vehicular pollution, a new employment avenue had sprung open that had generated jobs on a large scale, farmers were getting higher prices for their produce and millions of rupees had been invested in installing ethanol plants. All of this was undone by a single order by the government. Although the present Narendra Modi government has taken some steps to reintroduce the use of ethanol, I shall always regret the damage caused to the nation by the reversal of my decision. My view is that the wheels of progress should not move backwards, even if there is a change of guard at the Centre.

Hydrocarbon Vision 2025

Prime Minister Atal Bihari Vajpayee was of the opinion that a long-term plan should be drawn up to make India self-sufficient in her oil and energy needs and a Group of Ministers (GoM) had been appointed to work on this vision. They consisted of the Ministers of Finance, External Affairs, me as Petroleum Minister and the Deputy Chairman of the Planning Commission. With the help of the experts in our individual ministries, we hammered out a twenty-five-year plan with this objective in mind. Had our 'Hydrocarbon Vision 2025' been implemented in earnest, today India would have been in a much stronger position in these two sectors. Similarly, the 'National Fuel Policy' study group headed by famous scientist, Dr. Raghunath Mashelkar submitted its report, but it was not followed through as it should have been.

Anti-Adulteration Drive

My deepest regret is that the Anti-Adulteration Cell created by me to ensure clean and quality fuel was scrapped. Every citizen is entitled to clean, quality fuel but adulteration in petrol and diesel sold at various pumps across the country is a bitter reality. The consumer is cheated not just monetarily, but their vehicle is put at risk of damage too, because of the inferior quality of fuel that powers it. Moreover, pollution increases as a result of adulterated fuel. I launched this Cell in 2001 to prevent adulteration. It worked smoothly since I had ensured that nobody be allowed to interfere in its operations, nor would any pressure be entertained from any quarter. The incidence of adulteration had gone down since it was feared that a surprise check could take place any time. The very first decision of my successor, Mani Shankar Aiyar was to disband this Cell. I don't have to go into the reasons for this decision.

Outstanding Performance of PSUs

The performance of the 12 public sector oil corporations during my tenure was outstanding. They had earned a profit of ₹ 23,255 crore on a capital of ₹ 5,200 crore in 2002-03. Of the dozen, 5 corporations were in the Nav Ratna category, while 6 were in the Mini Ratna class. A highlight of this performance was that 75 percent of the total profits earned by 242 government PSUs in that year had been on account of the public sector oil corporations. Of the 10 highest profit-earning entities, 6 were under my ministry. Moreover, the profit of over ₹ 10,529 crore earned by ONGC was the highest in its history. It is in this light that the years between 1999 and 2004 are said to be the Golden Era of the Petroleum Sector in India.

A great soul had once said that one should do a noble deed and forget all about it. Still, one cannot help but feel regret if the good work one does is wasted. During the decade under the then Prime Minister Manmohan Singh, the country has had three Petroleum Ministers and this sector went in the doldrums. The situation has begun to show some signs of improvement under the present Minister, Dharmendra Pradhan of Modi Government.

I wish him and our nation all the very best.

(December 6, 2015)

❐

Ram Naik inaugurating a LPG bottling plant at Andaman, accompanied by Andaman Lt Govenor S.N. Jha, Minister of State Santosh Gangwar, Andman MP Vishnupad Ray and others

STORIES OF BLACK GOLD

As the Petroleum Minister, not only did I travel around the world, but also throughout India, from the very southern tip to the northernmost Himalayas. India is known as a country that has unity in diversity. Therefore, the problems faced by people in different regions vary. The residents of the hilly regions of Kashmir, Uttarakhand and Himachal Pradesh were finding it difficult to obtain LPG cylinders due to the regions' difficult terrain. Even in fair weather, reaching remote destinations in these mountains is tough. During winter, delivering the cylinders was almost impossible. As the cylinders had to be hefted onto one's shoulders, their fourteen and a half kilo

Ram Naik with Himachal Pradesh Chief Minister Prem Kumar Dhumal and others at the inauguration of distribution of 5 kg LPG cylinders

weight was proving too heavy for most people to handle. To overcome this problem, we installed a gas bottling plant of Indian Oil Corporation at a height of 5753 metres at Leh in Ladakh. This was a daunting task, but we completed it successfully. We also introduced smaller five-kg cylinders within a year's time. This provided great relief as they were easy to carry on heights.

Bottling Plant at Andaman

The Andaman and Nicobar Islands are at the foot of India and the grievance of its residents was altogether different. Andaman's BJP MP, Vishnu Pad Ray, always complained that though they were citizens of India, they had to shell out more money for cylinders than citizens in other parts of the country. There was a general impression that there was no remedy for this as the cylinders had to be transported by ship to the islands from either Chennai or Kolkata – a travel that took several days. This additional cost of transportation compelled the oil companies to increase the end-price of each cylinder paid by the consumer. However, it was unfair on the part of the government to extend the same facility to these people at a higher price. Finally, we decided to erect a bottling plant at Andaman. It was inaugurated on 20 April, 2003. Pending its commissioning, the cylinder prices were brought at par with the rest of India.

I have already narrated my sentimental association with the Cellular Jail at Andaman where Veer Savarkar was incarcerated for eleven long years. The Eternal Flame of Independence installed there has figured in an earlier chapter. Andaman is among my favourite places. It has pristine, beautiful beaches and an unending sea on the one hand and a thick jungle on the other, making it a fascinating spot. Frolicking deer, rabbits and squirrels greet a visitor every now and then. The tribes like Jarawa who have retained their ancient lifestyle add to the colour. It is an exotic world in a class of its own. The social situation is also unique. The residents are the offspring of the prisoners or workers brought here many decades ago under the British rule. Because it is a remote island, contact with the mainland is not easy. As a result, most of the marriages among the residents take place without caste or religious barriers. BJP MP, Vishnu Pad Ray's wife is a Muslim. The controversy surrounding the terms like 'intolerance' and 'sensitivity' in our society somehow seems so distant and absurd at Andaman. Whenever I watch heated debates on these issues, I invariably remember the cordial social relations I experienced in Andaman.

Ram Naik releasing a commemorative postal stamp on the occasion of the 2000th birth anniversary of Jesus Christ along with (L-R) Bishop Thomas Dabre, Father Francis D'Britto, Vicar-General Father Francis Correa and Post Master General Bhalchandra

2000th Birthday of Jesus Christ

My experience is that tolerance and sensitivity towards others can be conveyed through your words, the treatment we give to others and our body language. I recall a pleasant experience in this regard. When the 2000th birthday of Jesus Christ was to be celebrated on 25 December, 2000, massive preparations were underway around the world. Knowing the liberal attitude of the Vajpayee government, I received a novel suggestion from my friend, Father Francis D'Britto, who is also a renowned Marathi writer. He had suggested that the Indian government may issue a special postal stamp to pay its tributes to Christ. Though I was not handling the Post and Telegraph portfolio, he had conveyed this suggestion to me since Vasai, his hometown, was part of my Parliamentary constituency. An additional factor was that he knew my nature well. Therefore, he had proposed this to me without any reservation.

When I put this suggestion before the cabinet, it was welcomed enthusiastically and the special stamp was

Ram and Kunda Naik at a function to mark electricity supply to Arnala fort along with (L-R) Satish Pradhan, Ram Kapse both MPs and Padmasingh Patil, Maharashtra Energy Minister

released on that historic day. Customarily, such special stamps are released in Delhi, or in an important postal directorate. However, this release function was held at the Bishop's House in Vasai in D'Britto's presence. I remember this incident every Christmas.

Electrification of Arnala

Although the ocean and beaches in Andaman are unparalleled in their pristine beauty, I find Arnala, tiny fishermen's village dotting the coastline in my North Mumbai area equally fascinating The Portuguese demolished an old fort on the Arnala island and built a grand sea fort over five hundred years ago, which presently houses about six hundred families. At a stone's throw from Mumbai, the fort can be reached only by wading through sea water. However, even after five decades of Independence, this fort was without electricity. I decided to end this darkness.

The estimated expenditure for getting electricity across to the fort was ₹ 1.75 crore. The authorities thought that this was excessive in view of the small beneficiary population. Also it was needed to take electricity across the sea. This put me in a bind.

As the Petroleum Minister, I discovered a solution. Corporate Social Responsibility (CSR) has become a familiar term. A law has now made it obligatory for corporate firms to allocate a portion of their profits for CSR expenditure. However, even in the past, public-sector corporations under the Petroleum Ministry would spend some amount for select social causes from their enormous profits. I realised that unfortunately many companies spent the money as a legal obligation. I suggested to use these funds with serious considerations. ONGC had been extracting oil and gas worth billions of rupees from the sea near Vasai in the Bombay High oilfield. So, I suggested that a little bit of its profits be spent for the electrification of Arnala. Although the idea was out of the box, ONGC officials concurred with the idea and even lent the technology of installing transmission towers in the sea to the state electricity board. The project was completed very soon. When I went to inaugurate it along with my wife, we were taken in a procession. Forty years earlier, our marriage was a simple affair sans any form of fanfare which is typically done during Indian weddings. The Arnala procession took care of that one lacuna from our life. We both were conducted in the village in a grand procession. My satisfaction at seeing the residents' beaming faces is difficult to describe in mere words.

Sea-bund at Satpati

The fishermen's community is a big celebrant by nature. On special occasions, the fishermen and their families express their joy spontaneously. The affection they shower on me at Satpati, yet another coastal village of my constituency is really special. Satpati is famous for its catch of pomfret, which is also an item of export. Still, the local residents were in a constant state of fear due to the vagaries of nature. The coastline had been fast eroding due to high tides and the existing bund was broken, making it almost non-existent. Here too the construction of a breakwater wall – seabund was beyond the budgetary capacity of the Thane District Planning Committee. Fishermen living along the coast keep their crafts nearby and dry their catch in the same area. But in absence of a bund, the sudden rip tides would wash everything away. Moreover, no relief was forthcoming despite their repeated petitions. Now as if

Ram and Kunda Naik proceeding for inauguration of the breakwater wall at Saptati alongwith Union Minister of State Dilip Gandhi and MLA Manisha Nimkar

Ram Naik felicitated at Satpati on becoming Governor by (R-L) Rambhau Patil, Chintaman Vanaga, MP and Narendra Patil

the oil companies were in friendly competition in building innovative CSR projects; here Bharat Petroleum Corporation came forward and spent ₹ 2.85 crore to construct a 1380 meter-long retaining wall.

The village was in a celebratory mood when I arrived to inaugurate the wall and the streets were decorated with buntings. I was carried to the dais in a procession. When it became necessary to extend the wall by another 180 metres at a cost of ₹ 40 lakhs, Bharat Petroleum again came forward to discharge that responsibility, too. Many officials openly remarked, "This is the first time we are seeing a Petroleum Minister who asks us to spend for the public good. We feel that we should support him." Even after I became the Governor of UP, and during the ten years that I did not hold any post, fishermen from Satpati continued to meet me and invite me for various functions. After delimitations of the constituencies, the village is now part of the Palghar Parliamentary constituency, but my association with Satpati remains unchanged.

For the People

Crude oil is called black gold and I tried my best to add a golden hue to the lives of the people at large, trying to find innovative solutions to help them out, redressing their grievances by getting to know them at my own initiative. May be because my father was a teacher, I was uncomfortable that cooking gas used to be supplied to educational institutions at commercial rates. When I became the Petroleum Minister, I dealt with this matter, too. Sikh Gurudwaras serve visitors with free food called 'langar', but had to pay commercial rates for the cooking gas they used. I made an exception in this case since the gas was used for a social purpose. By applying the same yardstick, gas supplied to academic bodies that cook food for their students, their hostels, civic hospitals and homes for the aged began receiving gas supplies at domestic rates in place of the commercial tariff. It is their right, I believe.

Ministerial posts are not a permanent feature of anyone's life, but the true wealth one earns as a minister is the blessings of the people whom he helps. It gives me immense contentment and inner satisfaction that I was given the opportunity to be useful to society during my tenure as Petroleum Minister. I am certain that the people also view my achievements from the same perspective.

(December 20, 2015)

❐

Ram Naik campaigning during his first election on his scooter with Vikas Agvekar on the pillion

THE FRENZY OF ELECTIONEERING

I contested ten elections, winning eight in a row and lost two. My political career consisted of becoming an MLA, MP and Minister. I learned a lot through the process of electioneering. It was the most frenzied period of my life, yet it remains a treasure trove of experiences, full of constant activity, hustle and bustle and occasionally riddled with anxiety, but above all, always teaching me something new every time.

Today's political worker may find it inconceivable that for the first two Assembly elections, my mode of transport was my Bajaj scooter, which I rode myself. The general impression that a candidate must be surrounded by a bevy of followers existed even then, but I did not follow that practice. My Borivali Assembly Constituency was over ten km away from my Goregaon residence. My young associate, Advocate Vikas Agavekar would arrive at my doorstep at 7.00 am from his Borivali residence, so that we could begin our campaigning early in the day by reaching Borivali before 8.00 am on my scooter. After the day's electioneering, I would return to Goregaon late in the night. Some worker invariably accompanied me. After dropping him at Goregaon railway station for his return journey, I would arrive home alone by midnight. This practice continued throughout the first two elections' campaigning.

Partners in Victory

Any victory or defeat is always identified with the candidate, but the unseen hands working for him are numerous. In the good old days, mostly women workers wrote the election cards by hand, which mentioned details such as the voter's name, serial number and home address. Away from the hurly-burly of actual campaigning, they even cooked for the workforce; particularly on the days of voting and counting. Until 1995-96, printing technology was rather primitive, complicated and expensive. At present, any type of campaign materials like posters and flex banners can be printed in less than an hour. There are even services to set them up for display at strategic locations in the constituency. But in those days, every banner had to be painted by hand, then kept aside to dry. My wife and many housewives, whom I didn't even know, would stitch cloth banners on sewing machines in their homes. Once dried, they were attached to wooden sticks and hung everywhere. The cost of printing colourful posters was prohibitive and time-consuming. Until the 1990s, most campaigning would be through simple unostentatious black-and-white posters printed on ordinary paper. Workers would cook a thick mulch of wheat or rice flour which they would use to glue the posters onto public walls after midnight.

During my early elections, one of our party workers, Suresh Babar, met with a fatal accident while returning home after completing such an assignment while crossing a rail track. Suburban trains stop running for a few hours after midnight. Presuming that it would be safe to cross the tracks, Suresh was walking leisurely across and failed to notice an oncoming train. His untimely death pains me even today.

Assiduous Campaign Days

A candidate has to toil day and night during the campaigning. But this suffering is a unique type of intoxication. Though I used to be up and about at 5.30 am, the landline at my home would be already busy. The calls were from the workers, the media and from those workers facing some tricky problems, all rolled into one. The routine obligations as an elected representative were inescapable, despite an impending election. After scanning the newspaper headlines, I would venture out. Public corner meetings were held from 8.00 am till noon. The frequency of holding meetings was of about every twenty minutes. This was followed by interactions with prominent workers of the area and meetings which were of political importance. Meetings with Election Commission (EC) officials, fund raising visits, interactions with social service organisations

A boot-polish boy mobilizing funds for Ram Naik's election

and media had to be crammed sometime in between. Public campaigning would again resume at 4.00 pm. Time had to be alloted for meetings addressed by important leaders, for press conferences and to resolve disputes which arise in every election. Difficult tasks, like conversing with some visitors whose hidden agenda was to showcase their own importance, had to be discharged diplomatically. Assuaging the feelings of some aggrieved individuals was another delicate task that a candidate was needed to face. An added activity was to attend the meetings organised for fellow candidates in other constituencies. As if all this was not enough, a review of the next day's preparations was compulsory every night. Then I used to return home bone-tired.

Statutory requirements, such as police, civic and EC permissions for holding meetings, signing hundreds of documents to authorize party workers to attend polling duties and sundry other responsibilities, left very little time to rest. But our workers, too, exerted as hard as I did. The general public sees only those workers who appear on streets, or at rallies. However, there are countless others who work assiduously behind the scene. They plan the campaigning, make arrangements for the meetings of prominent leaders, secure various permissions, submit daily expenditure statements to the EC, insist that the local workers get cash memos and receipts for every expense, maintain accounts, look after the office work, prepare press releases and even deliver them. Another silent army is always busy ensuring that the printing schedule is observed, polling booths are manned properly and that there are no loose ends. It is only owing to endless and dedicated efforts of all that a candidate wins an election.

But no election can be fought without money. Besides political workers, those contributing towards my election expenses included even the boot-polish boys at railway stations who gladly parted with their day's earnings. The coolies and those working on tea and newspaper stalls at the stations also helped. Knowing their voluntary sacrifice, their patrons would willingly pay them more than usual.

Foolproof Campaigning

These election practices have undergone a change in a very short time. In my final election of 2009, my mode of transport was a 'Parivartan Rath' (a Chariot for Change). This was an ordinary vehicle that I had designed as per my requirements, at minimum cost and with maximum facilities in its upper portion. It proved extremely convenient and many other candidates emulated its design for their vehicles.

A candidate needs to be in a standing position for long hours every day. He is accompanied by three or four workers or local leaders. Sufficient room is necessary to accommodate them all. During longer journeys, the candidate needs to rest. So, a comfortable seat is fitted for him. The vehicle is also equipped with a megaphone, so that a loudspeaker does not need to be arranged at every venue. A barrel is kept ready to deposit the garlands and bouquets the candidate receives in large numbers. One corner is reserved for storing election material, such as handbills and badges. A folding ladder is kept ready, so that gathered supporters and voters could come up to garland or wish the candidate. Considering all these necessary requirements and other factors, my associates like Ram Jorapurkar and

Ram Naik exiting a police station after High Court verdict declaring impounding of 'Ram Rath' as illegal

Arvind Nandapurkar had used their technical expertise to finalise the design. Another group of workers decorated my Parivartan Rath with some eye-catching slogans and pictures – all their own creations. A senior colleague, Advocate Nana Pawar, had obtained the permission of the regional transport officer (RTO) to ply the vehicle on roads. He had used his keen knowledge of the Motor Vehicles Act to get the nod of assent. The posse of workers who would accompany me throughout my campaign would be hand-picked well in advance. At least, one of them would be an expert in handling the microphone. In all, our preparations used to be foolproof and reliable.

The practice of naming such vehicles began in the 1991 Parliamentary elections. Some names were quite unique and imaginative. My first such vehicle was named 'Ram Rath', so that the name complemented my campaigning. During the same electioneering, after the first phase of voting, Prime Minister Rajiv Gandhi was assassinated. Due to this tragic development, there was a sudden surge of support for Congress Party and many BJP candidates were unexpectedly defeated, though until then their prospects had looked bright. I was fortunate to win in spite of this odd. My workers felt that omen was brought by 'Ram Rath' and they insisted to retain the name of my vehicle during next elections.

Impounding Ram Rath

It was my view that the name was nothing more than an ordinary campaign tool, so I had not given it any serious thought. Other parties, too, did not find the name objectionable since by then, all of them had begun using such specially designed vehicles. But it was with the administrative officials that I had to fight a battle on this count. It is a known fact that some officials create uncalled for complications in an otherwise smooth process. This happened in my case during the 1996 Parliamentary election campaigning.

As per EC rules, no public meeting can be held after 10.00 pm. I was at Goregaon at a campaign meet one day at around 8.30 pm. Without any warning, an EC official arrived at my residence, flaunting an order to impound the Ram Rath. The order said that the vehicle should be seized. The intent behind serving the notice was to send the police to take possession of the vehicle, wherever it was. I had obtained prior permission of the EC and the RTO to use the vehicle and so far, it had been used for about ten days. Long after the permission had been given, the EC official had

Ram Naik also used a horse cart for campaigning at sea-shore villages

decided that the name of the vehicle had some religious appeal. The order threatened that the vehicle would be seized if the name was not changed forthwith. Had it been impounded, precious time would have been lost in preparing another such vehicle. Moving a court of law would also have consumed considerable time. This meant we would lose at least two to three precious days in completing all these formalities and the campaigning process in my hundred and ten km-long Constituency would be hampered.

My daughter, Vishakha and some prominent workers were busy discussing certain election matters when the bearer of the order arrived at my home. They showed great presence of mind, however, spending much time in perusing and discussing this letter, making the bearer wait. Vishakha signed an acknowledgement only after an hour. Matters became quite hectic after that. At 9.50 pm, even as I was delivering my speech atop the Ram Rath, the police seized it. The police guard who had stayed by my side till then as part of his election duties left feeling rather embarrassed, as he, too, had travelled in it with me. The workers were enraged. I showed great restraint during this bedlam, for had I shown the slightest bit of anger, the situation would have gone out of control.

I remained calm and reassured them, "Let them take away Ram Rath. We will bring it back with full honours." By then I had sent messages to my associates like Nana Pawar, Jaiprakash Mishra and Vinayak Bichu, all of whom were legal experts. They arrived at party office almost immediately and we sat through the night, deciding our line of action and preparing the documentation for filing a court petition. The next day, a writ petition was filed in the High Court, which accepted our contention and released the Ram Rath.

However, it suggested that it should be renamed 'Ram Naik Rath' so that the situation would not be aggravated.

We had already lost valuable campaign time and I did not want to waste any more time repainting the vehicle to change the name. So, the name 'Ram Rath' was concealed under paper for a day. A new board proclaiming the name 'Ram Naik Rath' was received and the renaming took place next day. Prima facie, the plot to impede my campaigning had succeeded. But, in reality, it worked in my favour. The media played up the story in a constructive manner, which actually proved beneficial to my campaign. The plot hatched by an official was foiled and I was elected for a third consecutive term. Moreover, I polled the maximum number of votes. It is still a mystery to me as to why the official, then Mumbai Suburban District Collector, Uttam Khobragade, had decided to seize the Ram Rath.

Campaigning and Publicity

Ram Rath was an object of attraction for the voters due to its decoration with catchy slogans and pictures. However, it is not easy to campaign in such a vehicle. Standing in it for a month in the scorching sun literally burns the skin. Standing for long hours leaves the feet swollen. I did not use sports shoes since I was in robust health. I tried to ignore the pain and swelling of my right hand, due to the non-stop hand-shaking with the supporters. Even eating two meals was virtually impossible on many days due to the paucity of time. The workers could take time off to eat by rotation, but I could not. Many a time, just a single meal was all I could manage throughout the day. One morning, I left home without breakfast. My workers were aware of this. When they realised that the campaigning was not likely to conclude in time, they began to get restless. Unable to control his concern for me, Vikas Agavekar furtively handed me a bar of chocolate, thinking that nobody noticed us. He knew my love for chocolates and the urgency for some form of sustenance for me. Vikas had done this out of love and concern, but this precise moment was caught on camera by a smart reporter of a Gujarati newspaper. He captioned his picture thus, "Ram Naik campaigns eating chocolates which his workers feed him." Vikas was livid since the reporter was his friend. I dismissed the episode as insignificant. I have narrated this incident merely to bring home the privations suffered by a candidate.

There are many anecdotes I can recall concerning the electioneering. I was the first candidate to campaign in a suburban train. Commuting in Mumbai is not everybody's cup of tea, but I love it and did it extensively during campaigning too. It is important to campaign, irrespective of the tools one has to resort to. There is no option but to walk when campaigning in Mumbai's slums. In coastal villages, I had to ride a horse cart during low tides. Even a solitary pedestrian needs to be greeted, lest he feels ignored. On occasions, people's response is such that a campaign procession resembles a victory march.

The spontaneous response of the voters during my campaign tours always guaranteed my success. Such a response was received in 2004 and 2009. Even then, I was trounced on both occasions. Nonetheless, I am overwhelmed when I come across strangers who still feel sorry for my defeats and compliment me for continuing to remain socially and politically active.

(January 3, 2016)

❒

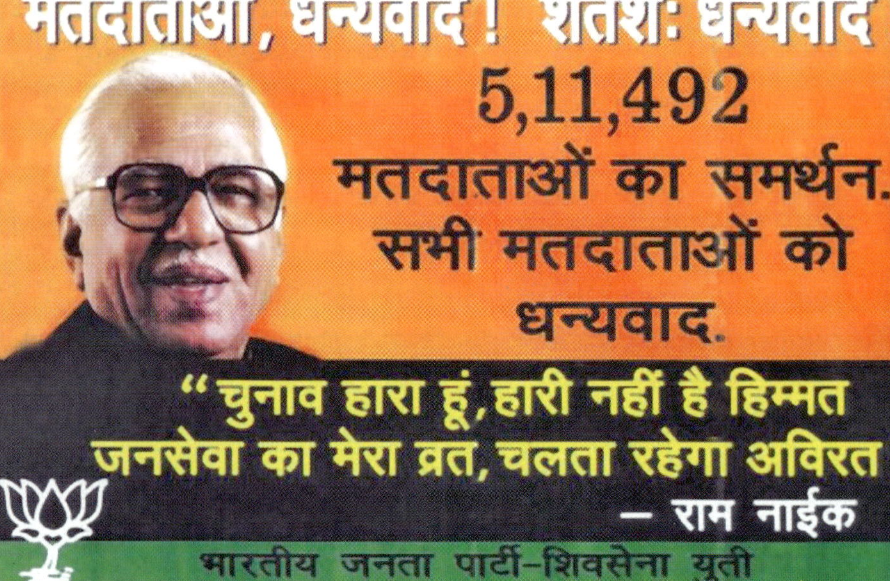

Ram Naik conceded his 2004 defeat by reiterating his pledge to continue to serve people through such hoardings declaring 'I have lost an election but not my resolve to serve the people'

FRIENDS IN VICTORY, FRIENDS IN DEFEAT

One of my favourite poems by Atal jee may be translated as, "I am not deterred by defeat, nor elated by victory. Whatever comes my way on the path of duty is right."

I had never imagined that this would resonate within the reality of my own life – that I would ever be defeated. But I had to swallow two election defeats. These unexpected losses were not a deterrent, since I had entered public life with the firm conviction that the electoral process offered one an effective medium with which to serve the people and I faced this reality with Atal jee's pragmatic words; 'not deterred by defeat'.

I had been elected an MLA thrice in a row, after which I had won five consecutive Lok Sabha elections. So, I was determined to perform a double hat-trick of wins in the Parliamentary elections in 2004. I was under the impression that my performance as Petroleum Minister was outstanding and my North Mumbai Constituency had benefited due to my work. It was not just I, but my entire workforce of colleagues which was confident that my victory was a foregone conclusion. However, I lost the election to film star Govinda by a small margin. I had polled over half-a-million votes in 1999 and had won the election. But, I lost the 2004 election, as my tally had declined by just six thousand votes.

When Govinda's name was announced as a Congress party candidate, The Times of India published it with a caption that read, 'Bade Miya versus Chhote Miya' (Big Boss against Small Boss). Caricatures of us accompanied the news item. My daughters found this rather amusing, greeting it with much laughter, though it left me somewhat puzzled. The heading was based on a hindi movie in which I was depicted as superstar Amitabh Bachchan (Big Boss), while Govinda, who had played the minor role, was Small Boss. My knowledge of the film industry is very negligible, though I was aware that my opponent was a famous personality and popular cine actor. But, till date, I have had no inclination or time to glean much about the silver screen. The last movie I watched was a Marathi film 'Shwaas' because Arun, the son of a fellow RSS worker was part of the starcast and the show had been organised by the BJP and RSS workers. But I am aware that I belong to a minority, since movies are the favourite pastime of the multitude and actors have their ardent fans among the audience. Of course, Govinda too had such a fan-following. The fans were fed a constant stream of propaganda against me through a TV channel named ‘Zee’, since I had opposed its owner’s entertainment park, ‘Esselworld’ at Gorai in Borivali, in order to protect the interests of the local people and the environment.

The ‘Indian Express’ and its sister publication, the Marathi daily ‘Loksatta’ began a campaign against me. The reason was an unjust controversy into which my name had been dragged. Before I took over the reins of the Petroleum ministry, the allotment of petrol pumps and cooking-gas agencies were distributed according to the whims and fancies of the Minister and top officials. When I took charge of the ministry, I too received hundreds of letters recommending some name or other for these allotments. Dr. Manmohan Singh, then the Leader of Opposition, had recommended the case of a woman professor for allotment of a petrol pump. I made it a policy that no allotment would be made under my discretion. Rather, I formed selection committees in every State. Every such committee was headed by a retired judge and comprised of two senior officials from two of the oil companies. The allotments were made after diligent screening. This system was meant to ensure transparency in the allotment process.

About eight per cent of the allottees had some connection with the BJP or the RSS. But some newspapers launched a campaign to indicate that I myself had indulged in corrupt practices, while completely ignoring the fact that the allottees included a senior Congress party leader, Girija Vyas. Not a word about the allotment to her was mentioned. I offered to resign due to the unseemly turn of events. But, Prime Minister Atal jee once more backed me firmly, stating adamantly that the question of my resignation did not arise, as he was confident that I had not indulged in any malpractice. However, he did cancel all the allotments against which objections had been raised. Those aggrieved by this decision moved the courts against their cancellation and the matter was adjudged only after the 2004 election results were declared. Most of the cancellations were reversed. But the biased media coverage might have affected my vote share adversely to some extent.

Matter of Prestige for Congress

The Congress had made the North Mumbai seat a matter of prestige. In 1984, the Party had fielded Amitabh Bachchan from Allahabad to ensure the defeat of UP's then prominent leader, H.N. Bahuguna. Many people recalled this tactic when Govinda's name was declared. The Congress campaigning had became feverish on account of Amitabh's phenomenal popularity, while Govinda was in a much lower league on this chart. No national-level leader of the Congress had ever visited my constituency before the 2004 elections, but for this election, Party President, Sonia Gandhi herself appeared. Her public meeting was convened at Vasai. The reason was that Vasai has a substantial Catholic population. Till then I was receiving their good support, since the residents were fed up with the strong-arm tactics of the local leader, Hitendra Thakur, whose elder brother, Bhai Thakur, was a dreaded name. As Sonia herself came to Vasai, a covert rumour was in circulation that the Pope had ordained the victory of the Congress candidate, Govinda. The most shocking stance was that of Socialist leader, Mrinal Gore, who having opposed the Congress party all her life, now joined the campaign against me. This was perhaps the only and last time that she was to step onto a Congress dais. We were well prepared to fend off such attacks. Still, some gaps remained due to unforeseen circumstances, such as the sad demise of my prominent colleague, Amarkant Jha, who had been very familiar with this very large Constituency.

Of course, I do not accept that my defeat was based solely on account of such developments. Although they may have been instrumental in the final outcome, the main reason for my defeat was an unholy nexus between the builder lobby and the underworld. The reported affinity between Hitendra Thakur of Vasai, international terrorist Dawood Ibrahim and Govinda was a matter of much speculation. The intimidation factor that had furtively insinuated itself within the electoral scene, came to light much later. The terror had established its stranglehold in the Constituency a couple of days prior to the voting day. Till then, I had scored substantial margins in all six Assembly segments which formed my Parliamentary Constituency. But, during the 2004 election, I was able to maintain the margin in just two segments. I was lagging behind at the Vasai and Malwani

Ram Naik addressing the media after submitting a complaint to the electoral officer regarding largescale irregularities in the electoral rolls

segments due to this intimidation factor. When the counting of votes began, there followed a repetitive state of flip-flop. The lead position kept alternating between Govinda and I, and at one stage, he became so exasperated that he walked out of the counting station.

But being a seasoned candidate I was apprehensive in the very first hour of the counting, preparing myself for an adverse verdict. However, I continued to maintain a confident demeanor so as not to dampen my counting agents' morale. They had only been accustomed to victories so far. The final result stunned them all, some being unable to control their tears. BJP leader and the then President of my Constituency, Jaiprakash Thakur stood up to thank the workers and request them to disperse. But, when he tried speaking to them through the megaphone, he broke down. Finally, I took over and addressed them. "You are the elixir of my life," I said. "When I am blessed with such dedicated colleagues, what is a single defeat to me," I continued, speaking to them in the same vein, till they finally regained their composure, recovering from the unexpected shock and distress.

The next morning, banners were displayed all over, carrying my message, "I have lost an election, but not my resolve to serve the public." It had been picked out of my speech the previous evening. I thanked the voters for their overwhelming support.

But the defeat had been a hard pill to swallow. My colleagues and supporters were despondent, as were the RSS activists who had ceaselessly toiled for me. Initially my wife had not betrayed any emotions at our defeat, but when veteran RSS leader, Kaka Damle came to my house to console us, she broke down, unable to control her tears.

"How long should we RSS workers continue fighting to create something out of nothing," asked the morose octogenarian. "Is this struggle never going to end?" He was referring to the lifelong, selfless struggle that thousands of RSS workers had been waging to win the trust of the people and the popular mandate.

I soon resumed my normal political activity, consoling myself that even a towering leader such as Atal jee had to face electoral defeat. In comparison, I was a small fry. It is true that I was grieved, but my sadness was of a different kind. It is said that victory has many fathers, but defeat has none. It has been over twelve years now, but I still meet people who lament that loss. I feel fortunate that I am privileged to hear such sentiments after all this time. My friends and well-wishers have remained loyal to me, through victory and through defeat.

Even women voters enthusiastically gathered to meet their favourite candidate Ram Naik during campaigning at Malad Railway Station

Voters' response was so overwhelming that even handicapped joined Ram Naik's campaign rally in big number

Duplicate Voters

During the 2004 election, a major scandal had come to our attention. This too, played its part in my defeat. The voters list had shown an unnatural spurt of a quarter of a million names. It was a fraud, but could not be rectified since it was already too late by the time we noticed it. I took up the job of this rectification after the election, employing a computer data expert to check the list. His investigation revealed that nearly four lakh names had been entered twice. We submitted a list of all these names to the Chief Electoral Officer of Maharashtra.

But, though we pursued the matter, the authorities did not do much about it. The 2009 Parliamentary elections were announced, even as this matter remained unattended. Not surprisingly, the number of the voters whose names were registered twice was very large. Even my daughter's name had appeared thrice on the list. It was obvious that this factor was going to influence the final results. But, we were prepared to tackle it. Following the reorganisation of the Constituencies, Vasai and Palghar had been merged in another Parliamentary Constituency. The remaining four Assembly segments were reorganised to form six segments. Geographically the Parliamentary Constituency had diminished, as a consequence of which, also the number of voters. My success seemed certain. Govinda's tenure as the local MP had disillusioned the people due to his lack of performance. On the other hand, I had continued unabated with my work even after my defeat. This contributed to the general sentiment that I would return to the Lok Sabha.

The Congress had a problem finding a suitable candidate to take me on. There was no dearth of hopefuls, but the Party chose former Rajya Sabha (Upper House of Parliament) member, Sanjay Nirupam, who had them deserted the Shiv Sena to join the Congress. A Hindi journalist, Nirupam had been elected to the Rajya Sabha twice on a Shiv Sena ticket. The BJP and the Shiv Sena were fighting the election as an Alliance. At that time, a television serial titled the 'Big Boss' had brought him into the limelight. It was very evident that the Shiv Sena workers would try their best to ensure Nirupam's defeat because of his betrayal, especially since he had been a long-time editor of the Shiv Sena mouthpiece, 'Hindi Saamna'. Every Marathi-speaking voter turned against him.

Ram and Kunda Naik being felicitated by L.K.Advani on his completion of 75 years while (L-R) Jaywantiben Mehta, Nitin Gadkari, Ramdas Athavale and Uddhav Thackeray look on

Skulduggery of MNS

Another major factor in the election was the Maharashtra Navnirman Sena (MNS), a new political party, founded by Raj Thackeray, the nephew of Shiv Sena Chief, Bal Thackeray. Raj had walked out of the Shiv Sena. He is a powerful orator and emulates his uncle. His mission was to project himself as the sole custodian of the interests of the Marathi-speaking people. Many Shiv Sena workers had joined the MNS. A misleading campaigning had begun against me, with false propaganda to the extent that Ram Naik, though a Marathi, would not protect the interests of the sons of the soil. As the day of voting approached, several young job aspirants from UP and Bihar who had

come to Kalyan near Mumbai, seeking jobs in the railways were mercilessly manhandled by MNS workers. This ugly incident projected the impression that Nirupam, who was born in Bihar, would be their true protector.

The motto of the MNS was to guard and enhance the interests of Marathi people. Still, it had fielded a candidate against me, a fellow Marathi. Had there been no BJP Marathi candidate, the MNS decision to contest such a seat could well be understood. It was easy to see that the entry of the MNS candidate into the fray would be detrimental to my prospects. But, the average voter is not privy to such skulduggery in the election scene.

It was conclusively established that the MNS had caused the victory of a non-Marathi candidate under the garb of its love for Marathi. My second defeat was evidence enough to prove this. Not a single MNS candidate could win the 2009

Parliamentary election, even though the new outfit was extremely successful in splitting the Marathi votes. I lost the election by a margin of 5,779 votes, while the MNS candidate polled 147,502 votes. My defeat was by a slender margin of just 0.84 per cent of the votes. Had there been no MNS candidate, all or most of these votes would have been in my favour, resulting in my win. Pretending to be pro-Marathi, the MNS was actually instrumental in the win of Nirupam, a non-Marathi candidate.

My colleagues recovered quite swiftly after this defeat. The MNS factor had made its presence felt and the BJP-Shiv Sena alliance candidates had suffered avoidable defeat in many constituencies. During all this happening, I had turned 75. My colleagues, followers and well-wishers organised a lively function to celebrate my birthday. Leaders of almost

Senior citizens invited Ram Naik to Dada-Dadi Park and celebrated his birthday during election campaign

all political parties attended the Borivali event, for which the public turnout was huge.

New Resolution

All the same, my platinum jubilee celebrations gave me much to brood about. I wondered what the future has held for me. I had been blessed with robust health and was confident of being elected in 2014. The workers wanted me to contest and avenge my defeats with victory. But why stand for another election, I asked myself. Being elected was never the objective of my life. I had decided at an early age to work for the Party and the public. But somewhere along the path came the electoral agenda and I embraced it as being part of my journey. As these thoughts swirled through my mind, I decided that my very first priority at that moment was to strengthen the North Mumbai Parliamentary Constituency, so that it could be easily bagged by the BJP in 2014. My Constituency was a BJP fortress from the day the Party was formed in 1980 and I was determined to bring back its lost glory. As far as my own candidacy was concerned, a decision could be taken at an opportune moment. I wanted to create such a situation that the Constituency would return to a BJP candidate, whoever he or she may be and I would consider the possibility of not contesting only after creating such a comfortable situation. I spared no effort in keeping to my decision between 2009 and 2014, although the BJP was not in power either in Maharashtra or at the Centre, nor was I holding any official post or position.

Still, I continued to work untiringly.

(January 17, 2016)

❐

Ram Naik ending his 48-hour hunger strike launched for demanding a fair deal for rehabilitation of the people affected by the Tarapur Atomic Power Project

ADIEU, ELECTIONS

I had announced my resolve to continue working for public causes while accepting electoral defeat and I soon had an occasion to prove it.

The Tarapur Atomic Power Project (TAPP), in my constituency, had drawn up an expansion plan, to which the local people were opposed. The main reason for this opposition was that the project affected persons (PAPs) had not been rehabilitated satisfactorily when TAPP was established decades earlier; hence people were apprehensive. I took the initiative to persuade them to withdraw their resistance since this 1080 MW power, station under the expansion project was in the interest of the nation. The locals reciprocated positively, trusting that I would remain with them to ensure their adequate rehabilitation.

I had laid the foundation stone of expansion project, i.e. TAPP III & IV as the Union Minister of State for Planning and Programme Implementation on 10th October, 1998. The Vajpayee government adopted a new rehabilitation policy so that all PAPs, including those under TAPP, would be adequately rehabilitated. The 2004 Parliamentary elections were announced before a decision could be taken to implement this policy with retrospective effect.

I lost the election. Moreover, a Congress government came into power at the Centre, adding to the existing woes of the PAPs. Their concern was not unfounded, for now they did not know if I would continue to be in the vanguard of their fight for the rehabilitation – or even if I did, whether the government at the Centre would heed my plea. Troubled by these uncertain circumstances, they filed a writ petition in the High Court at Mumbai. It was my honour-bound duty to keep my word and stand by them, even though I was no longer an elected representative. Against this backdrop, I decided to intervene in their Writ Application and became a party to it. In a remarkable development, the High Court Bench permitted me to plead the case myself. I was fighting on twin fronts – the judiciary and the State and Central governments.

But the government of Prime Minister, Dr. Manmohan Singh was insensitive. When Dr. Singh came to inaugurate the expansion project, which was completed before the deadline, he did not grant the PAPs an appointment. The fact that the project had been completed early only because of their cooperation and sacrifice was conveniently ignored. Instead, they were ignominiously driven away. At one stage of these developments, I sat on a hunger strike for forty-eight hours as the PAPs were forcefully evicted from their homes, but it did not move the government an iota. Eventually, the judiciary gave the PAPs some form of relief in phases. I attended over sixty court hearings, but had to discontinue after taking over as Governor of UP. Though most issues have been resolved, a final decision is still pending. I urged the Court to allow another PAP to become intervener in my place, due to my inability to continue, and it was granted. I am satisfied that I kept my word and pursued the matter persistently.

Besides the Tarapur case, I pushed the matter of Andaman's Eternal Flame of Independence. I am repeating this episode just because it will illustrate how busy I continued to be.

Mumbai Floods

Another milestone achieved in the 2004-14 decade came as a result of the disastrous floods in Mumbai on 26 July, 2005. Thousands of households had been washed away, leaving behind nothing. Losses ran into billions of rupees. One heart-rending tragedy was the death of a large number of buffaloes at Goregaon stables. They had drowned as they had been tethered to stanchions in their stable and were unable to escape. This flooding disturbed me very much. I remembered a flood at the Dahisar River in my Constituency that had claimed 21 lives 25 years earlier. It had been caused on account of unbridled encroachment along the river's banks. And now, the 2005 floods had been a result of the same menace – encroachments of natural channels, nullahs and outlets. Rivers in Mumbai are rapidly vanishing due to such encroachments. I was worried that the

Ram Naik inspecting a flood-hit locality

calamity could recur and, so, decided to undertake a study of this situation first-hand. The Maharashtra government, too, appointed a one-member study committee under internationally acclaimed water expert, Dr. Madhav Chitale. I have mentioned my friendship with him in an earlier chapter. My colleagues and I had prepared a list of measures that could be taken to prevent future floods occurring in Mumbai. This was submitted to the committee, which took due cognizance of the suggestions. Some of them have since been implemented.

Railway Bomb Blasts

A year later, Mumbai was shaken once more, though this time for a different reason. A series of bomb blasts took place on 11 July, 2006 at different railway stations, claiming 209 lives and injuring people in the hundreds. Once more, we got down to work. To add to their grief, unfortunately, the railway administration was causing emotional torture to the injured by its callous attitude, rather than helping them.

Its approach towards paying compensation or medical assistance was most inhuman.

It was announced that those who have become permanently disabled due to the blast injuries would be given compassionate appointments. These blasts had left some of the injured severely handicapped. Instead of employing them compassionately and promptly, the railway administration adopted a strange stance; it decided it would employ only those whose earning capacity had dropped below forty percent disregarding their earlier professions. The result was that even the blast victims whose disabilities were obvious to the naked eye were refused employment.

Several such unfortunate individuals approached me. One of them being a family earner named Hansraj Kanojia, had lost a leg in the blasts. He was a car mechanic, but it was now impossible for him to work. A happy household had been destroyed in a second. The railway administration refused to accept that a victim, who had survived miraculously, and was a physically challenged person, has lost his earning capacity. It was difficult to understand the logic behind such refusals. But they had not counted on Hansraj having such a strong determination. Placing all his faith in me, he continued to meet me thereafter. I travelled to Delhi to plead his case, meeting with the Railway Minister and Railway Board Chairman time

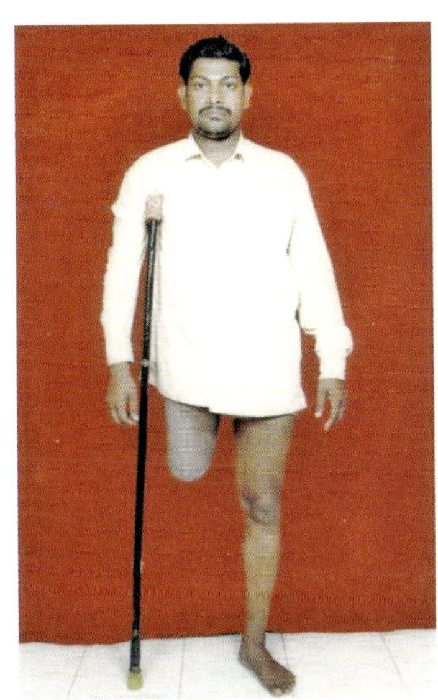

Hansraj Kanojia who lost a leg in a railway blast

and again to secure justice for him. Finally, because of my persistence, the orders were revised and Hansraj and many other physically challenged victims were given employment. My stint as a Minister of State for Railways in the past had proved very valuable during this prolonged struggle since I was well-versed in the working of the railways.

Simultaneously, a variety of social causes were claiming my attention. As mentioned in a previous chapter, I had been trying to bring together various organisations working for the welfare of leprosy victims from around the country, so that they could coordinate with ease, increasing their efficiency. Owing to a Petition I had submitted to the Rajya Sabha, this cause had also begun making some headway. It was through this initiative that I was elected as the President of the International Leprosy Union. This responsibility was quite different from holding a political office. Such social work energised my spirit, even as I continued my political work.

Ram Naik as a convener of MP MLA Development Cell addressing training camp of BJP's newly elected MPs at New Delhi

Roles at National Level

The BJP kept adding to my work, entrusting me with one responsibility after another and I continued to discharge them scrupulously. I became President of the Party's Disciplinary Committee and in this capacity, I had to take stern action against some colleagues. Firebrand leader, Uma Bharti, and former Delhi Chief Minister, Madan Lal Khurana, were suspended after I held an inquiry against them and submitted my findings. My adherence to duty and the truth brought in many accolades since I had not spared anyone if there was a breach of discipline.

The BJP had set up a Cell for developing quality in the working of the MPs and MLAs/MLCs on the floor of the house and in the constituency. This was in preparation for wresting power back. I was asked to head the Cell. I travelled all over India, convening workshops for the MPs and MLAs/MLCs in different States. After 2009, the BJP came to power in many states. A Good Governance Cell was then created in the Party with me as the National Convener with the objective to ensure that people got a government that fulfilled their aspirations. My effort was to share my experiences as an elected representative of over twenty-five years and as a Union Minister for seven years, so that the emerging leadership across the States could benefit.

Harbinger of Success

In spite of my preoccupation at the national level, I remained focussed on my North Mumbai Parliamentary Constituency. After the May 2004 Parliamentary elections, the Maharashtra Assembly elections were declared in October. I combed the six Assembly segments, appealing to voters to support the BJP-Shiv Sena alliance candidates and we were able to regain our earlier success, since the voters wanted to atone for their mistake in the previous elections. The four Assembly segments which were with BJP – Shiv Sena alliance earlier were retained.. It was not an easy win in Vasai, contesting against Hitendra Thakur for the reasons I have already listed. But the loss in the Kandivali Assembly segment was by an extremely narrow margin. Yet the overall outcome was a sign that people had reinstated their faith in us – a harbinger of days to come.

But this victory did not make me complacent and I could not rest on these laurels. Those who were aggrieved at MP Govinda's apathy continued to approach me and my response and ardour to assist them was the cement that bonded us further. Meanwhile, the parliamentary and assembly constituencies had been reorganised across the country. The North Mumbai Parliamentary Constituency had contracted in size, making it easier to keep in touch with the electorate. Our victories were resounding ones in the 2007 BMC election, the 2009 Assembly election and the 2012 BMC election and this reassured me of the future disposition of the people. It was almost a foregone conclusion that the BJP would stage a comeback in North Mumbai in 2014. My colleagues, local MLAs Gopal Shetty and Yogesh Sagar, the Mumbai Municipal corporators of our Party and the workers had all been working united. This pleased me. The trail of success was crowned in the Gujarat Assembly elections, where the BJP won with an overwhelming majority. My experience told me that based on this great achievement, Gujarat Chief Minister, Narendra Modi, would be very capable of handling the BJP's national leadership. Moreover, his charisma was captivating the voters around the country. Hence, the BJP's march to

Ram Naik always believed in principle of accountability to voters. Even after the defeat in 2004 he continued his practice of publishing Annual Performance Report

हर पल.. हर पन्ना... लोकसेवा में!

Ram Naik along with (R-L) Jaywantiben Mehta, Gopinath Munde and Jayprakash Thakur during publication of Performance Report for year 2005-2006

Ram Naik along with (R-L) Gopal Shetty, Rajnath Singh, Manohar Joshi and Gopinath Munde during publication of Performance Report for year 2006-2007

Ram Naik between Ravi Shankar Prasad and Manohar Joshi and others during publication of Performance Report for year 2008-2009

power at the Centre in the 2014 elections was going to be unstoppable.

Full Stop to Elections

I weighed the pros and cons – I surmised that there would be no better time to hand over the baton of my precious North Mumbai to a successor. A timely decision on my part would permit the Party enough space to consider a proper replacement. The workforce that would be disturbed by my decision would recover in time, resuming work as before for my successor. Moreover, if I myself urged the voters to support my successor, it would promote a seamless transition, so that my stepping away would cause no disruption.

My wife was the first to be consulted before making this decision. She was very amenable to my decision, saying, "You did not begin your public life to contest elections. So, not contesting any more elections won't matter. By God's grace, you are as capable as before and you will continue to be busy." She concluded this rhetoric with a slight dig at me. "At least, I will now have some of your time," she quipped. Her endorsement brought to mind my first election in 1978, even though it was a Party fiat and not my own decision. With this in mind, I thought it prudent to obtain the Party's consent before declaring my decision not to contest any future election.

At the time, Rajnath Singh was the BJP's national president. The Maharashtra BJP was headed by Devendra Fadnavis, while Ashish Shelar was the Mumbai BJP chief. The first person I consulted was Gopinath Munde, a former Deputy Chief Minister of Maharashtra and a state BJP veteran. He was not ready to accept my point of view. "Where is the need to decide this?" he asked emphatically. It was a difficult task to make him see my point of view. I found some lame excuse and remained non-committal. But I had realised that it would be pointless to discuss my decision with colleagues in Maharashtra, since their affection for me would make it difficult for them to consider my proposal dispassionately. I then contacted Rajnath Singh, who seemed baffled, too. He said, "You are well aware of what is good for the Party, so I am certain that you will not do anything contrary to it. But I can't decide in this case. You are a senior leader. Therefore, we will abide by your decision." Following this, I considered it judicious not to discuss the matter anymore with anyone and accordingly set a date to announce my decision.

There could have been no better day to announce this decision than 25 September – the birth anniversary of Pandit Deen Dayal Upadhyaya, a Jana Sangh mentor and an idol for millions. I regard such days as a Muhurta – an auspicious moment – to make an important decision or announcement. I decided to make my announcement at a press conference that afternoon and conveyed this decision to the Maharashtra and Mumbai unit BJP presidents in advance.

Devendra Fadnavis said to me, "Rambhau, as you have already made your decision, I will honour it. I am not happy with it, but I must congratulate you for creating a laudable example for the rank and file. We are fortunate to have a leader like you in our Party." I was overwhelmed by his appreciation of my years of toil for the Party. I was confident that under the new leadership of Devendra, the state would be led into an era of progress and prosperity. He represents the fact that the younger BJP leaders are aware of what is good for the Party and what needs to be avoided. His appreciation reaffirmed my resolve to quit electoral politics.

It was expected that the media would bombard me with many questions, but its response amazed me. On the one hand, the media regretted my decision, but on the other, they welcomed it since I was creating a healthy political precedent. Ever since the announcement, an unending stream of visitors began to pour into my home. These included my colleagues, workers and members of the public. It was an unpalatable situation for most, since they loved me sincerely. But, I remained steadfast in my decision. I conveyed to everyone that my work would continue in the future as before.

Welcoming New Era

The Parliamentary elections of 2014 were announced and the BJP decided to field Borivali MLA, Gopal Shetty, from North Mumbai. I shouldered the responsibility for his campaigning as the Election-In-charge, working day and night. His victory was already guaranteed due to his splendid performance as an MLA, because of the strong BJP network and owing to the wave created by our Prime Ministerial candidate, Narendra Modi. My campaigning for Shetty enhanced the faith of the voters in the BJP, amply proved by the outcome. I had won the 1999 Lok Sabha election with the highest number of votes in Maharashtra. Shetty repeated the feat.

I had also been requested to help an introductory workshop that was organised in Haryana for the BJP's newly-elected MPs. Soon after, I was appointed Governor of Uttar Pradesh. In light of this, I did not play any role in the Maharashtra Assembly elections held later that year. The highlight of this election was that the BJP's alliance with the Shiv Sena was terminated, prompting the BJP to contest the election on its own strength. Nonetheless, the Party won four out of the six Assembly segments in North Mumbai. They were Vinod Tawde (Borivali), Manisha Choudhari (Dahisar), Yogesh Sagar (Charkop) and Atul Bhatkhalkar (Kandivli East). Moreover, our candidate, Vidya Thakur won from Goregaon (part of my constituency before delimitation), defeating Shiv Sena leader, Subhash Desai, whose stronghold it had been until then. As I have mentioned earlier, Goregaon was where I had begun my political work. I was happy to see my dream of North Mumbai becoming a BJP fortress once again was realised.

Tawde and Thakur are now members of the Council of Ministers in Maharashtra – tidings that I warmly welcome.

(January 31, 2016)

❐

Maharashtra Chief Minister Shri Devendra Fadanvis and Minister of State Smt. Vidya Thakur paying courtesy visit to Ram Naik at Raj Bhavan, Lucknow with their respective better halves

Ram Naik inspecting Guard of Honour as Governor of Uttar Pradesh

CHARAIVETI! CHARAIVETI!!

I still have a long way to go.

The 2014 Parliamentary elections installed a stable BJP government at the Centre under Prime Minister Narendra Modi. I was thrilled with the vision of a future India emerging as a global power. What more could an average Party worker like me hope for? "We have achieved a lot in life," I confided to my wife Kunda. "Our only regret is that we had not been able to spend much time together. Now that I am free, just ask me and I shall be available. But spare me for one thing," I cautioned her. "I have to go to Delhi on 8 July to participate in the election of the BJP's national president. After that, I am entirely at your disposal,"

I explained. Expressing mock anger at my words, she replied, "You were born a wanderer. How will you be able to do something you have not been able to do in the last fifty four years? I will consider myself lucky if we are able to go somewhere for even a few days before July ends." Kunda has brought me great luck. Perhaps unknown even to her, she was making a prophecy about a new phase that was to make a change to yet another facet of my life.

BJP leader Amit Shah was elected the Party president. During my stay in Delhi, I met a large number of senior leaders and media friends. "Why did you not contest?" was a familiar question that greeted me. "You are gifted with such good health. You should have been in Delhi at this time," many said. I simply replied that I would be available for any assignment as and when required. No sooner had I landed in Mumbai then Union Home Minister Rajnath Singh called, saying, "We are going to recommend your name as a Governor to the President of India. It is an enormous responsibility and we hope you will accept it." There was no question of refusing. The President announced my appointment as Governor of Uttar Pradesh on 14 July, 2014. A new era had begun, even as I completed my 80th year.

New Era

Though my wife wanted to go out of Mumbai for a few days, I decided to take her along for a prolonged stay in UP. A close friend, always more attuned to her nature, chided, "At least now enjoy yourselves as a couple, else you will immerse yourself in the affairs of UP and find no time for her." My wife's response followed pat on this. "That is exactly what is going to happen," she remarked resignedly.

Chief Justice of UP Dhananjay Chandrachud administered the oath of office to me on 22 July, 2014.

I already had a close association with UP, as my North Mumbai Constituency had a substantial north Indian population. In addition, working for the BJP and in the Union Cabinet had brought about numerous occasions in dealing with the State. I accepted this onerous responsibility as a challenge. I did not want to spend my days in UP in an ivory tower since most Raj Bhavans (Governor's Abodes) are called homes for the aged in India and most Governors behave as if their appointment is meant to enjoy rest and leisure. I had no wish to join this bandwagon. UP is far behind on the scale of various social development indicators. I want to bring it on par with other important and developed states in India. The first challenge for me was to convey my determination to serve society. A Governor is usually placed on a pedestal. I experienced this attitude at the oath-taking ceremony. The UP Chief Secretary while politely seeking my permission to conclude the ceremony addressed me as 'His Excellency'!

No 'His Excellency' Please!

I had thus far been accustomed to being addressed as Rambhau, Naik jee or Ram Naik jee all my life, no matter which post I held and I was comfortable with it. This new sobriquet made me rather uncomfortable – almost as if I were a different person. The tradition of addressing the Governor or the President as 'His Excellency', is a British imperial legacy. What is the need to follow it now so thoughtlessly? In fact, I myself had observed this etiquette and addressed many an 'Excellency' in such a manner. Still, having the term applied to myself made me most uneasy.

Having decided that this term be stricken off any mode of greeting, I publicly declared this at the maiden press meet that had been arranged after my oath-taking. I followed it up with an official order that the custom be banished from governmental correspondence as well.

At the press conference, I was asked to enunciate my agenda as a UP Governor. "UP is the State in which Lord Ram was born," I responded. "It houses the most sacred temple of Kashi Vishveshwar. The Ganga and the Jamuna, our most revered rivers flow in UP, Shravasti, a blessed city where Lord Buddha had resided, is in this State. The 1857 War of Independence had been launched from here. I will make every effort to convert it into Uttam (ideal) Pradesh and the very first step in this direction will be to throw open the Raj Bhavan gates for the general public."

I have just completed the second year of my tenure as Governor. I have proceeded as I stated. Though I had been certain from the very start that there would be much to do as Governor, I soon realised that there is much more than meets the eye and it is not a light responsibility. I shared the general perception about the unsatisfactory law and order situation in UP. I found that there is ample scope for improvement. Senior Indian Police Service officers are routinely shuffled around every few months. How could a stable situation be expected from such a routine?

Testing Times

It was not too far into my tenure as Governor that I met my first acid test. The State government had sent an Ordinance for my signature. An Ordinance is a tool to introduce an interim law till the final legislation is duly adopted by the Legislature. The practice is that a Governor signs an ordinance without asking too many questions. It is also routine to issue ordinances for certain urgent matters that cannot wait until a Legislature session is held. However, the ordinance sent to me did not fall within this category. It was regarding bestowing the status of a Cabinet Minister to the Chairman of the Minorities Commission. Almost every State in India and the Union government have minority commissions, but nowhere is its chairman at par with a cabinet minister. Moreover, bestowing such a status is unconstitutional. The Supreme Court and several High Courts had delivered verdicts to this effect, making it improper for me to sign the Ordinance. A natural query would be about the urgency of granting that status. In this light, I sought an explanation for its urgency and did not sign it. My decision caused quite a stir. Opinions varied on the stand I took and were expressed vociferously. Some found that I was indulging in politicking. Others felt that I was not allowing the State government to function, while some were of the opinion that the Governor should sign it without any reservations. On the other hand, many supported my stand. I was under an obligation to go by the Constitution, in letter and spirit and I stood my ground, despite the cacophony of criticism, satisfied that I had allowed nothing unconstitutional to happen.

But this was only the beginning. A bigger storm was brewing ahead.

Appointments of MLCs

The Governor is empowered to nominate some members in the Legislative Council – the Upper House of the Legislature. The practice, however, is that the Chief Minister selects some individuals, who have a distinguished career in different fields like literature, science, fine arts, co-operation and social work. The list of such names is then endorsed by the Governor before the candidates are nominated. I had received a list of nine names, only four of which fulfilled the criteria and they were nominated immediately. However, the reasoning for the selection of the remaining five was far from lucid. I, therefore, sought an explanation from the State government. Simultaneously, my office began a scrutiny of their antecedents. Certain quarters were furious because not only had I refused to endorse the nominations but had asked for an explanation and they expressed their anger publicly.

The reaction to this response was quite amusing. Some of these five had been convicted for various crimes by courts of law. I received correspondence in this connection, supported by documentary evidence. Several newspapers ran stories which described how flawed the process of selection was. My stance shook those who had presumed that the Governor would be a puppet figure. But, a Governor is obliged to protect the interests of the State and while discharging this obligation, the improper nomination proposal had been stalled. This was the first gubernatorial refusal of its kind in the country. But, I took every precaution to forbid anything that would be contrary to the Constitution and so remain alert at every step. These names were subsequently changed by the Government.

Reports of Lokayukta

Allow me to mention two such cases: While one involved the appointment of the Chief Minister as Chancellor of the medical colleges in the State, the other concerned the termination of two MLAs on the basis of a report by the Lokayukta. My adherence to the law, my discretion and my determination to do my duty without fear or favour has constantly been tested due to such challenges.

According to the law, the Lokayukta submits a report to either the Chief Minister or the Chief Secretary after investigating the complaints he receives against public servants. Due action is then initiated by the state government. If no action is taken within three months, the Lokayukta is expected to bring this lapse to the attention of the Governor, who seeks an explanation from the State government. After the explanation is received, it is tabled in the Legislature. The Lokayukta had submitted twenty four reports, on which no action had been taken by the state government. When I initiated action, some quarters opined that I was an 'active' Governor, insinuating that I was interfering in the working of the government. Alas! Some expect the Governor to be in passive and mute mode all the time!

One of the reports of the Lokayukta dealt with was a sensitive issue. According to this report, two MLAs one belonging to the Bahujan Samaj Party (an erstwhile ruling party in UP) and the other to the BJP had been convicted for grabbing government contracts. Therefore, it was essential to terminate their MLAship. When I received this report from the Chief Minister, I sought the view of the Election Commission. On the basis of its response, I terminated their membership. Subsequently they approached the UP High Court.

Owing to such incidents, the Raj Bhavan and I have been regularly in the news. But, the common man on the street applauded my decisions, creating more and more affinity between us.

Appointment of the Lokayukta

The appointment of the UP Lokayukta hit the headlines across the country and generated a raging controversy. The one in office had been granted inordinate extensions. As per the law, his tenure was of six years but was increased to eight years by amending the law. Even that extension had concluded before my appointment as the Governor. The Supreme Court had directed that a new incumbent be appointed within six months. Despite this, no new appointment had been forthcoming even after I took over. As per the Act, it was expected that the name of a new incumbent would be recommended by the Chief Justice of the High Court, the Chief Minister and the Leader of the Opposition in the Assembly. However, they did not do so even after my repeated reminders. The reason was that they were unable to arrive at a consensus. Hence, the ruling Samajwadi Party amended the law by using its majority in the Assembly and dropped the Chief Justice from the recommendation process. When I refused to give my consent to the amendment, all the three met again to decide about the Lokayukta.

Meanwhile, a public interest litigation had been filed in the Supreme Court as a new Lokayukta was not yet appointed. Even after the apex court granted a grace period of one month, no decision was arrived at. Ultimately, the Supreme Court ordered the State government to submit the list of the names considered, selected one of them and announced its appointment. When it was brought to its notice that the UP Chief Justice was against this name on account of the integrity factor, the Supreme Court withdrew this name and directed the appointment of Justice Sanjay Mishra, a former High Court judge. This verdict was pronounced on 28 January and I administered the oath of office to Justice Mishra on 31 January. A prolonged controversy in UP had finally ended. This was the first time in the country that the Supreme Court had to intervene in the appointment of a State Lokayukta.

Governor as a Chancellor

Most of the Governor's time is spent supervising the working of various universities in the State, since he is the Chancellor of these universities. This is among the Governor's most important duties. In UP, I have to devote my time for many more activities but the universities are my area of minute attention. There are twenty-five universities under me. The overall academic level in UP is lamentable.

I gleaned that no regular convocation ceremonies had been held in some of them for quite some time. The first thing I did was to ask the authorities to hold the convocations so that thousands of graduates could get their degree certificates. It was an ordeal for me and the recipients alike to manage the flowing gown and black headgear while giving away and receiving the medals meant for meritorious achievers. That relic of the British academic tradition is most inconvenient. There is no emotional attachment to that pompous garb but it is used as a tradition. I suggested that special attire for convocations would be most welcome,

Pakistani ghazal singer Ghulam Ali was felicitated by Ram Naik at the Lucknow Festival

but asked why it could not be Indian? Taking the cue, all the universities have now Indianised their convocation attires. The student community has also welcomed this. Though seemingly a trivial matter, this change has played an effective role in inculcating the national ethos among the students.

The students in UP have developed a special affection for me, though for very different reasons. When I arrived in Lucknow, campus atmosphere was not healthy in many universities. The menace of copying was widespread. Even MLAs and ministers were involved in this racket. I decided to initiate stern action against it. As part of this exercise, I suspended one Vice Chancellor and one Registrar in two separate universities. After this, the students began looking to me as their saviour. I began convening periodic meetings with all the Vice Chancellors. One of my proposals envisaged extending their term to five years from the existing three years.

Ram Naik with Chief Minister Akhilesh Yadav handing over a monthly assistance certificate to a leprosy affected woman at the Raj Bhavan in Lucknow

Charaiveti! Charaiveti!!

For me, the Raj Bhavan has not been a place of rest or retirement. This forty-seven acre landmass has a beautiful garden, numerous trees, a cowshed and tiny farms. The building is about two hundred years old and is a heritage structure. The weather here inspires me to work, so that the reputation of this precinct is enhanced. A Governor can really while away time and no explanations need to be given. But, I cannot enjoy such luxury, for the work is my tonic.

When we arrived here, I was quite amused to find separate bathrooms readied for me and my wife, as was the wont. Every bathroom in Raj Bhavan is larger than my first two-room residence in Mumbai, with the trappings fit for a king. It would not be exaggerating to say that Raj Bhavan is like a palace. But I am unable to relish these luxuries, as I prefer being a commoner, to be among people. While I have opened the Raj Bhavan to the public, I also visit different districts as and when possible. In my first year-and-a-half, I must have met more than seven thousand visitors and attended over five hundred different events in the State. They included the visits of VVIPs, like the President and the Prime Minister and also felicitation of dignitaries like Pakistani Ghazal singer Ghulam Ali. People appreciate the variety in such functions. Locals often mention that they have not seen such a Governor before.

Raj Bhavan employees work throughout their lives in this palatial enclave but live in the staff quarters on the premises. These were two different worlds. But now, the picture is changed. Unlike in the past, they now invite the Governor for their family functions. On my request, the State government has sanctioned a monthly grant of ₹ 2500 each to the leprosy affected persons in the State. Chief Minister Akhilesh Yadav suggested me to host the function at Raj Bhavan for the first disbursement.

What better acknowledgement can one look for?

Of course, I don't feel like taking a pause or a stop. I need to keep working as I still have a long way to go. Charaiveti! Charaiveti!! Marching Ahead! Marching Ahead!! However I am putting a stop to this series of my memoirs. Bye-bye!

(February 14, 2016)

❑❑❑